Cryptography For Dummies®

Cheat Sheet

The Ten Principles of Cryptiquette

1. If someone sends you an encrypted message, reply to them in kind.

2. Don't create so many keys for yourself that it confuses users.

3. Don't trust someone simply because he/she has a key.

4. Always back up your keys and passphrases.

5. Be careful of what you put in the Subject line of encrypted messages.

6. If you lose your key, revoke it and update the public key servers.

7. Never publish someone else's public key to a server without their permission.

8. Don't sign someone else's public key unless you have a need to.

9. Send a copy of your public key to someone you are corresponding with for the first time.

10. Be choosy in what you encrypt.

The Basic Differences in Encryption Algorithms

- *Symmetric algorithms* use one key to encrypt and the same key to decrypt.

- *Asymmetric algorithms* use one key to encrypt and a different key to decrypt.

- *Stream ciphers* are algorithms that encrypt each bit in sequence.

- *Block ciphers* are algorithms that encrypt a finite block of bits and then go back and encrypt the next block.

- *Hash* and *Message Digest* are one-way ciphers that encrypt but can't be decrypted. They are mainly used to create "fingerprints" of data.

Wiley, the Wiley Publishing logo, For Dummies, the Dummies Man logo, the For Dummies Bestselling Book Series logo and all related trade dress are trademarks or registered trademarks of John Wiley & Sons, Inc. and/or its affiliates. All other trademarks are property of their respective owners.

For Dummies: Bestselling Book Series for Beginners

Cryptography For Dummies®

Cheat Sheet

Some of the Most Commonly Used Algorithms

- **DES (Digital Encryption Standard):** A symmetric algorithm that uses block encryption.

- **3DES (Three DES or Triple DES):** A symmetric algorithm that uses block encryption.

- **RC4 (Rivest Cipher #4):** A symmetric algorithm that uses stream encryption.

- **RSA (Rivest, Shamir, Adelman):** An asymmetric algorithm that uses block encryption. (Actually, there are a couple of subsets of RSA. Check the RSA Security site for more information.) This algorithm is most often associated with its ability to exchange keys securely.

- **IDEA (International Data Encryption Algorithm):** A symmetric algorithm that uses block encryption. This algorithm is generally found in commercial versions of PGP.

- **AES (Advanced Encryption Standard, also known as Rijndael Algorithm):** A symmetric algorithm using block encryption.

- **SHA-1 (Secure Hash Algorithm):** A symmetric algorithm used only to create a message digest (fingerprint) of data. It's a one-way function and once the encryption string has been created, it cannot be decrypted.

- **Blowfish** (not an acronym): A symmetric algorithm that uses block encryption.

- **Twofish** (not an acronym): A symmetric algorithm that uses block encryption. This algorithm was one of those on the shortlist to become AES.

Encryption Cracking Software (Including Password Crackers)

I am including these links to software because I realize that there is a legitimate need for such products. Of course these products can also be used for nefarious purposes. Be careful how you use them and always have the permission of higher-ups within your company before installing them on any system.

- **WEPCrack** (http://sourceforge. net/projects/wepcrack): This program can find weaknesses in the RC4 algorithm used in WEP and break the encryption. You may want to use this on your own network to see if your encryption is up to par.

- **AirSnort** (http://airsnort.shmoo. com): AirSnort is one of the original WEP crackers and is frequently used by War Drivers. It gathers packets and, when it has enough, computes the encryption key for you.

- **Password Recovery Toolkit** (www.accessdata.com/Product00_ Overview.htm?ProductNum=00): This site has a software program that can crack the passwords of dozens of different software programs such as Word, Excel, Quicken, and so on. If you've forgotten your password, or a person has left the company without giving his password to anyone, this may save your lunch!

- **Password Recovery XP** (www.iopus. com/password_recovery.htm): This program is for recovering passwords from XP systems only.

Copyright © 2004 Wiley Publishing, Inc.
All rights reserved.

Item 4188-9.

For more information about Wiley Publishing,
call 1-800-762-2974.

Cryptography
FOR
DUMMIES®

Cryptography FOR DUMMIES®

by Chey Cobb, CISSP

WILEY

Wiley Publishing, Inc.

Cryptography For Dummies®

Published by
Wiley Publishing, Inc.
111 River Street
Hoboken, NJ 07030-5774

Copyright © 2004 by Wiley Publishing, Inc., Indianapolis, Indiana

Published by Wiley Publishing, Inc., Indianapolis, Indiana

Published simultaneously in Canada

No part of this publication may be reproduced, stored in a retrieval system or transmitted in any form or by any means, electronic, mechanical, photocopying, recording, scanning or otherwise, except as permitted under Sections 107 or 108 of the 1976 United States Copyright Act, without either the prior written permission of the Publisher, or authorization through payment of the appropriate per-copy fee to the Copyright Clearance Center, 222 Rosewood Drive, Danvers, MA 01923, (978) 750-8400, fax (978) 646-8600. Requests to the Publisher for permission should be addressed to the Legal Department, Wiley Publishing, Inc., 10475 Crosspoint Blvd., Indianapolis, IN 46256, (317) 572-3447, fax (317) 572-4447, e-mail: permcoordinator@wiley.com.

Trademarks: Wiley, the Wiley Publishing logo, For Dummies, the Dummies Man logo, A Reference for the Rest of Us!, The Dummies Way, Dummies Daily, The Fun and Easy Way, Dummies.com, and related trade dress are trademarks or registered trademarks of John Wiley & Sons, Inc. and/or its affiliates in the United States and other countries, and may not be used without written permission. All other trademarks are the property of their respective owners. Wiley Publishing, Inc., is not associated with any product or vendor mentioned in this book.

LIMIT OF LIABILITY/DISCLAIMER OF WARRANTY: WHILE THE PUBLISHER AND AUTHOR HAVE USED THEIR BEST EFFORTS IN PREPARING THIS BOOK, THEY MAKE NO REPRESENTATIONS OR WARRANTIES WITH RESPECT TO THE ACCURACY OR COMPLETENESS OF THE CONTENTS OF THIS BOOK AND SPECIFICALLY DISCLAIM ANY IMPLIED WARRANTIES OF MERCHANTABILITY OR FITNESS FOR A PARTICULAR PURPOSE. NO WARRANTY MAY BE CREATED OR EXTENDED BY SALES REPRESENTATIVES OR WRITTEN SALES MATERIALS. THE ADVICE AND STRATEGIES CONTAINED HEREIN MAY NOT BE SUITABLE FOR YOUR SITUATION. YOU SHOULD CONSULT WITH A PROFESSIONAL WHERE APPROPRIATE. NEITHER THE PUBLISHER NOR AUTHOR SHALL BE LIABLE FOR ANY LOSS OF PROFIT OR ANY OTHER COMMERCIAL DAMAGES, INCLUDING BUT NOT LIMITED TO SPECIAL, INCIDENTAL, CONSEQUENTIAL, OR OTHER DAMAGES.

For general information on our other products and services or to obtain technical support, please contact our Customer Care Department within the U.S. at 800-762-2974, outside the U.S. at 317-572-3993, or fax 317-572-4002.

Wiley also publishes its books in a variety of electronic formats. Some content that appears in print may not be available in electronic books.

Library of Congress Control Number: 2003105686

ISBN: 0764541889

Manufactured in the United States of America

10 9 8 7 6 5 4 3 2 1

1O/QY/QR/QU/IN

WILEY

About the Author

Chey Ewertz Cobb, CISSP, began working in computer security in 1989. Since then she has managed her own computer security consulting company, Cobb Associates, working for such clients as Apple Computers and Sun Microsystems. She later worked for the government, creating a secure network at Cape Canaveral, assisting in the security at Patrick Air Force Base, and later as a technical security officer for the National Reconnaissance Office (NRO), which is more secretive than the NSA.

During her work in security, she had the opportunity to evaluate and manage cryptosystems for private industry and the U.S. Intelligence Agencies.

Chey now writes books on computer security (*Computer Security Handbook, 4th Edition* and *Network Security For Dummies*), writes articles for magazines, and speaks at computer security conferences.

Dedication

To R. W. Ewertz, Jr. He was my role model and inspiration when things got tough.

Acknowledgments

First of all, let me thank Andrea Boucher and Melody Layne who saw me through thick and thin and never lost faith in me (at least they never let on that they did!). I enjoy working with them both, and any writer who has the opportunity to work with them should count himself/herself lucky!

Secondly, I want to thank Dave Brussin, Ryan Upton, Josh Beneloh, Jon Callas, and Dave Del Torto for setting me on the correct path when my explanations strayed. Thanks so much for lending me your brainwork!

Last, but not least, Stephen. My love, my life, and my everything.

Publisher's Acknowledgments

We're proud of this book; please send us your comments through our online registration form located at www.dummies.com/register/.

Some of the people who helped bring this book to market include the following:

Acquisitions, Editorial, and Media Development

Project Editor: Andrea C. Boucher

Acquisitions Editor: Melody Layne

Technical Editor: Tim Crothers

Editorial Manager: Carol Sheehan

Media Development Manager:
Laura VanWinkle

Media Development Supervisor:
Richard Graves

Editorial Assistant: Amanda Foxworth

Cartoons: Rich Tennant (www.the5thwave.com)

Production

Project Coordinator: Maridee Ennis

Layout and Graphics: Joyce Haughey,
Andrea Dahl, Stephanie D. Jumper,
Jacque Schneider, Melanee Wolven

Proofreaders: Andy Hollandbeck,
Carl William Pierce, TECHBOOKS
Production Services

Indexer: TECHBOOKS Production Services

Publishing and Editorial for Technology Dummies

Richard Swadley, Vice President and Executive Group Publisher

Andy Cummings, Vice President and Publisher

Mary C. Corder, Editorial Director

Publishing for Consumer Dummies

Diane Graves Steele, Vice President and Publisher

Joyce Pepple, Acquisitions Director

Composition Services

Gerry Fahey, Vice President of Production Services

Debbie Stailey, Director of Composition Services

Contents at a Glance

Table of Contents

Introduction

Congratulations! You've successfully navigated through the gazillion computer books on the bookstore shelves and finally found just what you were looking for — a book on cryptography that you can read and actually understand! Just thumb through some of the chapters here and you'll soon realize that you don't need a degree in advanced mathematics, nor do you need to be the world's biggest brainiac to understand this stuff. If you have a basic understanding of computers and networking, and you have an interest in increasing your data and communications security, then this is just the book for you.

What I'm talking about here is cryptography — you know, *crypto, geek talk, secret coding, cypherpunk'n*. If you have heard of the word *cryptography,* you'll know that it is one of those subjects that many people are aware of, but very few people can actually tell you what it's all about. Frankly, just the mention of the word cryptography scares the heck out of people — even experienced network administrators! And to be honest, a lot of the books on the subject are more suited as college textbooks than business "how-to" guides or intros to the subject, and have contributed to the atmosphere of *FUD — fear, uncertainty, and doubt* — about cryptography. Yep, the subject can be scary as all get-out.

So, how do you decide whether or not you should use cryptography? I'll help you answer that question with questions and checklists. Before you go on to that chapter, however, there are many situations in which cryptography could or should be used. Here's a preview of some situations:

- Your company relies heavily upon its trade secrets to gain a competitive edge over your competitors. If an unauthorized person got access to those trade secrets, it could spell disaster for your entire company.

- You work in the health care industry and are required by the HIPAA legislation to protect personal information. You get notice from a federal authority that your protection methods are about to be scrutinized because there have been complaints about the way you have handled personal information.

- You're an attorney who has been charged with prosecuting someone guilty of war crimes, drug trafficking, or any situation where witnesses and evidence need to be fiercely protected. Obviously, you wouldn't want your evidence or your witnesses compromised.

Cryptography is a complex subject, I won't kid you there, but it could definitely save a lot of headaches if it were used in any of the situations mentioned above. Additionally, adding cryptography to your security doesn't necessarily have to be expensive or impossible to understand. That's why I wrote this book. I'm here to take the fear out of the equation and to help you get it right the first go-round. After you read through a few sections of this book, you'll be spouting the jargon like a true techno-geek and you'll even be able to understand what you're talking about.

I'll give you some advance warning, though: You'll be seeing a lot of information about *keys* in this book because (and excuse the cliché) the key to cryptography is the keys. That is perhaps the most confusing thing about cryptography — that the word "key" can be used to mean more than one thing. I wish I could change the terminology so it wouldn't get so confusing, but I have to consider the real world, too. The terminology used in this book is based on what you are really likely to encounter.

About This Book

As I just mentioned, the subject matter covered in this book is what you are most likely to encounter in real life. That means that you can obtain enough information here to help you make decisions on cryptography: Is it right for you? What type of programs should you use? How do you set things up appropriately? After you have installed your chosen system, you can always refer back to this book to refresh your memory as need be.

Every time I introduce a new concept, I start out with really basic explanations with some analogies to help you get the idea and then, as the chapter progresses, I explain things in more detail. I promise not to get to the uber-geek level of detail on any particular subject because I certainly haven't intended for the book to act as a substitute for a sedative.

How to Use This Book

It's quite simple, really. You hold the book in one hand, and use the other to turn the pages! Alternatively, you could use the book to prop up a broken table leg. To be honest, though, I don't recommend the last usage because you really won't receive the benefits of the book if you can't open it to read it.

Seriously, I suggest that you peruse the Table of Contents and have a look at the headings and subheadings. When you see something of interest, dive right in; I promise it won't hurt. If nothing else, you can also flip through the book and have a sneak peek at all the cartoons.

What You Don't Need to Read

Occasionally I include some deeper technical detail on certain subjects. When I include this sort of information, I make it obvious by putting a special icon called "Technical Stuff" next to the section. It isn't really necessary that you know this stuff, but I thought I'd include it just in case you were interested.

So, if you see the Technical Stuff icon, you can just pass it by. Or, if you want to impress your boss, you can memorize the information and impress him with your knowledge!

Foolish Assumptions

When you are writing for a mass audience (as I am here), it's difficult to gauge the level of aptitude. Because I didn't know ahead of time what you know and what you don't know, I've had to make certain foolish assumptions. So as not to insult your intelligence, here are the assumptions I've made:

- You'd really like to know more about cryptography.
- You're not intimidated by computers, computing, or networks.
- You are connected to an Internet, whether through your job, DSL or cable modem at home, or a dial-up account.
- You are interested in security and, in particular, securing your data and communications.
- You are aware that your e-mail messages can be read by almost anyone in the world (besides the intended recipient).
- You're aware of the fact that unauthorized persons can get access to your computer and read, steal, and change your files.
- You're capable and/or authorized to install computer software programs.
- You don't expect this book to make you an instant expert; I give you enough information to get you started and to be able to speak intelligently with others on the subject.

How This Book Is Organized

I've assembled this book into distinct and separate "parts" and each part focuses on a particular aspect of cryptography. This will help you to find the correct level of explanation for the questions you need answered. It's not necessary to read each part completely in order to get an idea of what's going on. Here's a brief description of each of the parts.

Part I: Crypto Basics & What You Really Need to Know

The title says it all! Algorithms and ciphers explained. An introduction to keys and how they are used in cryptography. Help with deciding what you really need. And I discuss keys in depth (because they are really, really important!).

Part II: Public Key Infrastructure

Public Key Infrastructure, also known as PKI, is as it says, an *infrastructure*. That is, basic facilities, services, and installations needed for the functioning of a cryptographic system. It's not something that comes complete in one box; you generally have to build this system with servers, software, and connections to a public network like the Internet.

This part goes into what PKI does, how it does it, what you need to do it, and why you would want to build such a system.

Part III: Putting Encryption Technologies to Work for You

Now that you've decided that you really should be using cryptography as an additional security measure, here are all the things you can use it for. I discuss e-mail systems, file storage, and authenticating users of your systems. In addition, I have a look at e-commerce on the Web, the use of VPNs, and last, but not least, wireless security. Wireless security is a hot topic right now!

Part IV: The Part of Tens

Do you like lists? Do you like tips, tricks, and resources for additional information? Included in this part is lots of information that is sure to inform and amuse you! I've included Web sites, software, and common mistakes, among other goodies.

Part V: Appendixes

Here you get three appendixes with even more information! In addition to a handy glossary of terms you'll read about, I also tell you all kinds of stuff about crypto attacks and encryption export controls.

Icons Used in This Book

You'll probably notice that I put a lot of these in the book. If you really want to impress your geeky friends, this is the stuff to read. It's not really necessary that you read every one of these, but you might be amazed at what you'll learn.

These are the things you always want in a hurry. They sometimes make the job easier or faster by suggested short-cuts for common tasks.

Basically, this icon means *Don't Do This!* Tread softly, pay attention, and be very, very sure of what you are doing. Always have a back-up plan in case things don't go well.

We all need a little nudge now and then to jog our memory. That's exactly what these sections do. After a while you won't need these reminders as tasks become second nature to you.

Where to Go from Here

Start flipping through the book and dive in where something catches your eye. Like I've said before, it's not necessary for you to read this book in any particular order, so you're free to dive in anywhere to get your feet wet.

Occasionally I suggest software that you may want to try. Go to the site I mention and download the file and install it on your system. I recommend that you install these programs on test machines first, to see how they work and to see if they conflict with anything else you already have. Playing around with the software is one of the best ways to underscore the knowledge I impart here. In any case, enjoy yourself!

Part I
Crypto Basics & What You Really Need to Know

The 5th Wave   By Rich Tennant

"We take network security very seriously here."

In this part . . .

This is the part to get you started — get you started so you can attend that meeting on cryptography and encryption products and sound like you know what you're talking about. This is the section that will make your boss realize that you're an indispensable employee. And if you *are* the boss, this part will give you the information you need to work your way through the labyrinth of confusing jargon and new technology.

In addition to giving you the basic information to be able to understand what the software and hardware vendors are throwing at you, the basics of algorithms and keys are explained. There's also a complete chapter to help you decide what you need by giving you situations in which encryption is used and the technology needed to make it happen. You don't have to start here if you don't want to, but if you've never encountered cryptography or encryption before, I suggest you at least give it a browse.

Chapter 1

A Primer on Crypto Basics

Computers and use of the Internet have fostered new interest in cryptography partly due to the new emphasis on personal privacy. Little did I realize that in our efforts to make it easy for computers to share stuff, it would make it easy for other people to see all of our personal stuff, too. Perhaps you've discovered for yourself that it is far too easy for unknown persons to read your e-mail, private documents, love letters, financial information, and so on. The Internet is truly the Global Village . . . a village where everyone can see what you do and hear what you say. The good news is that you can use cryptography to protect yourself from the eavesdroppers and Peeping Toms of the village.

Not only can cryptography scramble your files, but it can also be used to prove who you are (and maybe who you aren't!). Cryptography can be used to alert you if the contents of a file have been changed, attest to the identity of the person who sent you a message, keep online communications safe and secure, and, of course, hide important data. And the best news of all is that not every cryptographic solution is expensive, and you don't need to be a rocket scientist to incorporate crypto solutions into your network.

It's Not about James Bond

There's no need for fancy gizmos, fast cars, or beautiful women. As nice as those may be (for some!), the world of cryptography can be used on even low-tech systems. Forget the cloak and dagger and put away your raincoat and fedora — most cryptography is done out in the open now. The special programs and codes used to scramble data are available for all the world to see. In fact, having them out in the open helps make cryptography more secure because more people can test for weaknesses.

Because cryptography is usually associated with spies, secret messages, and clandestine meetings, you might have thought that cryptography stopped being used at the end of the Cold War. Believe it or not, its use is actually on the rise. I think that's partially due to more awareness of personal identity theft and also because more is being written in the media about how data needs more protection that a common PC gives you.

Cryptography is about scrambling data so that it looks like babble to anyone except those who know the trick to decoding it. Almost anything in the world can be hidden from sight and revealed again. The magician David Copperfield has made his living from hiding enormous things from plain view — like elephants and the Statue of Liberty — and then magically revealing them again. Any magician will tell you that in order to make things disappear and appear again, you have to have a plan of action — a formula or recipe — to make the magic work. Although you can't directly equate magic acts with cryptography (although cryptography may seem like magic), there is a similarity between magic and cryptography in that they both need to have a formula in order to work correctly time after time.

Go with the rhythm

In cryptography, the magic recipe for hiding data is called an *algorithm*. An algorithm is a precise set of instructions that tells programs how to scramble and unscramble data. A simple algorithm might read like this:

```
Step 1:Delete all instances of the letter "e" in the data
Step 2:Replace the letter "t" with the number "7"
Step 3:Reverse the order of the data and rewrite it from the
        end to the beginning
```

Now, this is just me playing around with what a simple algorithm *might* look like, just so you can get an idea of what I'm talking about. The steps above are not an actual algorithm; it's my pretend algorithm of the week. Algorithms used in programs today are mathematical functions with the instructions written in programming code.

Here's just a portion of a real algorithm called *DES* (Data Encryption Standard) that was adopted by the government in 1977. DES is a block cipher that transforms 64-bit data blocks under a 56-bit secret key by means of permutation and substitution. (You're not meant to understand that last sentence yet!) So, here is just a tiny, tiny bit of the DES algorithm:

```
Get a 64-bit key from the user. (Every 8th bit is consid-
        ered a parity bit. For a key to have correct
        parity, each byte should contain an odd number of
        "1" bits.)
Calculate the key schedule.
Perform the following permutation on the 64-bit key. (The
        parity bits are discarded, reducing the key to 56
        bits. Bit 1 of the permuted block is bit 57 of
        the original key, bit 2 is bit 49, and so on with
        bit 56 being bit 4 of the original key.)
Permuted Choice 1 (PC-1)
57 49 41 33 25 17  9
1  58 50 42 34 26 18
10 2  59 51 43 35 27
19 11 3  60 52 44 36
63 55 47 39 31 23 15
7  62 54 46 38 30 22
14 6  61 53 45 37 29
21 13 5  28 20 12  4
```

In actuality, the remainder of the DES algorithm could easily fill six or seven pages! What I've shown you is just a small portion of the entire recipe. Interestingly, although DES is complex, it was found to have serious flaws that were exposed in 1998. These flaws lead teams of cryptographers to re-work DES because the original algorithm could be cracked and was no longer considered safe to use. The algorithm the cryptographers came up with to replace DES is called *3DES (Triple DES)*. I' tell you more about 3DES in Chapter 2 about algorithms.

Rockin' the rhythm

The reason that algorithms are so complex is to ensure that they can't be easily broken. It wouldn't do a spy any good to send out a secret message if everyone in the world could crack the code and read it. The algorithms we use today have been tested by crypto experts to check their strength, but sometimes it takes years to find the fatal flaw. When this happens, notices are sent out via vendors and the media to let users know that they may need to make some changes in encryption programs they are using.

Most algorithms are mind-numbingly complex mathematical equations — or at least they appear that way to me! Fortunately, you normally don't have to deal with the algorithm itself — the encryption software does that for you. For that reason, I'm not going to dwell on the math behind the science. Just like you don't need to be a mechanical genius to drive a car, you don't need to be a mathematician to be able to use encryption products. (Hooray!)
For most encryption products, the most difficult part is the initial setup. After that, the scrambling and unscrambling is mostly done without your interaction.

There are tons of different algorithms used in the world of cryptography. Why? For the same reason you use different recipes to make a cake. Some recipes are better, some recipes are easier, and some recipes depend on time and care to make them turn out right. The same thing happens with algorithms — we need to use faster, easier, stronger algorithms, and some are better than others at accomplishing the task. It all depends on your needs as to which algorithms you'll eventually use in your system.

There are also tons of arguments as to what makes a good algorithm and what makes a bad algorithm. Get any three crypto geeks in a room to discuss the differences and, chances are, they'll still be arguing a week later. Good algorithms are generally referred to as *strong crypto* and bad algorithms are called *weak crypto*. You'll find arguments galore in newsletters and mail lists that attempt to describe why one algorithm is better than the other. You'll need to know at least the basics on how to tell one from the other, so you'll be seeing information on good versus bad later on in this book. Often the problem has more to do with the installation and setup of the software than problems with the product or the algorithm.

Starting with this chapter, I give you the plain, old-fashioned basics that are good for you to know. This subject is really complex, and humongous tomes have been written by others, but that's not what I'll be doing here. I know you're not trying to get a college degree on the subject — you just want to know enough to buy the right stuff, install it correctly, and be able to use it. If that's what you want, then you've got the right book!

Getting to Know the Basic Terms

I'm going to start you off with some introductory terms. These are not meant to confuse you; rather, they are meant to gradually introduce you to some of the lingo used in cryptography.

- **Encrypt:** Scrambling data to make it unrecognizable
- **Decrypt:** Unscrambling data to its original format
- **Cipher:** Another word for *algorithm*
- **Key:** A complex sequence of alpha-numeric characters, produced by the algorithm, that allows you to scramble and unscramble data
- **Plaintext:** Decrypted or unencrypted data (it doesn't have to be text only)
- **Ciphertext:** Data that has been encrypted

Cryptography through the ages

Making secret messages and then sending them on to someone else to figure out is nothing new. The ancient Greeks used ciphers to send secret messages to their armies in the field. Benedict Arnold used a cipher based on a book called Blackstone's *Commentaries* (a book of essays about the law). In one sense, the Egyptian hieroglyphics can also be considered to be ciphers.

Ciphers really came into their own during WWI and WWII. Entire military and government departments were dedicated to the tasks of coming up with new methods of making secret messages. In addition to making secret messages, these offices also had to figure out how to decrypt the enemy's secret messages. It was from that base of intelligence that modern cryptography has come to be. The government soon discovered that, war or no war, they still had to create secret messages.

I want to mention *keys* at this point because they are all-important to cryptography. A *key* locks and unlocks secret messages — just like a door key locks and unlocks doors. Because keys are central to good cryptography, you can be sure that you'll be learning much more about them in Chapter 4. For now, though, I'm going to keep focused on ciphers and discuss some of the common cipher types.

What Makes a Cipher?

Over the ages there have been as many ways to hide and change data as there have been changes in clothing fashions. Likewise, some of these ciphers have fallen out of fashion while others have become classics.

Generally, ciphers are much simpler forms of algorithms than we use today. Many of these early ciphers were very easy to crack. In today's algorithms, we use the principles of these early ciphers, but much complexity has been added to make them harder to crack. Here, then, are some of the basic ciphers from which our modern cryptography has emerged.

Concealment ciphers

Concealment ciphers have been used for centuries to hide a message in plain sight. They have been used to give orders to troops at war, to tell spies where to meet their contacts, and to even help people like Mary, Queen of Scots, coordinate rendezvous times with her admirers.

The next paragraph is an example of a very old concealment cipher that was given to a prisoner in England during the time of Oliver Cromwell. Hidden within the message are the instructions to the prisoner on how to escape:

> *Worthie Sir John: Hope, that is the best comfort of the afflicated, cannot much, I fear me, help you now. That I would saye to you, is this only: if ever I may be able to requite that I do owe you, stand not upon asking me: Tis not much I can do: but what I can do, bee you verie sure I wille. I knowe that, if deathe comes, if ordinary men fear it, it frights not you, accounting is for a high hounour, to have such a rewarde of your loyalty. Pray yet that you may be spare this soe bitter, cup, I fear not that you will grudge any suffereings; onlie if bie submission you can turn them away, tis the part of a wise man. Tell me, as If you can, I do for you anything that you can wolde have done. The general goes back on Wednesday. Restinge your servant to command. R.J.*

I don't know how the key was given to the prisoner so he could decrypt the message, but the key is, "the third letter after every punctuation mark." If you follow that key, you will find that the concealed message is:

"panel at east end of chapel slides"

And, yes, the prisoner did escape! He asked to go to the chapel prior to his execution so he could pray for his soul. The guards left him in the chapel and manned the entrance. When they figured he had had long enough and went in to check on him, surprise! No prisoner! How do you explain that one to the King?

Substitution ciphers

Just as it sounds, a *substitution cipher* substitutes one letter or character for another. As a child you may have gotten a secret decoder ring from an offer on a cereal box or chocolate milk powder. The decoder ring consisted of two dials, both containing all the letters of the alphabet. The trick was to twirl one dial around the other so that the letters of the alphabet did not match up. Then you found the letter you wanted to use on one ring and substituted the letter on the other ring. Carry on letter by letter and then you have a secret message. Although this is technically not a ring shown below, here's an example of how the substitutions would line up:

```
A B C D E F G H I J K L M N O P Q R S T U V W X Y Z
S T U V W X Y Z A B C D E F G H I J K L M N O P Q R
```

Using the graph above, you would locate your letter and then substitute it with the letter directly below it. Therefore, the phrase:

```
ATTACK AT DAWN AT THE NORTHERN BRIDGE
```

would become

```
SLLSUC SL VSOF SL LZW FGJLZWJF TJAVYW
```

Of course to decrypt your message, your intended recipient would also have to have a decoder ring and he would need to know how far to twirl his dial so it matched yours. This number would indicate the switch in letters — and it is also the key to decrypting the message. In the example above, the switch is 18 letters to the right of the letter *A;* therefore, the key is "18." This cipher is probably one of the best known in the world and is also referred to as the "Caesar Cipher" because of historical references linking Julius Caesar and this type of cipher.

Transposition ciphers

One of the oldest known ciphers is called a *transposition cipher*. This type of cipher changes the order of the letters of the original message. One method is to write the message in a series of columns and rows in a grid — or you could write the message backwards. One of the oldest transposition ciphers is the Spartan *scytale* (also spelled as *skytale*). This information comes from Plutarch, who was an ancient Greek priest and scholar. Plutarch tells how Lacedaemonian generals exchanged messages by winding a narrow ribbon of parchment spirally around a staff or a spear. The message was then written length-wise across the wound-up parchment. When the parchment was unwound, you could only see parts of words or phrases that were written and the pattern of the words seemed random. This cipher could be read only by the person who had a spear of exactly the same circumference, who could rewind the parchment, so that the letters would reappear in their original order. If the spear used was too thick or too skinny, the words would not match up when the parchment was wound around it. So, in this case the receiver had to be aware of two secrets — or two keys — to read the message.

The German Enigma cipher machine

The most commonly known substitution cipher is the Enigma machine that was used by the Germans in World War II to encrypt their secret military messages. The Enigma machine looked roughly like a typewriter except that it had a number of different rotors, sort of like the odometer on your car. These rotors were placed next to one another on a shaft and then spun to set the shift in letters for substitution. But because there was more than one substitution involved, the messages were even more scrambled than using the single substitution I used in the example above.

The Enigma machine was one of the first usages of a strong cipher. It took the concerted effort of many nations, many minds, and a number of years to finally crack the Enigma code.

He had to know to wind the parchment around a spear of some sort, and he also had to know how thick the pole should be.

While substitution ciphers preserve the order of the letters used in the message, transposition ciphers reorder the letters. Transposition ciphers are rarely used nowadays, but they have been very important in the past. Although there are literally hundreds of different types, I'm going to show you one of the simpler ones. You can do this one yourself — all you need is paper and a pencil.

The encrypted message gets to you looking like this:

```
GRYSO IISAU  VNTFS EKOEE EEAHX
```

The key to this cipher is a block grid. If you know how many rows and columns are on the grid, then you can decrypt the message. Looking at the grid below, can you see how the message was created and what the message really says?

G	I	V	E	E
R	I	N	K	E
Y	S	T	O	A
S	A	F	E	H
O	U	S	E	X

Solution: if you read *down* the columns, you see the encrypted message. If you read *across* the rows, you can decrypt the message, which reads: *GIVE ERIN KEYS TO A SAFEHOUSE X.*

You may have noticed that the encrypted message did not match the same spacing as the decrypted message. That's done on purpose to (hopefully) confuse you further. If you don't know where one word starts and another begins, it makes it harder for a casual viewer to make any sense of what's written. In many old encrypted messages you'll note that the messages are in all caps and are written out in groups of five letters. In fact, it has become a standard to type a message in groups of five letters for simple encrypted messages.

Hash without the corned beef

A small departure from the ciphers I've been discussing comes under the heading of hashes. A *hash* is not meant to be decrypted. "What," you say? That's right. A hash is what is referred to as a *one-way function* — you use a hash to encrypt something, but the result is never decrypted.

The purpose of a hash is to create a "fingerprint" of your data. The hash algorithm goes through its permutations, and the result is a bunch of alpha-17 fixed lengths.) The purpose of a hash is to prove the integrity of the data (encrypted or not) that has been sent. When you receive the data, the hash is included at the bottom of the data. You can run the same hash algorithm against the data you receive, and if the data has not been changed en route, you will get the same set of alpha-numeric characters. If your result is not the same, then something happened during the transmission and the data you received was changed from the original.

Many software companies include a hash value with their programs. That way, you can check to see if the software you got matches the value the software vendor sends you. If they don't match, then you need to get another copy of the software. Any software can be hijacked and have Trojans or other malicious programs inserted into them. A hash helps you detect whether or not this is a possibility.

I have much more information on hashes in Chapter 4.

XOR what?

Now I'll probably be slammed by all the brilliant crypto-geeks in the world for putting XOR here because it is not really a cipher. It's actually a mathematical *operation*. I'll justify putting it here because a majority of modern algorithms use the XOR operation during the encryption process.

Yes, the operation is pronounced just like it looks: *Ex-Or*. When I first heard this uttered, I thought there might be something missing from the person's statement. Was he trying to say, "Ex, or else" or "X or Y"? I finally asked "Ex, or what?" and soon discovered that XOR stands for *Exclusive-Or*. Although the name of this operation does sound silly, it's one of those things that you are bound to hear associated with modern cryptography.

When you see an algorithm diagram, you'll see the symbol for XOR, shown here in Figure 1-1.

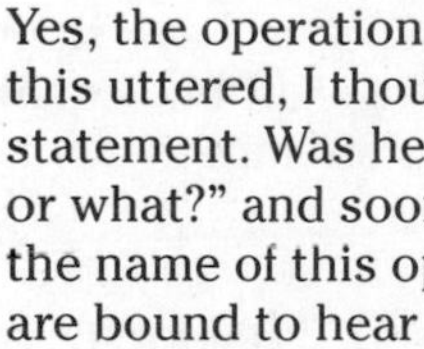

Figure 1-1:
The symbol
for XOR.

= XOR

You'll often hear snake oil salespeople tell you that their software encrypts data with XOR. These salespeople either don't know what they are talking about or they are out to deceive you. Many buyers have discovered, to their dismay, that a simple XOR operation is practically no encryption at all, and it's very easy to break. So if you hear someone tell you that their product "encrypts" with XOR only, you'll know that person is selling nothing more than snake oil — in other words, nothing worth purchasing. On the other hand, if XOR is done numerous times throughout the encryption process, it has the possibility of making the algorithm stronger.

XOR is possible because of binary code. You know, that code where the characters on your keyboard are converted to ones and zeroes, which correspond to the ASCII code for the characters on your keyboard? Yeah, that's the one. The binary code of 01100001 = 97 = a. Likewise, 01100010 = 98 = b. What XOR does is compare each of the zeroes and ones, in sequence, and, if the numbers are the same, it marks the spot with a zero. If the numbers are *not the same*, it places a one in that spot. It's kinda hard to explain completely in text, so I'll give you a visual example:

```
Plaintext  = baby = 01100010 01100001 01100010 01111001
XOR key    = data = 01100100 01100001 01110100 01100001
Ciphertext = ????   00000110 00000000 00010110 00011000
```

You've probably at least heard of *binary code* — the series of ones and zeroes in the example above are characters in their binary code form. Basically, a computer understands the electricity that passes through miniscule "gates" on its chips. If the gate is closed and no electricity can pass through, that's a zero. If the gate is open and the electricity can complete the connection, that's a one. But how do these ones and zeroes become characters that you can recognize?

First of all, the binary codes are limited to eight spaces. Each single space (a one or zero) is known as a *bit*. A combination of eight bits equals one *byte*. A byte also corresponds (in a computer's understanding) to a character.

If you count the ones and zeroes in the example above, you'll see that each has only eight ones and zeroes in a block of space — that's a byte. Before those ones and zeroes can be changed to a character, their numeric value is calculated first. Rather than go through the entire mathematical explanation of how to count in binary math (also known as Base 2 or 1^2), I'll give you an example you can relate to.

Not to give away my age, but I was taught how to use an abacus when I was in grade school. If you travel to Asia today, you'll see that many shopkeepers still use an abacus as a calculator to figure out how much you owe them. An abacus simply uses beads on a dowel that are used as a place-maker to help you count and add. Believe it or not, binary code numbers can be counted and added the same way. Here's how:

128	64	32	16	8	4	2	1	Value of each bit in a byte
0	1	1	0	0	0	1	0	0 = Don't Count
								1= Do Count
0	64	32	0	0	0	2	0	64 + 32 + 2 = 98

So, what you see is that each one or zero is a place holder or a marker for the numbers along the top of the table. If you see a 0 in the row below the number, it means "Don't count this number." If you see a 1 in the row below the number, it means "Yes, count this number."

You count from left to right in this case, first looking to see if there is a one in the 1 column; there isn't, so I don't count the 1. However, there is a 1 beneath the 2 column, so I do count that. As a went along, I found that I needed to count the numbers 2, 32, and 64. When you add those all together, you get the number 98.

Now comes the easy part, and that's called *ASCII* (American Standard Code for Information Interchange). This is simply a table that assigns a keyboard character to the numbers 0 to 256 (if you added all the numbers in a byte, the maximum number is 256). As it so happens, the number 98 corresponds to the lower case "b" on the ASCII table.

There are a number of Web sites that explain the ASCII table and can do conversions for you. Here's the one I used to look up the codes for my example: www.ascii.cl/index.htm.

The encrypted data in my example actually comes out as ^F^@^V^Z, which are actually control codes used by your computer (holding down the Ctrl key and tapping another key produced a control code). I know if I got a message in the mail that looked like that, I wouldn't have a clue as to what it really was!

What's really cool about XOR (or maybe not, depending on whether you are using it for security or for fun) is that you can see how easily you can get back to the plaintext by reversing the operation:

```
Ciphertext = ????   00000110 00000000 00010110 00011000
XOR key    = data = 01100100 01100001 01110100 01100001
Plaintext  = baby = 01100010 01100001 01100010 01111001
```

Of course the key to decrypting the message is knowing what characters were used for the XOR key. In this example I used the word *data*.

That's all there really is to XOR. It's just magical enough to be fun for people who were never good at math (like me!) For cryptographers, coding in XOR is easy and, if there are a number of iterations of XOR throughout the algorithm, it's pretty effective at giving data a good jumble.

Breaking Ciphers

One big problem with ancient ciphers is that they were easily figured out, and the secret messages weren't secret for very long. As cryptography got more complex, the secret messages stayed secret for a longer period. As I mention in a sidebar earlier in the chapter, the Enigma machine took several years to break and it was finally cracked through a combination of eavesdropping, engineering, pattern recognition, human laziness (on the German side), and some sheer luck. The Enigma team listened and heard clacking and clicking, which told them they were dealing with a machine, and then they managed to make a duplicate machine themselves (and got it right with luck). They noticed that some messages started with the same grouping of letters and were very lucky that the Germans used the same phrases many times to synchronize remote machines.

Not-so-secret keys

If you leave the keys to your car in the ignition and the doors unlocked, what do you think the chances are that it will be stolen soon? (If it's a new Mercedes SL55 AMG valued at over $110,000, I'd say the chances are pretty good that it would be gone by morning.) The point is, if you leave the keys where other people can find them, you're the one to blame. One of the biggest weaknesses in cryptography has been the poor use or sharing of keys. Like your password, you don't write it on a sticky note and put it on your monitor. (Do people still do that?)

The art of cryptanalysis

Cryptanalysis is the art of breaking ciphers, and the National Security Agency (NSA) is renowned as one of the world's largest employers of crypt-analysts. The CIA is also very into crypto (which makes sense, as they are the home of spy versus spy), and they have a crypto challenge for anyone who wants to give it a try. When the new CIA headquarters was built in 1990, a sculpture called "Kryptos" was installed in front of the main entrance. The sculpture is an encrypted message. Part of the code has been cracked, but the man who got it spent more than 400 hours on it before he even got close to cracking just the first part. He finally managed all but the last 97 characters. If you want to give it a try, visit www.odci.gov/cia/information/tour/kryptos_code.html.

Key-length is mentioned a lot in books and articles about cryptography. That's because the longer the key (drum roll, please), the harder it is to guess what the key is! All the examples of keys I've given you in this chapter are very short, very easy keys. Even if these keys weren't already common knowledge, they still wouldn't take long to guess. You could probably even do it with plain old paper and pencil.

The job of keeping keys a secret has been one that has plagued us for centuries. You have to share the key at some point in some manner, or the recipient won't be able to decipher the message. This is such a major job that I've devoted all of Chapter 7 to the subject of managing keys.

Known plaintext

If you know for certain both a plaintext word and its ciphertext mate in a message, it can make cracking the message a piece of cake. For example, if you look at an encrypted message with a string of characters like XROL and you know that it means CAKE, you can go through the entire message substituting all the Xs with Cs, Rs with As, and so on. If nothing else, it can certainly give you a clue as to what the words might be. It's kind of like playing *Wheel of Fortune.* If you play around with these variations long enough, you might just discover the key for the entire message.

Pattern recognition

The first thing you look for when you're trying to break a code is a pattern in the encrypted message. For example, the letter *E* is the most commonly used letter in the English language, so you look for a letter in the message that is used more than any of the others. That *may* indicate that that particular letter is actually the letter *E*. Failing that, the second most common letter in the English language is the letter *T*.

Finding a pattern was part of the solution for the man who has partially cracked the Kryptos sculpture at the CIA headquarters building (which I talk about a couple sections back). He looked long and hard for a grouping of letters that would correspond to the word *the*. Because *the* is extremely common in the English language, it's usually a safe bet to start there, and many cryptanalysts do.

What a brute!

If you've failed to decrypt a secret message by trying to figure out the key or by looking for patterns, you might just try banging your head against the wall. Brute force might just work.

I'm kind of joking and kind of not when I list *brute force* as a method of breaking an encrypted message or file. Actually it's done quite often thanks to computers getting faster and the ability of linking computers together for strength and will power. In some cases, computers working in parallel can be more powerful than one of the most powerful computers used by the NSA.

Brute force is a trial and error method of trying every possible combination of characters against the encrypted data in an attempt to discover the key. That's one of the reasons I always stress that you use the longest keys possible. For example, a 56-bit key has 2^{56} possible keys. That's more than 72 quadrillion keys that must potentially be tried in order to find the correct one. You might think that, given those numbers, a 56-bit key would be pretty safe then. Wrong. In 1997, a distributed computing effort cracked the RSA's 56-bit RC5 encryption in less than 250 days. One of the more famous brute force cracks was that of the DES algorithm. Many people didn't think it was possible to crack DES by using brute force, and everyone in the crypto world was talking about it when it happened.

Cryptosystems

By definition, a *cryptosystem* is the combination of three elements: the *encryption engine, keying information,* and *operational procedures* for their secure use. In other words, almost every encryption program can be considered a cryptosystem because it has everything together in one package. The encryption engine is the part of the software that starts the encryption with the selected algorithm, and the keying system is the portion of the software that creates (and sometimes manages) the keys needed to encrypt and decrypt data. The operational procedures are how all of these parts interact and how the output, or result, is formatted and what file extension (if any) is used. So, almost every encryption product you buy off the shelf is, in a sense, a cryptosystem. Some people may argue that a cryptosystem is the complete infrastructure of encryption programs, hardware, and network connections, but I'll stick to the more traditional definition.

Many of the self programs include more than one algorithm for you to use for encryption. Usually these programs give you a one type of algorithm — such as symmetric or asymmetric algorithms — for you to decide upon. Sometimes you'll see a drop-down list of the algorithms for use, or there will be a configuration setting in which you choose which you care to use. The differences between the algorithms are discussed in detail in Chapter 2, but it's safe to say that they come in two types: *symmetric,* which means one key is used, and *asymmetric,* which means two keys are used.

Because symmetric algorithms work much faster than asymmetric algorithms (again, more on that in Chapter 2), some cryptosystems use both types in their software package. This is referred to as *hybrid cryptosystems*. Usually with this type of system asymmetric algorithms are used to exchange two keys between sender and recipient, and a symmetric algorithm actually does the encryption.

That's all you need to know for now as I'll get into all of this stuff in much more detail as you read through this book, and I'll have many examples to help get the point across.

Everyday Uses of Encryption

Whether you realize it or not, there are a lot of ways that you deal with some form of encryption every day. As businesses now rely heavily on the Internet and other forms of networks to buy, sell, organize, inform, provide services, and form alliances, they also have to deal with the fact that sometimes these networks are transmitting very sensitive data. Some businesses decide on their own that protection of this data is a good thing, and others have either learn that through bad experiences or have to comply with new laws that deal with the protection of personal data.

Computers have become so insidious that many of us don't even realize sometimes that we are interacting with them. Most of these systems are encrypting the data as it goes across the wires. Have you used your debit card to buy gas at an automatic pump lately? Read on for some other examples of everyday encryption.

Network logons and passwords

When you log on to a network, either at home or at work, you are normally asked for your UserID (or User Name) and your password. When PCs first appeared, they didn't have the capability of networking, so there was no need for such security. But when networking software became generally available, businesses especially realized the need to keep unauthorized users off the networks and to compartmentalize which sections of a network the staff were allowed to roam. Hence, the UserID and password was the logical choice for controlling access.

Because there were (and are) various networking applications, not all the logon procedures were developed the same way. It's the same old story — all the vendors make their own version of networking, hoping that theirs will become the standard. Alas, we run into something very common in computing and networking, and that is applying the lowest common denominator in order to achieve interoperability.

At first, passwords were passed from the user's computer to the server in plaintext. Definitely not a good idea, but who would have thought that people would want to do harm with computers? Some sort of encryption had to be used to protect the passwords, so each of the vendors developed their own algorithms or hashes for accomplishing this task. The first encryption hashes were pretty dismal and could easily be cracked. To make a long story short, password encryption got better, but some elements of the older, crackable hashes had to be included for backward compatibility and other interoperability issues.

The remaining bad apple in the batch is called *LANMAN,* which stands for Local Area Network Manager.

LANMAN is a method of storing your password that Microsoft included so that your password could be exchanged with other non-Microsoft networks such as Novell. The trouble with LANMAN is the way that it is encrypted and stored on the computers. To be frank, it's the worst password encryption method I've ever seen — the passwords can be cracked in less time than it takes to blink an eye. Here's how the LANMAN encrypts and stores passwords:

- Passwords are converted to all uppercase characters.
- Password length is a maximum of 14 characters. If your password is longer than 14 characters, LANMAN shortens it. If your password is less than 14 characters, LANMAN "pads" it with extra character.
- When LANMAN "pads" a short password with extra characters, those extra characters are *always the same characters*, no matter what the original password is.
- The password is split into two, seven-character pieces.

So first of all, LANMAN breaks the rule of using upper- and lowercase characters in your password by changing all the characters to uppercase. For example, if your password was cATclaW, LANMAN stores it as CATCLAW. Secondly, because the next set of seven characters is always the same set of characters, hackers know they can just throw that portion away and concentrate on the first seven characters. Thirdly, the algorithm that Windows uses to encrypt the character is extremely weak and any password cracker worth its salt can crack them in no time.

Windows, by default, stores your password both in the LANMAN method and a stronger encryption method. Hackers don't have to bother much with the stronger stored version since the LANMAN is so easily cracked.

Although most Windows networks no longer have a need for LANMAN support, Windows still stores LM password hashes (also known as LANMAN hashes) by default on Windows NT, 2000 and XP systems (but not in Windows 2003). There is an article on Microsoft's support site on how to disable

LANMAN which can be found at: `http://support.microsoft.com/default.aspx?scid=kb;en-us;147706`.

If your system has LANMAN enabled and you don't absolutely need it, please disable it soon!

Secure Web transactions

The odds are in your favor that if you've ever purchased something from an online shop with your Web browser, you've interacted with at least one form of encryption. In fact, you should ensure that any shop you order from is using at least 128-bit encryption because otherwise, all of your personal information is probably not being protected — or at least not being protected to the fullest extent possible.

As I mention earlier, having your credit card number and personal data travel across the wires in the cleat is *not* a good thing! However, prior to 1995, there was no technology in place to ensure secure Web transactions. All personal data was sent in the clear, and you couldn't even verify who you were really sending that data to. Because it's very easy to hijack a transaction between your computer and a Web site without you even realizing it, you could be sending your credit card number to an imposter and you'd have no idea it happened.

In order to correct the problem of the Web sending and receiving data in the clear, some fixing had to be done to the HTTP protocol that handles the sending and receiving of data. *S-HTTP* (Secure HTTP) was created so messages and files could be sent encrypted. S-HTTP doesn't actually provide the encryption; it just makes it possible for encryption to be added on. But vendors competing against each other again resulted in the fact that not all Web browsers and servers can use S-HTTP. There go those standards again. . . .

Another fix created to solve the security problem was the creation of *SSL* (Secure Sockets Layer). SSL is designed to allow a secure connection between your browser and a Web server, and all data that travels between the two can be encrypted, not just individual messages like S-HTTP. Again, SSL doesn't actually provide the encryption; it just makes it possible for encryption to be used. SSL has become sort of a de-facto standard, and all Web browsers and servers are capable of using it. There are two levels of encryption available: 40-bit and 128-bit. The *bit* is the size of the key and, — and I'll keep harping about this — the longer the key, the better the security.

SSL and S-HTTP have very different designs and goals, so it is possible to use the two protocols together — and some merchants and banks do use both. You'll know when a secure connection has been established when a small key or lock appears in your browser's status bar (see Figure 1-2) and the URL has changed to "https" instead of just plain "http."

Figure 1-2:
When you
see the lock,
you know
you're
secure.

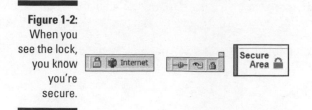

There's much more on secure e-commerce and encryption in Chapter 11. I tell you there how to check that 128-bit encryption is being used for secure transactions. I also talk about examining Web site certificates to check that they are authentic to verify a merchant or bank's identity.

ATMs

Ahhhhh, what would I do without ATMs nowadays? It's wonderful to be able to go downtown or travel overseas and not have to worry about stacks of bills in your wallet. No need to rob a bank; just stick your card in the hole in the wall, and the machine makes money on demand for you (or at least it seems that way).

A lot of famous stories and movies are about big bank robberies, and people seem to always cheer when the crafty robber gets away will millions and lives happily ever after. But, hey! That was your money the robber stole, too! Obviously, security is a big issue here. Banks have had to add much more physical security to their ATMs in the past few years, but they are also pretty good at keeping up on the back-end security through the use of encryption.

The magnetic strip on the back of your ATM card contains a wealth of information that is picked up by the bank's computers when you slide your card into the slot (or in a merchant's point-of-sale machine). One of the bits of data on the strip is your account number, encrypted of course. When you enter your PIN, an encryption key is compared to an encrypted account number to see if they match. If they do, you're in luck. Punch in the wrong PIN too many times and the machine slurps up your card.

But just because your bank utilizes encryption when handling transactions, don't be lulled into a false sense of security. The *implementation* of encryption has to be good or the security can be breached. In 2001, two university student researchers in England found a huge hole in the way most systems were handling encryption of the account number. It wasn't the banks' fault — the vendor who sold them the systems for handling their ATM transactions had goofed. It turned out that the first four digits of the account number were always sent in the clear! The students used this information to eventually get the 3DES key used for encryption, and they were able to demonstrate that they could then crack up to 7,000 PINs per hour.

This didn't get too much media coverage in the United States, but luckily the amount of press this was getting overseas forced the computer vendor to come up with a fix for the system.

Music and DVDs

If you haven't heard of the *DMCA* (Digital Millennium Copyright Act of 1998), then you probably don't get into copying DVD movies or downloading music from the Internet. I don't want to get started on whether the DMCA is a good thing or not — that's a huge and contentious issue in itself and doesn't really have anything to do with cryptography except that the DMCA allows film and music companies to protect their copyrights with encryption.

Each DVD player sold has a computer chip in it that contains a decryption key so it can read the encrypted portion of a DVD disc. The computer chip is also contains a country code that matches where the DVD player will be sold and used (assumedly, in any case).

When the DVD discs are made, a section of the disc is encrypted by the music industry's proprietary system called *CSS* (Content Scrambling System). This system encrypts part of the disc with a country code — sort of like the country codes for the telephone system. One code is used for North America, another for the South Pacific, and so on.

Now comes the fun part. If you buy your DVD player in Japan and try to play a DVD bought in America, the disc won't play. That's because CSS is an access control system that prevents the playback of discs on players that don't have the decryption keys that the movie industry provides to authorized manufacturers. Many, many people don't know this and have found out the hard way when they try to play the movie they bought while vacationing in England orsomewhere other than the United States.

There's a young man in Norway who owned some DVD movies and wanted to watch them on a computer he built, but the computer did not have the ability to read the encrypted code on the DVD discs. So, he wrote a program he called DeCSS and installed it on his computer. It worked! He could now watch his movies on his computer. The young man was so pleased with it, he put it on the Internet to distribute for free. That was probably his first big mistake.

Part of the DMCA says that the manufacturing of or trafficking in technologies capable of circumventing technical protection measures used to restrict access to copyrighted works is highly illegal. Well, the young man did circumvent the technical protection on DVD discs, and he made it available for distribution. The guy has been tried and acquited for this crime once, but it looks like another trial may be coming up soon.

I'm not arguing who's right or who's wrong here; I just wanted you to be aware of the fact that sometimes the use of cryptography gets just a little bit sticky.

Communication devices

Until about 10 years ago, everything you said over a cell phone could be picked up and listened to over a simple, inexpensive Radio Shack radio scanner. There were huge scandals in the UK when tapes of Princess Di's cell phone conversations were released to the tabloid press. It seems a lot of people like to eavesdrop on others' conversations. Even Newt Gingrich was stung when his cell phone conversations showed up in the press.

The majority of cell phones in America have their phone numbers and voice transmissions encrypted, but only to a certain point. The part of the call between the cell phone and the tower is encrypted, but as soon as the conversation reaches your provider's gateway to the land-line phone system, it's decrypted. That's right, all land-line telephone communications (with the exception of government and military systems) are unencrypted. If you know how and where to place a gator clip and a phone receiver, you can listen in on anyone's phone calls.

The GSM (Groupe Speciale Mobile) wireless phone is the standard in Europe and is the world's most widely used cellular technology. More than 215 million digital phones use it worldwide, including more than 100 million in Europe and 5 million in the United States. GSM transmissions are encrypted, but the A5/1 algorithm keys, which are used to scramble and unscramble the data, are much shorter than advertised and thus much easier to break.

Why Encryption Isn't More Commonplace

Until fairly recently, it was unlawful for average American citizens to even own encryption technology. That was the realm of the NSA, and all encryption products were tightly controlled. In the early 1990s, a number of privacy activists and cryptographers helped loosen the restrictions on who could own encryption, and the courts have since ruled that we have the right to privacy in our communications and storage of our own data. Given that our right to own and use encryption is so new, it's not surprising that not many people know much about it.

Now the market is burgeoning with new products and encryption technologies, which makes it even more difficult for people to decide what to buy and implement — if they decide on encryption at all! However, some states are passing laws stating that companies that store personal information need to use cryptography to protect that information. It's likely that we will see a wave a new laws like these over the next five years.

Another thought that comes to mind is the Internet. Again, until recently, we trusted the Internet and saw no need to protect ourselves. But with hacking and identity theft becoming more common, it makes sense to start looking at ways to protect ourselves and our information.

Difficulty in understanding the technology

By and large, encryption programs have suffered from a lack of intuitive interfaces — if people don't understand how to use the software, they won't use it. Period. This is the fault of the developers. They seem to have forgotten that cryptography is new to most users.

The graphical interface to many encryption programs was almost indecipherable, even to people like me who know what they are doing. It's no wonder then that people who have bought encryption products have never gotten around to use them. They don't know how to work the commands and menus.

Another reason people find cryptography so hard to understand is that the creators of cryptosystems — usually mathematicians — are the same ones who have written most of the textbooks explaining the subjects. Now, I don't want aeronautical engineers explaining to me how a plane flies because I won't understand what they are saying. For that same reason, I don't want a mathematician to explain to me how to encrypt my e-mail. Because of this I have taken the non-mathematical route to explaining how cryptography works.

Luckily, things are changing in the world of cryptography. User interfaces for encryption products are becoming easier to use, and publishers are seeing the need for easy-to-understand books (like this one) for these products. The vendors themselves are also helping by putting large amounts of "How-To" information on their Web sites with FAQs (Frequently Asked Questions) to help you find the answer to your problem.

You can't do it alone

One of the biggest problems with cryptography is that you can't do it alone! You need at least two people — a sender and a receiver. Otherwise, the encrypted files or messages just sit there. It's sort of like when the first video phones appeared — there was no sense in buying one for yourself if you didn't have anyone to call who had one, too. What's the point in showing your face on the telephone line if there's no one on the other side to see it?

If you're going to be receiving encrypted files and messages, you need to have the same software, or compatible software, as the sender. That's simple common sense. Likewise, if you are sending encrypted files or messages, you need to be sure that the people on the receiving end have some means of decrypting what you've sent.

Luckily, many products operate on similar standards and can be made to work with similar products. It may take a bit of trial and error to get it working correctly, but the good news is that you usually have to do that only once.

Sharing those ugly secrets

If I ask you to water my houseplants while I'm on vacation, you'll obviously need the key to get into the house. If I don't have the opportunity to hand you the key in person, I'll have to hide it somewhere and then let you know where it is. I can't leave a message on the front door — that would be too easy for someone else to intercept. I shouldn't put the key under the doormat because that's usually the first place a thief looks. I could call you on the phone and tell you the location of the key, but how do I know that I'm really talking to you?

That last scenario may be a bit far-fetched, but I'm sure you can see my point by now. How do you share a secret without letting the whole world know? That, in a nutshell, is the largest problem facing cryptography — how do you safely and securely share the keys? There are tons and tons of papers and books covering this subject alone. It's safe to say that modern cryptography products do have ways of safely sharing the keys, but it takes some effort and common sense on the users' part, too.

I'll be covering keys and the correct methods of sharing them in Chapter 4. In fact, there will be so much about this subject that I'm likely to get you all keyed up! (Ouch!)

Cost may be a factor

Although there are free crypto products available for use, few of them are suitable for a business environment. Then, as with all business decisions, whether or not to employ cryptography comes down to the question of how much it will cost. As I mention earlier, you can't do it alone, so you also have to make sure that your solution will interoperate with what your partners and customers are using.

In addition to the cost of the crypto products themselves, you also have to take into account the man-hours spent just coming to a decision. There's a lot of research to do (much of which I help you with), and you may need to add servers and sub-nets to your existing network. There is time and money involved in the setup and configuration of the system, the training of users, and personnel to handle maintenance of the system.

This may seem like an overwhelming task at first, but I help you break it down so you can make a decision that you can ultimately afford. When it comes to crypto products, newer is not necessarily better, as I discuss throughout this book. The last thing you want to do is to buy crypto products solely based on their "gee-whiz" appeal.

Special administration requirements

Crypto products require special handling, which means that you need to have experienced staff to operate and maintain the systems. This is not something the accountant can do as an adjunct to his or her normal duties; you need a skilled professional. Why? Because if your crypto systems are not set up and maintained correctly, you run the risk of exposing all of your secrets. In addition, your staff will lose their keys and forget their passphrases, and new users need to be added to the system and trained on its use. If you're trying to increase the security of your system and protect your company's assets, you might as well do the job as well as you can. In this case, "good enough" sometimes *isn't* enough.

You'll find information on identifying your requirements, deciding what you need, and telling good products from bad products in the following chapters. I also give you sneak peeks into various products you may encounter, and I give you a really good description of that incredibly elusive beast, *PKI* (Public Key Infrastructure). I explain more about PKI in the chapters in Part II.

Thanks for staying with me so far — now let the journey begin.

Chapter 2

Major League Algorithms

*I*n Chapter 1, I discuss some of the ancient methods of encrypting messages that needed to be kept secret. While all of those methods were effective at the time they were created, the decryption method was eventually discovered, and the secret messages were not so secret anymore. In all of these situations, both the method of encryption (the algorithm) and the key were discovered. What did that mean? It meant that the interceptor of the message was able to find the key, and with that was able to decrypt the message.

Over the decades, many agencies, companies, and individuals developed more and more sophisticated algorithms. Of course they also developed more complex keys to go with those algorithms so the secret messages could be decrypted so easily. In every case, whether the algorithm was made public or not, someone figured out the algorithm and published the results. It turned out that it is relatively easy (for cryptanalysts or very experienced programmers, that is) to crack algorithms. The algorithms can be reverse engineered, and the internal workings can be made known.

In 1987, RSA Data Security developed an algorithm called *RC4*. They had cryptanalysts test it, and the tests proved that RC4 was a good algorithm. Now, instead of publishing the algorithm, RSA decided to keep the inner workings of RC4 to themselves in the hope that they could license it and make money off the algorithm itself. In 1994, the inner workings of RC4 mysteriously appeared on the Internet for all the world to see. Because the secret was out, RSA could no longer sell the algorithm, and it was back to the drawing board for them.

What the RSA/RC4 example proves is that the internal workings of an algorithm *are always discovered*. Talented people can reverse-engineer software that uses an algorithm. Even if the entire workings are not immediately evident, cryptanalysts can make some very educated guesses. Well, if that is true, how do you keep the data safe if everyone knows how it's done? The solution is in the key. The key to unlocking the algorithm, that is. If you can keep the key unknown and unknowable, that goes a very long way in keeping the data safe from prying eyes.

Look at it this way: We all know how the lock on a door works. There are a series of small round bars called tumblers that, when lined up correctly, drop out of the way, removing the obstruction, so you can turn the key and open the door. But, just because you know *how* a door lock works does not mean that you can find the right key. (I'm not talking about locksmiths and burglars; I'm talking about average folk here.) It takes a lot of time and trouble to find the correct key. Yes, that is a simplistic view, but I think you get the point.

In modern cryptography, the developers of algorithms are quite happy to release information on how the algorithm works because they have created new ways of making stronger keys. Keys nowadays are made from very long prime numbers and the longer the key, the better the security. (Prime numbers can be divided only by the number 1 and the number itself. For example, 7 is a prime number.) In addition, some keys are also encrypted themselves. So, even if you find the key, you have to figure out how to decrypt it. It's important to know, too, that the keys are just data files, so they look just like the rest of the encrypted data. It takes a degree of skill to be able to recognize a key and separate it from the rest of the message or file.

Beware of "Snake Oil"

In most software and hardware markets, the latest and greatest product is the one that everyone wants. People like all the bells and whistles in the new product, and they gobble up the marketing literature that gives you 101 reasons why this product is the answer to all of your prayers. In the world of cryptography, almost the exact opposite is true — nothing new is trusted until it has been extensively tested by the outside world.

Snake oil refers to any crypto product that vendors oversell as a cure-all. It harkens back to the frontier days when pharmacists and traveling salesmen sold products of a dubious nature that were supposed to cure everything. They wouldn't tell you exactly what was in it, but they assured you that it worked.

Cryptographic software and hardware has sometimes been sold the same way. The makers of this magic stuff all assure you that it works in "new and previously untried ways." The salespeople will make promise after promise of all the wondrous things the software is capable of, but will not be able to provide you with one verifiable test that upholds their claims. Nor will they give you any technical data on the inner workings of their product. These things should be enormous red flags to potential buyers. If you can't get hard data on how a cryptosystem works, it's very likely to be snake oil. Buy it and you will get bit by the snake.

Here are some things you should look out for when reviewing cryptosystems for signs of snake oil:

- The marketing literature and technical literature are full of technobabble. If you can't make sense of what is being said, how can you expect to be able to implement it? Run it by your IT Department to see if they can make sense of the hype. These types of cryptosystems are trying to baffle you into thinking they are brilliant.

- The company tells you that the algorithm is *unbreakable*. Believe me when I tell you that every algorithm is breakable. It may take 100 years or 10,000 years, but someone will find a way of breaking the algorithm.

- They claim that their product uses *military-strength* encryption. Do you really think that the military would tell the general public which algorithms they use? Exactly how safe would the military's secret be if every terrorist group in the world knew what they were using? Of course, some sales people confuse the term "military strength" with the fact that the encryption has been reviewed by the military. Just because the encryption has been reviewed by the military (or the NSA) does not necessarily equal military strength.

- They claim to use *secret algorithms*. That's right up there with "military-strength" encryption as a red flag indicating snake oil. All the crypto experts will tell you that for an algorithm to be determined good, it has to be tested by people who had nothing to do with the development of the algorithm. It's a commonly known fact that writers can't see their own typographical errors — that's why there are editors. In the same vein, developers of algorithms can't see their own errors, and it takes an outside expert to discover them. There are scores of mathematicians who are ready, willing, and able to test algorithms. Some of them even do it for a living.

- The claim that *You don't need to know what the product is doing* or the *Trust Us* plea is a good indication of snake oil. This usually means that either the vendor doesn't know how the product works or they are just lying to you.

✔ The claim that the algorithm has been *tested by hackers* is totally bogus. Excuse me, but hackers don't know much about algorithms; they know operating systems, network protocols, software, and programming. This does not make them experts in cryptography.

✔ They claim that *experts* evaluated their product and found it safe or strong. If a vendor is using experts, they won't mind listing the papers the experts have written. These papers are often used to establish who is an expert and who is not. Chances are that if you've never heard of the expert and the expert has never been published, that person is not an accepted expert on the subject.

✔ The claim that the software and/or algorithm are *exportable from the U.S.* is also a red flag. For those who are not aware of it, the U.S. government restricts the export of strong encryption to many foreign countries. If the encryption used in the product you are considering is "export strength," it could mean that it's not very strong (like only 40-bit encryption). If the encryption is "strong" and the vendor states that it is "exportable," that could also mean that you may have to comply with a number of government rules and regulations concerning its export. (For more on this, read Appendix B at the back of the book.)

You should take all encryption products' marketing literature with a grain of salt. They are all in the market to make money. You should look at their list of claims and compare them to the snake oil flags listed above. If the marketing brochure contains only one of the claims above, it could well be that the marketing staff is clueless about encryption products. On the other hand, if the marketing brochure lists many of the points mentioned above, the chances are pretty great that you are dealing with snake oil.

Although cryptography and encryption techniques and algorithms are complex subjects, the software and hardware vendors are attempting to sell their products to non-experts. For that reason alone, the vendors should have materials that explain what their products do and how they do it in simple terms that the average user can understand. If you can't understand what the vendor is talking about, ask to see their installation guidelines or their user guides. You have to be able to understand how to install and implement a system in order to use it correctly. If you mess up the installation and implementation, the encryption will be flawed, which is almost as bad as not having encryption because it gives you a false sense of security.

As for the "new" algorithms, certainly there are new algorithms being created on a constant basis, but there are also many very good algorithms that have been widely tested and are freely available. You can get the source code for these algorithms for free at most university Web sites and other sites dedicated to cryptography. In this case, it's better to chose the devil you know over the devil you don't. There are always forums and newsgroups on the Internet dedicated to cryptography who are very good at steering newbies in the right direction.

But, enough of the bad news, let's get on with the good news: encryption techniques and algorithms that work!

Symmetric Keys Are All the Same

That's a bad joke, of course. What I really mean is that symmetric algorithms all use one key to encrypt data and the same key to decrypt it. That's why they are called *symmetric*. Your front door key is also symmetric — you use the same key to lock your door as you do to unlock it. The secret to the security of your front door is that you (hopefully) have the key with you at all times and you don't give a copy to anyone else. If you do trust someone else with the key, it will always be an exact copy of the one you have.

The success of the key is how *random* the number is that starts the process of generating a key. There's more on the randomness of numbers in a bit, but it's important for you to know that the success — and failure — of some algorithms is directly related to the randomness of the number in the key.

The key table

When the user of a symmetric algorithm creates a key, most symmetric algorithms create a *key table* from the original key. This is also known as the *key setup* or *initialization*. Not to make things more confusing than they need to be, but it's actually the key table that is used to encrypt the data. The trick is that the original key is mathematically tied to the key table so, as long as you have the original key, the key table can be created.

Think of the original key as a model or mold for all the other keys in the key table. It's kind of like making a batch of muffins — they are all made from the same recipe (the original key), but none of them are exactly the same. I'm oversimplifying, of course, and I don't want you to get too hung up on the key table concept. You're bound to hear about it when discussing crypto products with vendors, though, so I want you to at least have a basic idea of what they are talking about. By the way, if a vendor tells you that their product *reuses* the key table, that's a *bad thing!*

To better give you an example of how a key table works, I've created the following pretend key table. I'm using a portion of the alphabet as the key and then using the letters in that key to create alternate keys. Here's a short example:

KEY	KEY TABLE
ABCDEFG	GFEABCDGFE
	CDCDABFGEE
	AABBGCFFDE

You'll note that the keys in the key table are longer than the original key. That's because the keys in the table are *supposed* to be longer than the original key. It's just the way the algorithm was written. It's not really important that you understand how a key table works.

Key generation and random numbers

The key in a symmetric algorithm starts with a number. Of course, the longer the number the better. When you create one key for one message and then another key for another message, you want to make sure that the numbers are not in sequence. If the key for your first message was 109374629, the key for your second message was 109374630, and the key for your third message was 109374631, an attack on the keys would be very easy because you could figure out the sequence of the starting numbers. But how do you make sure that the numbers are not in sequence or otherwise related to one another? You make them *random*.

It's extremely difficult for the human mind to create truly random numbers because our minds are always trying to establish patterns from chaos. That's why we see clouds that look like rabbits or horses or old ladies. Our minds won't allow us to just accept the randomness of a cloud's shape; it has to match the shape to something we are familiar with. It's the same with numbers. We may start out with a random number or two, but eventually, we unconsciously start connecting numbers. For that reason, we give the task of creating random numbers to our computers.

A truly random number is based on an unknown quantity like the rate of radioactive decay, or the number of leaves that will fall off a tree today, or how many rust spots will appear on the hood of a car in a given month. These types of unknowns are referred to as *entropy* (EN-tro-pee). True entropy can produce random numbers that never return the same result twice in a row. In a computer, something that takes input from an entropic event and converts it to a number is called a *random number generator* (RNG). Intel makes a computer chip that reads the amount of thermal noise in your system to create a random number and other companies that manufacture cryptographic accelerators also use special chips as an RNG.

But, and here's the big but, true RNGs are expensive, and it's not economically feasible to include them in every computer. So, you do the next best thing; you devise a recipe — or algorithm — to create a *pseudo-random number generator* (PRNG). A PRNG generates random numbers, but it generates the same random numbers every time you run it. That's a contradiction, isn't it? Yet, it's true. If you install a PRNG on one computer and generate a number, and then install it on another computer and generate a number, the numbers will be the same. The trick to using a PRNG is to grab another random number from some other source and mix that with the number from the PRNG.

There is no fancy way to pronounce RNG or PRNG — you just say the individual letters.

To make the PRNG better, the PRNG takes some sort of other random input from your computer and mixes that up with the pseudo-random number from the PRNG to create another number. For example, the PRNG might use its number and then grab the time in milliseconds from your computer's clock and add the two together. Or it might look at the last 1,000 keystrokes, mouse movements, and cursor locations that are stored in RAM, turn that data into a number, and add it to the PRNG. Whatever the case, the PRNG takes data from your computer, throws away the non-random stuff (like the month and year from the date), and mixes it with the number that it created on its own. This other random number is also known as a *seed*. This seed is "planted" with the PRNG and used to "grow" a number that eventually becomes the key.

If (and this is the big IF) the PRNG algorithm is good, it produces a good number that, in the end, generates a nice strong key. The failure to do this properly has been the downfall of many vendors' attempts at creating strong encryption. Not to throw stones, but let's take a look at Netscape. In its first version of SSL (Secure Sockets Layer, used to make secure Web connections), Netscape gathered data from the computer as the seed. The trouble is that the data they took could be easily figured out. Part of the seed was the year, month, day, hour, minute, and second of the transaction. It was a no-brainer to figure out the year, month, day, hour, and minute because all you had to do was look at the time the data was gathered. Figuring out which second the transaction took place took a maximum of 60 tries to get it right (because there are only 60 seconds in a minute). In practically no time, this weakness was made public — Netscape didn't waste much time in getting version 2 out to market.

Protecting the Key

Now that you've created a long, strong key with which to encrypt your data, how the heck do you protect it? You can't send it to your recipient in the clear because someone could intercept it and steal it. If someone can steal your key, they can decrypt your secret messages. What about hiding it? Well, hide it where? If the key is hidden, you still have to tell your recipient where it is hidden, and how do you do that without other people finding out? Everyone hides door keys beneath the doormat or under the flower pot, so you can't do that. Even if it's hidden in a good spot, you still have to tell your recipient how to find it. Are you going to send that person on an elaborate scavenger hunt just to find the key? That doesn't make things very easy, does it?

The answer is to encrypt the key. Pretty simple when you think about it, but pretty difficult to crack. Even if you find the key, you still have to decrypt it to be able to use it. An encrypted key no longer looks like a number — it looks like a series of random characters from your keyboard, almost as if your cat had walked on your keyboard. There's a secret to encrypting the key, but I'm not going to go into detail about that here. I cover much more about keys and the methods used to protect them in Chapter 7. Because this chapter is really about symmetric algorithms, that's what I focus on now.

Symmetric Algorithms Come in Different Flavors

Although symmetric algorithms all use one key to encrypt data and the same key to decrypt data, that doesn't mean they all work the same. There are quite a few flavors of symmetric algorithms: IDEA, Twofish, DES, 3DES, and AES just to name a few. If all that looks like alphabet soup to you now, you'll be eating it up by the end of this chapter when you realize that it's not all that difficult. I go through the commonly used symmetric algorithms and explain their similarities and differences.

Making a hash of it

Not all algorithms are meant to be decrypted. Huh? That's right — some algorithms are used to encrypt data, but not to decrypt them. Such is the case with a *message digest,* which is also known as a *hash.* I'm not sure if "hash" is a nickname the algorithm got because it "hashes up" the message, but it certainly seems logical.

The most commonly used hashes are SHA-1 (pronounced *shaw-one*) and MD5. Hashes are not truly symmetric algorithms because the encryption works only one way. The end result — the encrypted data — is never meant to be decrypted. Instead, the end result is used sort of like a unique serial number. I include hashes in this section because the output is like a symmetric key.

Hashes take a message and pad it a bit by adding some extra data to the message. The hash then encrypts the message and uses a finite number of bytes from the encrypted portion to be used as a snapshot or fingerprint of the data. Hashes are used to prove that the data that has been transmitted is same as the original data and that *nothing has been changed en route*. How can it do that? Well, every time you use a hash algorithm on the same data, you'll get exactly the same result. On the other hand, if the data has been changed, even by one letter or a single space, the hash will change.

Figures 2-1 and 2-2 are two examples of what a hash looks like. I used a hash calculator (of which there are many available online) to compute two different text strings. The context of the text strings is exactly the same; the only thing that changes between the first figure and the second is the capitalization of one word: *hash*. Note that the hashes are completely different, even though the sentences are essentially the same.

Hashes are useful in ensuring that the software you download from the Web is the same software that the vendor released. It has not been uncommon for hackers to get the source code of software, insert a back door or a Trojan program, and then place it back on the Web for downloading. If you were to compute the hash for the altered software, it would not match the hash that the vendor made from the original software. In this way, hashes are used as protection mechanisms.

I cover hashes in more detail in Chapter 9. They are something you may want to consider for checking the integrity of data kept in storage and messages that can be used as evidence in court.

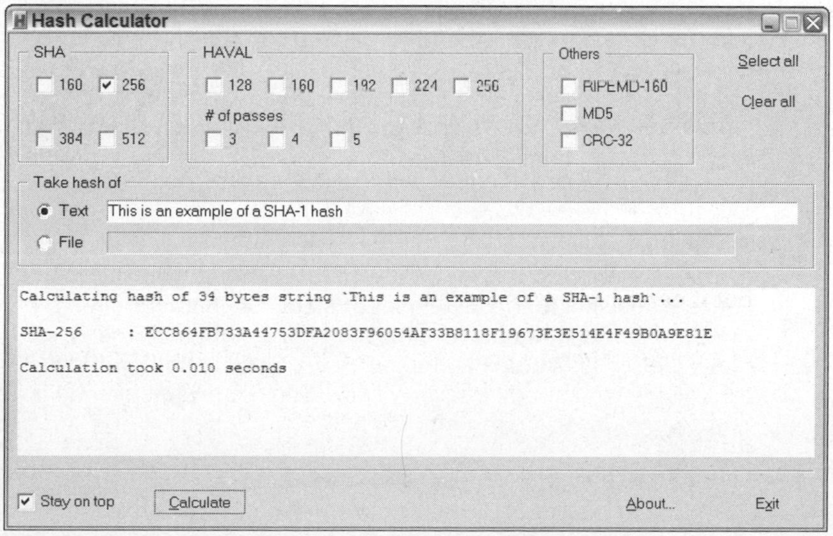

Figure 2-1:
First
example of
a hash.

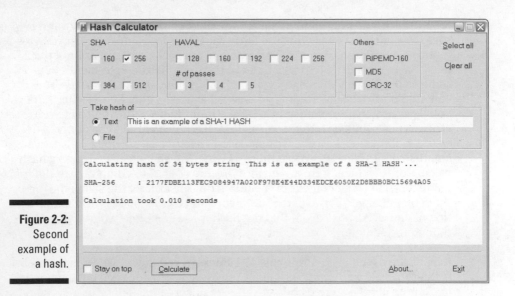

Figure 2-2:
Second
example of
a hash.

Defining blocks and streams

At first this may seem like a non-sequitur if you are just browsing the chapter, but block and stream ciphers are important subsets of symmetric algorithms. I'm not talking about walking around the block or paddling down a stream; I'm talking about the mechanisms of how the symmetric algorithms go about encrypting the data.

Block ciphers take exact chunks of data, encrypt them with the key table, and then take the next chunk, and so on. You can think of it as being a digital bucket brigade. In this type of brigade, however, every bucket must contain exactly the same amount of data. If a bucket is short and doesn't have the correct amount of data, the algorithm drops a bunch of bits in the bucket to even out the amount. The algorithm knows what was used to fill up that bucket, so it can throw those bits away when the decryption process begins.

There is a weakness in block ciphers, though. If two different chunks of data contain the exact same data, the ciphertext could be exactly the same. It's entirely possible that a statement or string of characters are repeated throughout a document, (like the name of a company or a product name) so block cipher algorithms had to be changed to fix this problem. They do that by starting with an *initialization vector* (IV). And what exactly is an initialization vector? It's more random stuff!

In one sense, an IV is similar to the seed data that is added to a PRNG. However, not every algorithm or encryption product uses the same method for creating an IV. Some systems can take random input from the computer's memory buffer and add that to the chunk of data to be encrypted. There have been some products that have been found to have flawed IVs; that is, they used the same string of data all the time instead of takings something random from the computer. To make you feel more at ease, I can tell you that this flaw is usually quickly exposed and the method of creating an IV is changed.

But we're not finished yet with the encryption process for a block cipher. In order to further obfuscate the ciphertext, the block ciphers currently in use create multiple loops of encryption called *cipher block chaining* (CBC). In a nutshell, here's how the whole thing works:

1. The algorithm creates some random data called an initialization vector (IV).

2. The IV is XOR'd with the first chunk of data. (XOR-ing is a bit-by-bit comparison that is explained in Chapter 1.)

3. The XOR'd data is encrypted with an entry from the key table.

4. The encrypted data is XOR'd with the next chunk of data.

5. The XOR'd data is encrypted with an entry from the key table.

6. Repeat Steps 4 and 5 over and over until the entire data file has been encrypted.

And there you have a block cipher that includes an IV and CBC. You're already beginning to sound like a crypto-geek!

Now we go on to *stream ciphers*. If you go back to my original analogy of a bucket brigade, you can think of stream ciphers as the full rush of water coming out of the fire hose. The difference is that instead of encrypting each bucket as it comes through, you encrypt each drop of water as it comes out of the hose. It may seem impossible, but modern computers have little trouble handling this type of speed.

Here is a short example of how a stream cipher does its tricks:

1. Generate a key to create a key stream (a very long key of random data that is at least as long, or longer, than the plaintext).

2. Grab one byte of plaintext and grab one byte of key stream.

3. Encrypt the plaintext with the key stream to create the ciphertext.

4. Start over from Step 2 and continue through Step 3 until all the data is encrypted.

As you can see, a stream cipher is quite a bit different from a block cipher. In one sense, the key stream can be considered the same as a one-time pad (explained in Chapter 1). As long as the pad (the key stream) is used only once, the encrypted data is secure. However, if the plaintext is longer than the key stream, then the algorithm will either have to create a new key stream or use the existing key stream again. After that key stream is repeated, the encryption becomes much weaker. Reusing the key stream makes it easier for an attacker to discover the key and may ultimately crack the encrypted data.

So is one type of cipher better than the other? I cover that next.

Which is better: Block or stream?

The simple answer to this question depends on what you need the encryption for. Stream ciphers are very simple to program and they process very quickly. The most commonly used stream cipher is RC4, which is used in SSL *(Secure Sockets Layer* in secure Web transactions). To date, that is the only stream cipher that has become a de facto standard.

I mention the possibility of a stream cipher having to use its key stream more than one time. This is a weakness and therefore you shouldn't use a stream cipher if you have a lot of data to encrypt; that is, unless you are willing to have the process interrupted to re-key every time the algorithm reaches the end of a key stream. This takes time and processing power, too. The only system I'm aware of that has overcome this problem is the secure telephone unit used by the government and the military for secret communications. This particular phone is called a *STU-III* (Secure Telephone Unit #3). It uses a stream cipher because it is easier to change a conversation into a continuous digital stream and mix the digital conversation with a stream cipher. Because there is no way of telling how long a conversation might last, the STU-III constantly remixes the stream cipher as it encrypts the voice transmissions. Listening to the encrypted conversations on these systems is a hoot because it makes everyone sound like Donald Duck on helium speaking some alien language.

Block ciphers are slower to process but more block ciphers have become standards than have stream ciphers. Take almost any encryption program available and you'll discover that they are set to accept DES, 3DES, and AES. That's because those ciphers are accepted standards. If you are concerned about interoperability with other encryption programs, you're better off using block ciphers.

If you need to reuse keys, a block cipher is better. That's because the key table that is created by the algorithm can create a huge number of keys to use. There is very little likelihood that you would get the same bunch of random numbers to encrypt your data.

Neither cipher type is really "better" than the other; it's more a question of meeting your encryption requirements.

Identifying Symmetric Algorithms

If you were to do a Web search on the term "symmetric algorithms," you would receive thousands of pages in response and discover that there are scores of symmetric algorithms. The main difference is that some of the algorithms have been extensively examined and tested by cryptanalysts and found to be good and others are not as well known or have not been heavily scrutinized. The algorithms that I mention here are considered standard and are commonly used by commercial encryption software. Of course you don't have to go with the standards — you are free to create your own software with other algorithms. If you are using something new and untested by the cryptographic community, you could be compromising your security without even realizing it. For that reason, I strongly advise you to stick with the algorithms that have become accepted standards.

DES

DES stands for *Digital Encryption Standard* and was created in 1975 with some assistance from the National Security Agency (NSA). In 1981, DES became an accepted standard and was widely used. DES is a block cipher that uses a 56-bit key to create the key table. Then it goes through the process of combining a key from the key table with the block of plaintext. After the key and the plaintext have been combined, DES goes through 16 more changes (called *rounds*) to thoroughly mix up the ciphertext. To decrypt the data, DES just goes through all the changes in reverse order.

Given that a 56-bit key has about 72 quadrillion different combinations of numbers, most people felt that DES would be secure for a very long time. What people failed to consider was that computers got faster and cheaper and that it wouldn't cost very much to create a computer specifically to break DES. In 1999, DES was broken in less than 24 hours on a specially built computer.

Triple DES

Many years before DES was broken, cryptographers began working on its replacement. It wasn't that DES was badly flawed; it was that the crypto community could see the end coming and they wanted to be prepared. So Triple DES (also referred to as *3DES*) was created. Because a lot of software and hardware was already coded with DES, it made sense to make changes to an algorithm that was already in use, rather than creating an entirely new one. In that way, many of the older products were able to upgrade to 3DES (or a very similar variant) without having to completely rebuild the hardware or software.

As its name implies, Triple DES does something three times more than normal DES. That triple threat comes from using three keys on each block of plaintext. Instead of using one 56-bit key from the key table, Triple DES encrypts the plaintext with the first key, encrypts that ciphertext with another 56-bit key, and then encrypts the ciphertext with *another* 56-bit key. That may seem like overkill, but it works. 3DES is also able to work with longer keys to make it more secure. The most commonly longer key lengths (at present) are 112 bits and 168 bits.

In order to crack this algorithm you would need to figure out three separate keys. Not only that, but the ciphertext will decrypt only when all three correct keys are used and in the correct order. It might be possible to guess one key, but you'd never know if it was correct until you combine it with the other two keys. The number of permutations is outrageously high, and no one wants to spend that amount of time attacking something of unknown value. What if you went to all the trouble to find all three keys, in the correct order, only to find the data was an e-mail message reminding everyone that there was leftover birthday cake in the break area? A lot of effort spent on nothing, I'd say.

IDEA

IDEA stands for *International Data Encryption Algorithm,* and it's most often seen as a component of PGP (Pretty Good Privacy, a popular e-mail encryption program). This algorithm starts out with a 128-bit key. It then breaks up the 128-bit key into a total of 56 subkeys. How it does this is to divide the original key into eight, 16-bit keys. Then the bits of the original 128-bit key are shifted 25 bits to the left (sort of like everyone in a baseball stadium moving over 25 seats to the left). Now that the original key has been shifted and remade, it's cut up into eight 16-bit keys again. You keep shifting and cutting up until you have a total of 52 keys, each of them 16 bits in size.

Believe it or not, with all of this switching and cutting, the IDEA algorithm is processed about three times faster than DES. One of the reasons it's used is because it doesn't create as much of a load on the CPU of the computer. But, because IDEA is newer than DES and 3DES, it has not really been accepted as a standard. It has been analyzed by the military, but they're not saying what they've found. If there are any weaknesses in IDEA, no experts on the outside of the government have found them — yet.

AES

AES stands for *Advanced Encryption Standard*. Many expect this algorithm to be the heir apparent to DES and 3DES. It's the first algorithm that was created through organized competition.

The contest was announced by NIST *(National Institute of Standards and Technology)* in 1997 in an attempt to find a good algorithm that would become the next government standard. In 1998, the list of competing algorithms had been whittled down to 15 candidates. Then the heavy duty testing began. The contestants began dropping like flies as weaknesses were found in most of the algorithms under consideration. By 1999, the cast of players had been cut to just five and another round of testing began.

Late in 2000, NIST announced it had a winner — an algorithm called *Rijndael* (after Vincent Rijmen and Joan Daemen, pronounced *rine-doll*). It had survived all the tests, and people generally liked the way it worked. The government has called it their Advanced Encryption Standard (AES), but it isn't quite the standard in the real world yet. Again, because it's relatively new, there is some distrust and a feeling that it has not been tested enough for weaknesses. Regardless, there are products on the market that openly use AES and will continue to do so until it's proven weak or breakable.

Asymmetric Keys

Just when you thought you had keys all figured out, here I go and throw another one in the works. Where the previous section focused on symmetric keys and algorithms, this section takes a look at asymmetric keys and algorithms.

One of the biggest problems with symmetric key algorithms is that it is difficult to both share the key and protect it. Because you are using the same key to encrypt and decrypt the data, there's no way around the fact that you have to share the key. Like the key to your front door, it's possible for someone to steal the key or copy it.

Asymmetric keys take care of the problem of distributing keys by making two separate keys that are mathematically connected. You use a "private" key that you never reveal to anyone to decrypt the data you've received and the recipient uses their corresponding "public" key that everyone can have to encrypt the data. Actually, that explanation is a bit simplistic, but you get the idea. A similar idea is a bank safety deposit box. The bank has one key that they keep private, and they have a public key that they give to you. When you go to unlock your box to put your valuables in it, you need both the bank's key and your key in the locks at the same time to be able to open the door to the box.

Asymmetric keys use prime numbers as their starting point. The first part of the process is to create a very large number by multiplying two very long prime numbers together. Prime numbers, if you remember your high school algebra, are numbers that can be divided only by the number 1 or the number itself. One example of a prime number is the number 7. No matter how hard you try, 7 can be divided only by 1 or 7. Now let's say that you multiply two prime numbers together. If you multiply 5 x 7, you get 35. It's not too hard to work backwards from the number 35 to figure out which two prime numbers were used to create it. But, if you used a number that was over 100 numerals long, how hard do you think it would be to find the two numbers that were used to create it? Go ahead and get your paper and pencil. I'll wait.

You probably came up with the same answer I did: It takes an awfully long time! Even if you go through all this trouble, you have only one number. You still have a long way to go. From that long number, you derive a portion of it (via a mathematical computation) for the private key, and from the private key you derive a portion of it for the public key. The elegance in this process is that you can't reverse engineer the public key and obtain the private key.

Although this private/public key concept is considered strong, you need at least a –2,304-bit key to achieve the same level of security of a 128-bit symmetric algorithm. Asymmetric algorithms are slow in processing and it is impractical to use them to encrypt large amounts of data. Symmetric algorithms   can be approximately 1,000 times faster than asymmetric ones. Therefore, you usually see asymmetric algorithms used to protect small amounts of   data such as e-mail messages and - small data files such as attachments to messages.

RSA

This is probably the most recognizable asymmetric algorithm, due in part to the very large corporation that stands behind it — RSA Data Security. RSA comes from the last names of the inventors, Ron Rivest, Adi Shamir, and Leonard Adleman, who created the algorithm in 1978. To date, it is the only asymmetric algorithm in widespread general use that is used for private/ public key generation *and* encryption. Two other algorithms call ElGamel and Rabin also generate two keys and encrypt, but you don't see them used as often as RSA. Because most of the other asymmetric algorithms generate only two keys, many programs use a combination of asymmetric algorithms and symmetric algorithms to protect data.

RSA uses prime numbers to create each of the keys (private & public), but using those keys to encrypt a large amount of data is impractical due to the amount of time it takes a computer to process the encryption. More often than not, an encryption program that uses RSA encrypts the data with a symmetric algorithm such as RC4 (or DES, or IDEA, and so on). Then the symmetric key created by RC4 is encrypted with the recipient's public key. When the recipient gets the message, she uses her private key to decrypt the RC4 key, and when the RC4 key is decrypted, the bulk of the message can be decrypted.

Diffie-Hellman (& Merkle)

This algorithm is commonly known as *DH,* which represents the last names of two of the inventors. However, if you were to meet Whit Diffie or Martin Hellman, they would be sure to point out that they couldn't have done what they did without the work of Ralph Merkle. It was only bad luck that Diffie and Hellman's paper appeared in print before Merkle's did, even though they all arrived at the same idea about the same time. So, out of respect for the authors, please remember Merkle.

There is one huge difference between RSA and DH in that the DH algorithm is not used for encryption. Huh? That's right — DH is not an encryption algorithm; rather, it is a *key exchange* algorithm. Diffie, Hellman, and Merkle were more concerned with the problem of sharing a key over an insecure channel than they were about the encryption of data, so they came up with a solution that created a way to share a secret.

Here's how it works:

1. Natasha has a DH key pair consisting of a private key that she keeps to herself and a public key that she sends to Boris.

2. Boris receives Natasha's public key and uses the DH algorithm to create a temporary private key and a temporary public key for himself. (Note that Boris's keys have something in common with Natasha's public key.)

3. Boris now takes his newly created private key and Natasha's public key and has the DH algorithm generate a *secret number*.

4. Boris uses the secret number (instead of a RNG or a PRNG) to generate a key just for this transaction. This is called a *session key*.

5. Boris uses the session key to encrypt the data and sends it to Natasha along with his temporary public key.

6. When Natasha receives the encrypted message she can derive the session key because her keys and Boris's keys have the same derivative — her public key.

7. With the session key pulled out of the message, Natasha can now decrypt the message.

Please note that when I say, "Natasha does this," and "Boris does that," I really mean that they are using their encryption program to carry out these actions. Natasha's and Boris's only real actions are to respond to any dialog boxes that pop up during the process. Of course the encryption program has the DH key exchange algorithm included in it, or none of this would be possible.

Introducing Boris and Natasha

If you've ever looked through any other mainstream books on cryptography, you likely noticed that the sender and recipient are usually named Alice and Bob. This was found to be easier then saying "Sender A encrypts a message to give to Recipient B." There are other characters who play the roles of interceptor, hacker, and trusted third party.

I've decided to use Boris and Natasha simply to add some humor to the examples and because they are perfectly cast as characters who might use secret messages. Rocky and Bullwinkle may also appear, so watch for them!

PGP

Let me say this from the start: PGP *(Pretty Good Privacy)* is not an encryption algorithm, although many people tend to think of it that way. PGP is actually an encryption program that uses both symmetric and asymmetric algorithms to encrypt data. It is most often used for e-mail because it has some very nice e-mail program plug-ins, but it can also be used for disk encryption and to securely erase data from a disk.

PGP is a hybrid cryptosystem. When a user encrypts plaintext with PGP, PGP first compresses the plaintext. Then it creates a session key, which is a one-time-only secret key. This session key encrypts the data. When the data is encrypted, the session key is then encrypted to the recipient's public key. This public key-encrypted session key is transmitted along with the cipher-text to the recipient.

I cover PGP in more detail in Chapter 8, where you create your private and public keys, encrypt a message, and send it on to a friend who will then decrypt the message.

Elliptical Curve Cryptography

Elliptical Curve Cryptography, also known as ECC, is a very different form of asymmetric cryptography. It's not used very much but when it is, it tends to be used to encrypt large amounts of data. That's because ECC computes very quickly, and it doesn't tie up a lot of processing time. ECC is also newer and not as well understood as some of the other encryption algorithms. For that reason, fewer researches have spent very much time trying to attack them to find their weaknesses. I am mentioning them here because I've begun to see secure data storage programs use ECC to encrypt the huge amounts of data that sits in large server farms.

ECC starts with a curve drawn on a graph. Remember your high school math projects where you had to draw a curve and then plot its *x* and *y* axes? Well, ECC starts out the same way. After the curves have been created, lines are drawn to intersect with the curves. Have a look at Figure 2-3 to see what I mean.

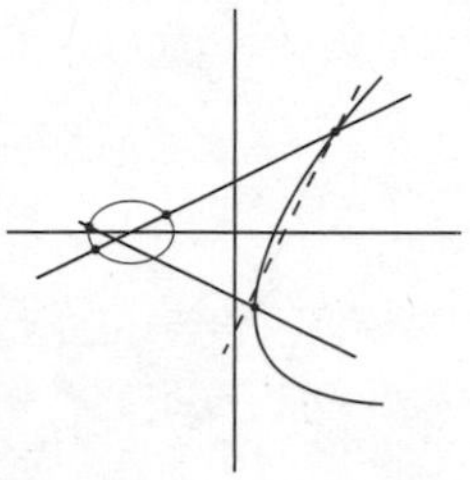

Figure 2-3:
An example
of an
elliptical
curve with
intersecting
lines.

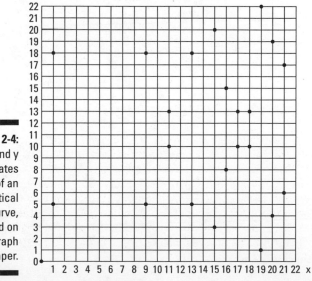

The intersecting points on the curve are given numbers. Of course they are plotted numbers, so there are two: the x-coordinate and the y-coordinate. Going back to school again, Figure 2-4 shows an example of the plotted points, without the curves and intersecting lines marked:

(0,0) (1,5) (1,18) (9,5) (9,18) (11,10) (11,13) (13,5)
(13,18) (15,3) (15,20) (16,8) (16,15) (17,10) (17,13) (18,10)
(18,13) (19,1) (19,22) (20,4) (20,19) (21,6) (21,17)

These points may be graphed as below:

Figure 2-4:
The x and y
coordinates
of an
elliptical
curve,
plotted on
graph
paper.

Now, add a bunch more dots to the graph as the seed, give them all numbers, and start adding and adding and adding all the numbers. The trick to ECC is that you have to know the shape of the original curve, the points where the lines intersect, and which point is the starting point for the addition to begin. From all of that you can create a large number and then compute a Diffie-Hellman key pair. ECC is simple enough to create, but it seems very difficult to attack.

Working Together

An issue with all algorithms is whether or not they are interoperable. The simple answer is that if you stick with the major algorithms, you won't run into many problems. Almost all encryption programs come ready to use DES, 3DES, AES, and RSA. Fewer are able to handle DH key exchange and even fewer than that handle ECC. If you are going to be exchanging encrypted data with a partner, customer, friend, or significant other, it's best to make sure that their programs are set up to use the same algorithms that your programs use. Not only do you have to worry about the interoperability or compatibility of the algorithms, but you also have to consider the file formats of the original data, too. For example, if you encrypt a graphics file as a .tif format and your partner can handle only postscript files, the decryption and viewing isn't going to work correctly.

Interoperability becomes much more of an issue when you move into PKI (*Public Key Infrastructure*). PKI systems can be complex and expensive, and if you are using this type of system to authenticate users, customers, and partners, it's very important that their systems and yours be able to talk to one another. I cover this aspect in detail in Chapter 6.

Chapter 3

Deciding What You Really Need

In This Chapter

▶ Getting management to listen to you

▶ Making your case with facts and figures

▶ Looking at situations that could benefit from the use of cryptographic systems

You wouldn't buy a car without first researching all the makes and models you were considering. Likewise, you wouldn't buy a truck if what you really needed was an economical sub-compact. The same considerations should be made when deciding what cryptographic systems or programs you need to protect your data and communications. You'd think that it would be obvious to do a little homework before entrusting your security to a new system, but you'd be surprised at how often it's considered just a necessary evil and the cheapest solution is considered good enough to do the job.

In this chapter, I give you the basis for making decisions about what you really need and offer some solutions that you ought to consider. I want you to also remember that it's not just the solutions you pick that will make your system work for you; it's also the personnel you need to manage and maintain the system. You wouldn't hire an inexperienced (albeit talented) teenager as a long-distance truck driver, and neither should you hire someone to manage your systems who has no practical experience in the field. Many systems require a certain amount of training of both administrators and users, so be sure to include that in your decision-making matrix.

Justifying the Costs to Management

Without a doubt, the most problematic area in almost any business is getting the management to approve the purchase. It doesn't matter if you're talking about office cubicles, copying machines, phone systems, or upgrades to the network. Whatever choices you give them, they always want to know if you can get the project done cheaper. It's a fact of business life that you just have to deal with, and I'm here to give you some tips.

First of all, you have to look at the situation from management's point of view. They have to make sure that the business shows a profit each year, and they may have a number of entities sitting in judgment of their business decisions — boards of directors, shareholders, and so on. This tends to make management very cautious, especially when dealing with a situation in which they feel insecure. How many managers do you know who really understand technology? So, in putting yourself in their shoes, you can often come up with persuasive arguments to make your case and covertly "teach" the technology to management so they can explain it to their higher-ups.

In simple terms, management responds to decisions that make good money sense — something that will either save them money or make them more money. Start up your spreadsheets, and I'll tell you which figures to start collecting.

Long-term versus short-term

Projects that will last a long time tend to pay for themselves over time. Consider solar-generated electricity for a home — it's very expensive in the short term, but in the long term you can eventually kiss your power bills goodbye. Not only that, but a homeowner can and will have power if a bad storm knocks out the power grid, and in some cases might be able to sell his excess power back to the power company. This foresight and planning is good for everyone in the long run.

Short-term projects generally take only a short period of time to complete, and the investment results are more immediate than with long-term projects. There are no rules that state that one type of investment is better than the other, but there are pros and cons to each.

Unfortunately, in this age of cut-backs and low employment, many companies are concerned only with short-term solutions for their problems. What they forget to figure into their equations is that the short-term solution may not look so attractive in the long run. Take the company who decided to purchase cheap desktop PCs with limited expansion capabilities and low amounts of RAM. In the short-term, that purchase probably saved the company a lot of money. But in the long-term, it also cost them a lot of money to expand and upgrade their system as the company grew. What initially looked like a good return on their investment turned out to be a waste of good time and money.

The addition of cryptography to your network can be seen as either a long-term or a short-term investment, depending on the size and scope of the project. If you are setting up SSL certificates on your Web server to accept secure transactions, that may be seen as short-term because it can be quickly implemented and the costs are generally low. On the other hand, if you are setting up a full PKI system for authentication, single-sign-on, and to protect the integrity of documents, that will probably be considered long-term due to the increased costs in labor and equipment. Neither of these situations — or others — need to be viewed with a negative eye, however. You just have to figure out what management's bottom line is.

Tangible versus intangible results

Sometimes the things that push management's hot-button are not necessarily dollar figures; sometimes they are intangible results. If you can come up with a scheme that will make your boss look like a hero in his superior's eye, you can often get what you want. Another intangible that often works well is to promote the positive effect your changes make in costumer confidence. Customer confidence is hard to put into dollars and cents, but the end result is loyalty — the customer is more likely to stay with you than to go to a competitor if the customer has confidence in your ability and your technical expertise.

Positive ROI

For those of you not familiar with the term ROI, it simply means *Return on Investment.* When you buy stock and the price goes up, you get a positive ROI because you've made money with your initial investment; a negative ROI is when the stock price goes lower than what you paid. Simple, isn't it? For a number of years, the term ROI has been the buzz phrase with management. They often don't even ask if the system will work — they just want to see a positive ROI (on paper in any case).

To be honest, there is no single, fool-proof method of determining a positive ROI. Although the concept of ROI is standard, the method of obtaining and tabulating the costs and figures is a bit like black magic. You can find hundreds of companies on the Internet who are more than willing to sell you special applications that are supposed to help you obtain ROI figures by messaging your numbers to fit your arguments. I don't recommend buying these programs, and I can't give you a definitive method of producing positive ROI figures for cryptography, but I can give you some helpful tips.

In order to argue that the use of cryptography in the workplace will give a positive ROI, you must collect data for the following:

- Cost of current security measures
- Effectiveness of current security mechanisms
- Cost of recent security breaches
- Current and future levels of threat
- Increased security

 ✔ New regulatory requirements for security

 ✔ Cost of cryptographic system(s)

When you have these facts and figures, you can start building a persuasive argument for the inclusion of cryptography into your systems. Remember that crypto is scary to a lot of people, so do your homework well.

Cost of current security measures

If your business is large and has IT departments scattered all over the country, it may be difficult to get an exact figure on the costs and effectiveness of current security measures. However, you can figure the cost of your own systems and use that as an average cost. If other offices are larger or smaller than your own, you can weight your figures accordingly and come up with a weighted average. Some of the figures you'll want to include are replacement parts for electronics that will inevitably die at some point. You'll also need to gather the salaries of the people responsible for network security. The reason that these costs are shown as a *negative* ROI is that they don't generate any income in themselves and they are recurring yearly costs.

To obtain some *positive* ROI figures, keep in mind, also, the cost of the cryptographic solutions you will be proposing. In some cases, the business can take accelerated depreciation and can write off the total cost of the system the first year. Because the costs of the cryptographic solutions can be viewed as an upgrade and their costs may be written off, the net result for the business is that the costs are balanced by the write-off. In some cases, it may also reduce the costs of your company's various insurance policies. That, certainly, is a positive result.

Effectiveness of current security mechanisms

This is somewhat of an intangible. If you haven't had any security breaches with your current security mechanisms, you can't really be sure if it was the security mechanisms that prevented breaches or if you have just been lucky not to have been targeted by hackers or other attacks. However, some real data can be computed by questioning the IT staff. Ask them how much time is spent reviewing firewall logs and responding to alarms sent by the firewall and intrusion detection systems. If the systems are sending out so many false-positive alarms that the IT staff no longer pays attention, then those security mechanisms aren't really effective. They've become the equivalent of the Boy Who Cried Wolf. Calculate the number of man hours spent responding to alerts and use that as a negative ROI figure.

If your new cryptographic system increases the effectiveness of your network security, that is a positive ROI. For example, if all of your important data is encrypted, the theft of that data may not be as serious as if it had not been encrypted. Your effectiveness is increased because you can spend more time trying to find out who was responsible for the theft and less time on damage control on the data that has been stolen. The hours saved responding to security breaches are positive ROI.

Cost of recent security breaches

The Gartner Group specializes in gathering data on network security, security policies, and the costs of security breaches. In a recent report, they found that a security breach costs medium- and large-size businesses $1 million for each security event. That figure is reached by calculating the amount of lost revenue (lost customers, drops in stock prices, labor costs to recover from the problem, and missed business opportunities). They also found that a significant number of businesses never recover from a serious breach. A serious breach is one that lasts three days or longer, and it must be noted that the average recovery time for most breaches is three days. Could your business survive three days with no network? Even viruses that don't do any harm cost businesses a lot of money because cleaning up the servers of virus infections is quite labor-intensive.

Use the cost of security breaches as a negative ROI. On the other hand, if you can show that the installation and use of cryptographic systems can reduce or eliminate costs of certain types of security breaches, put that cost savings down as positive ROI.

Current and future levels of threat

With the threat figures, you can extrapolate how much money the company would lose if it suffered a serious hack that was made public. You'd lose the confidence (and probably the business) of some customers, and negative press could adversely affect the stock price or the value of the company. Additionally, you have to include the cost of labor to stop the hack, reverse any damage done, and plug all the holes that let the hackers enter in the first place. If trade secrets or future product data were stolen, that could well mean the end of the company.

The new regulations on financial companies and the health care industries require that you be able to prove you have done all you reasonably can to ensure the security of your corporate network. There are other situations in which you might have to prove your network is secure, like an audit by the FTC stemming from consumer complaints. Regardless of the reason, you want to have the best security possible to avoid lawsuits and governmental fines. If you see that your company could be included in any of those situations, you must pull together figures for legal advice, trial lawyers, PR firm consultations, and more. These can be very convincing numbers to management, and the likelihood of being found guilty of disregarding possible security mechanisms is a lot less if your system includes encryption.

Conversely, if you were to introduce some type of cryptographic solution into your network, you could avoid certain types of risk and show a positive ROI. For example, if all the personal data of your customers is encrypted, you save yourself the cost of lawsuits that can occur when personal data is either inadvertently released or when someone steals those files in order to sell the information. It's pretty rare in the world of network security that you can say that a solution eliminates risk completely, but some crypto solutions can certainly help mitigate the risks.

Increased security

Many companies have spent tens of thousands — or even hundreds of thousands — of dollars on firewalls, intrusion detection systems, VPNs, and more. However, all of that protection works only on the data in transit. After the data lands on the servers, its only protection is access control. And we all know how easily access controls are subverted — old accounts, guest accounts, bad passwords, and sloppy administration allow unauthorized persons to access the data on the servers. This is the equivalent of connecting two wicker baskets with a steel pipe (see Figure 3-1). The steel pipe protects the data in transit, but almost anyone can get access to the wicker baskets (the data at rest).

Data in encrypted tunnels is protected

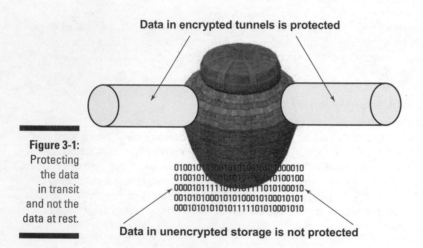

Figure 3-1:
Protecting
the data
in transit
and not the
data at rest.

Data in unencrypted storage is not protected

Intruders can and will get past firewalls, they can fool intrusion detection systems, and they can hijack network connections. In fact, if you read the stories and statistics, you'll soon see that most hacks have focused on the data at rest and have not attempted to pick up the data while it was in transit. Credit card numbers, personal financial data, trade secrets, and software are usually stolen right off the server.

Imagine a scenario where the data in transit is adequately protected with a VPN or SSL connection. Likewise, the data at rest (on the servers) is protected by encrypting it. It would be hard enough for a hacker to get access to the VPN, and he would be doubly thwarted by finding that all the data he got looked like gobbledygook. This is an example of increased security at its best. It's a bit like changing the wicker basket into a steel vault.

Increased security is always listed as a savings. Just look at the banking industry. By using encrypted SSL connections for online banking, the financial institutions have saved millions in the reduced number of staff needed to man phones for customer support. These companies have been able to let

the customer take care of his business without having to interact with someone at customer service. Certainly customer service calls are still important,
but Web transactions with SSL allow the customer service personnel to focus
on more important tasks, and the customer can take care of the smaller
chores such as transferring money between accounts and requesting more
checks.

Consider what reduction in man hours can be had by incorporating encryption into your systems. If nothing else, you may be gaining disk space as
some systems compress the data as they encrypt it. If the data is compressed
to even 25 percent of its original size, that may save you having to buy new
servers this year.

New regulatory requirements for security

California recently passed legislation that requires businesses to tell their
customers when unencrypted data has been released — whether that release
was accidental, intentional, or the result of a malicious act. If the business
does not tell its customers of a security breach and is found out, huge fines
could be the result. Notice that the law says *unencrypted* data. If your data is
encrypted, you may have nothing to worry about!

Both the Gramm-Leach-Bliley Act and the Health Insurance Portability and
Accountability Act (HIPAA) have certain requirements for companies to protect personal data. If the data is not protected adequately and personal information is released, the end result could not only be huge fines, but jail time
for top management, too. However, if all of that data has been encrypted, it's
very likely that you can show due diligence in trying to protect your data. If
you can show that you have done everything possible to protect your data,
you may be able to save yourself from lawsuits and cumbersome fines.

If you think the California law and the two acts mentioned above are the only
regulations you have to be concerned about, think again. The FTC has
recently taken on the mantle of the protector of privacy rights, and they are
not shy about prosecuting businesses. Even Microsoft has run afoul of the
FTC and now has to comply with imposed security regulations and audits for
the next 20 years. Think of the savings that would have been made if
Microsoft had implemented their own encryption technologies — it would
have saved them 20 years of submitting to audits and preparing reports. That
would have been a huge positive ROI.

Cost of cryptographic system(s)

This is the main figure to start from, and it's the one that management is
probably going to complain loudest about. Some solutions can be fairly
simple and not altogether expensive. For example, if you plan to implement
e-mail encryption only, you may consider S/MIME, which has many freeware
components. On the other hand, a full PKI system that handles secure e-mail,
encrypted files, and standard document exchange protocols is a very pricey
investment. However, you must consider any cryptographic system as an

investment in ensuring your network security. If something reduces your risk of catastrophic events, then that isn't such a bad thing.

In addition to the encryption software programs or suites that you plan to buy, you will probably need key servers and certificate servers, too. You may be able to utilize some existing hardware if it is currently in excess of your needs. Remember to add the cost of training and administration for the system, too.

To add a positive figure to the cost of the system, see if the increased security enables your business to enter new markets that were previously closed to you. For example, does encryption give you an edge over your competition that would allow you to take some of their business? Or does the use of encryption allow you to partner with or at least work with European companies that have a much higher standard for data security? Check out the Department of Commerce "Safe Harbor" program. You could get your network certified by the Department of Commerce so you could work with European companies.

Think of other benefits that are likely to come about through the company's use of encryption. There may be lots of opportunities you may not have considered. Brainstorm with others in the company, and search the Web for ideas. Then present your case to management with all the positive aspects highlighted.

Government due diligence

As I mentioned before, there is new legislation that requires increased security, especially for personal data. If there is a complaint against your company, the government is duty-bound to investigate, and you better bet that they will. The government is very paranoid about network breaches allowing terrorists to gain entry to personal information and other sensitive data.

If the government decides to take a look at your network, they will do a complete security audit of your system. In addition, they will want to see documentation of all the security measures and mechanisms that you have considered, whether they were implemented or not. The government considers encryption a very good thing for network security. If your company can prove that you at least considered cryptographic systems to enhance your network security, you will be well on your way to showing that you exercised due diligence in considering every possible security solution. Many of the companies who have been recently dinged by the government with fines and 20-year oversight would never have had a problem if their data had been encrypted.

Insurers like it!

And last but not least is the fact that insurance companies are beginning to offer discounts for proof of increased network security. Insurance rates for businesses take a big bite out of the money bag, and the bean counters like to get every break they can. Like the government, insurance companies will insist on a full security audit, and the use of encryption adds a lot of positive check marks in the "good practices" column.

Presenting your case

Management is in love with PowerPoint presentations that are clear and well-designed. Get the best person on your team to put together the slides and don't try to cram too much information into each slide. Try to stick to just the highlights and good points for your bulleted items. Remember, you are going to be the salesperson to get them to buy into an encryption scheme.

Prepare a spreadsheet with all the figures you've assembled. Here's an example of what you might do:

Risks, Opportunities, and Solutions	Cost
Cryptosystem for encrypted e-mail and encrypted data storage	–$50,000.00
Labor (yearly)	–$75,000.00
Labor savings in reduced staff requirements (yearly)	+$100,000.00
Savings in reduced requirements for new storage capacity (servers)	+$90,000.00
Labor costs for disaster recovery for this system (yearly)	–$5,000.00
Labor costs for key recovery and help desk assistance (yearly)	–$3,500.00
Increased sales due to increased security (average 15 clients annually)	+$600,000.00
Total cost of system	+$656,500.00

Those types of figures should bring you a round of applause and possibly a promotion as well. In the table above, the negative amounts (–) are outgoing costs, and the positive figures (+) are savings or income for the company. In case you don't have a calculator, the figure I used for increased sales was an average of $40,000 per customer. You can probably get those figures from your marketing department. Just ask them how much, on average, each customer is worth to the company.

In the following sections, I look at some of the situations that would benefit from the addition of cryptographic solutions to your current list of security mechanisms.

Do You Need Secure Communications?

There are many ways that we communicate with others on computers, and 95 percent of those communications are not secured against secret listeners. You won't even be aware of the fact that your communications have been intercepted until or unless you suffer a security breach that can be related directly back to the messages.

Secure e-mail

If you aren't aware of it by now, let me tell you in no uncertain terms that e-mail sent in the clear can be read by someone other than the intended recipient. E-mail goes astray. E-mail servers get hacked. E-mail traveling across the wires gets snagged like fish in a pond. If your e-mail isn't encrypted, woe is you.

Imagine that you are working with an independent programmer who is building a new software program for you. Maybe that person sends you new code files every few days. Because your company is relying on this new program to make money for them, do you think it's a wise idea to be sending these messages in the clear? What if your competition got hold of the code?

In another situation, imagine that you are an investigative journalist and you correspond daily with a number of sources who send you very sensitive material. Maybe it's documentation of war crimes or human rights abuses. Maybe the head of a Fortune 500 company is engaging in illegal activities. Maybe you're trying to track down the source of drugs coming into your community. All of these communications should be protected via encryption to ensure the confidentiality and safety of the informants. I could come up with a million situations, but you get the general idea.

Given all cryptosystems available, e-mail encryption is probably the easiest and cheapest system to implement. By "easiest" system, I don't mean to imply that the setup is without problems, but it is an awful lot easier than setting up a full PKI system.

The two most common solutions for encrypted e-mail are S/MIME *(Secure/ Multipurpose Internet Mail Extension)* and PGP *(Pretty Good Privacy)*. MIME was created as a standard for transferring or transporting different types of files attached to e-mails, such as GIFs, JPEGs, DOC files, and so on. The *S* in S/MIME indicates a standard for incorporating secure encryption standards into the protocol. In a perfect world this would work perfectly; however, as is usually the case, the various vendors have taken to interpreting the standards to meet their own needs. S/MIME works, but different e-mail clients use it differently, and the results are not always fabulous. On the plus side, S/MIME is cheap and is included in most e-mail systems and e-mail clients (such as Outlook and Eudora).

Because there are interoperability problems with S/MIME, it might be better to go with a vendor who has developed special implementations of S/MIME that have been altered to ensure better interoperability. Baltimore and ArcticSoft are two companies that come to mind with good products. These purpose-built systems tend to be pricey, but you get some good technical support in setting up and troubleshooting your system.

In Chapter 8, I show you how to set up S/MIME in Outlook and how to obtain the digital certificates needed to sign and encrypt your e-mail messages. You'll need a friend or co-worker to do it, too, so you have someone else to exchange messages with. (As I mention earlier, encrypted e-mail is like video phones — you need two people to participate!)

PGP has a very long and interesting history. To make a very long story short, it was created by a very non-techie person by the name of Phil Zimmermann at a time when the government was intent on keeping encryption technologies out of the hands of common people (1991). At that time, the only legal use of cryptography was by the military or government systems. The government filed charges against Zimmermann for violating export violations and six long years later, the government dropped the charges. Today PGP is a corporate entity, and its use has become a type of standard and is probably the most widely used e-mail encryption software in the world.

PGP is available as freeware (GnuPGP) or as commercial software (PGP Corp). It's an encryption and key-sharing protocol with a user interface to use with popular e-mail programs such as Outlook or Eudora. Its first interfaces were horrible and did a lot to scare people away from it, but the new versions are much nicer, and the program inserts buttons in the e-mail command bar of your e-mail program. However, for individual use it still takes some rooting around the manual to figure out all the intricacies of the product. The enterprise versions for company-wide installations are a good deal because of the ability they give the administrators to fix things such as lost keys. I give it a big thumbs-up because of its wide use and the relative ease of installation. It also interoperates well with older versions of PGP, so you don't have to worry that your correspondence can't be decrypted by the recipient. Another plus to PGP is that it has the ability to encrypt files and storage, where S/MIME does not have that capability. In Chapter 8, I give you some basics on setting up PGP.

Instant Messaging (IM)

Only a few years ago the world of IM belonged to teenagers. If Mom told her daughter she couldn't use the telephone to call her friends until her homework was done, she got on the computer and immediately initiated online conversation with all of her friends. Poor Mom didn't know her daughter wasn't doing her homework, and chances are that her friends' moms were just as clueless. Well, it doesn't take us old farts very long to catch on, and soon we took IM to work. Now your boss thinks you're preparing the big proposal that will land you millions, and you're actually berating your friend across the country over his poor choices in the football pool.

You'd better not be discussing this big proposal on IM, though, because IM in its default installation not only introduces all kinds of security holes into your network, but almost anyone can read your messages, too. Whoops. There went your million dollars to the competitor and, by the way, hackers used IM to get into your network and are using it to distribute illegal MP3s. There have also been cases of people in the IT department snooping in on IMs to get information about impending layoffs.

To the rescue are secure IM servers and clients. The market is currently flooded with competitors like JabCast, Jabber, Bantu, and Ikimbo, to name just a few. They are reasonably priced (sometimes even free), and some systems come with a secure IM server as well as secure clients. Some of the programs use symmetric key encryption (the same key encrypts and decrypts) while other programs allow you to use public/private key pairs (you encrypt with your private key; the recipient decrypts with your public key). If you use your own IM server, all text is encrypted as it travels across the wires and as it sits on the servers. If you are using a public IM server, be sure you trust that server and find out what its security policies are.

Secure e-commerce

Any Web server that collects private information from customers should be considered an e-commerce server, and all possible protections should be implemented. Traditionally, only Web sites that conduct sales or financial transactions have been considered e-commerce servers, but I want you to think outside the box. Because of new privacy regulations, it may be in your best interest (and your customers!) to make your Web site more secure by using encryption.

California declares encryption a necessity

The California Encryption Act, as it is sometimes referred to, is very interesting because it is the first in the nation to be passed. It went into effect July 1, 2003, and businesses and security experts are waiting to see if it will stand up in court. Basically the Act says that if you have names and other personal information such as addresses or Social Security Numbers, you must protect that data. Encryption is an acceptable form of protection, but encryption of the data in transit is not enough. In short, SSL and S-HTTP are not good enough. You must encrypt the database and/or servers containing the information. In addition, if the information is stolen or released, you must notify people of the security breach. The Act is strongly worded, and it remains to be seen if other states adopt this stance.

Most secure Web servers use SSL *(Secure Sockets Layer)* and/or S-HTTP *(Secure HyperText Transfer Protocol)*. Both of these options will encrypt the data as it travels across the wires to prevent the hijacking of information in the clear. On the other hand, these options do not encrypt the data that stays on the Web server or that is transferred to the database server. To be totally safe, you should encrypt the data on both the Web server and the database server.

Whether or not you use SSL and/or S-HTTP, you should know that the default installation of Web servers introduces train-sized security holes into your network. That's because traffic to and from a Web server is supposed to be anonymous and, if the Web server is behind a firewall, you have to allow this traffic through the firewall. The default installations also frequently include scripts and default directories that can be used against you. So, if you plan on going into e-commerce in the future, be very, very careful and implement the best security possible. If you already have e-commerce up and running, then you need to double-check your security policies and procedures — and you really need to consider encrypting the data at rest, too.

Why the concern? Well, there are departments within the Federal government and agencies within state governments that impose severe penalties on companies that even inadvertently spill personal data. If you accidentally send out a customer list with personal information to all of your customers, you will be caught and charged. If a hacker gains entry to your Web server, database, or other network server and can gain access to personal unencrypted data, you will be found out and prosecuted. In fact, a new California state law states that if you have the personal information of even one California resident on a server, it must be encrypted — even if your servers are not located in California.

Online banking

Online banking is just another form of e-commerce. You're collecting and disseminating personal information across the Internet. The Federal Gramm-Leach-Bliley Act of 1999 laid down regulations on safeguarding personal information collected, especially if the collecting is done online. And you don't necessarily have to be a bank to fall under the shadow of this Act, either. If you handle information for banks, or if you counsel people on debt reduction, you will have to provide the following to the government:

- ✔ Risk assessment results
- ✔ Risk management decisions
- ✔ Results of testing for security weaknesses in your systems
- ✔ Attempted or actual security breaches or violations
- ✔ Responsive actions taken to breaches or violations
- ✔ Recommendations for improvements to the information security program (on a regular basis)

That's a lot for some small companies or nonprofit organizations to bite off and chew. Again, encryption of your data in transit should be imperative, and you'll have to show that you gave strong consideration for encrypting the data at rest. If you suffer a serious breach and you can't show that you did all you possibly could (with the technology available at the time), then the FTC is going to take a big bite out of your bank account and certain company executives could end up wearing special jumpsuits for a long period of time.

In addition to protecting the data coming, going, and resting, you should also be making sure that the user logon IDs and passwords/passphrases are encrypted. It won't do you any good to install all kinds of fancy security mechanisms if people can get the UserIDs and passwords with little or no effort.

Virtual Private Networks (VPNs)

When businesses communicate over the Internet, there is no protection promised or implied. Everything is done out in the open and can be seen, captured, destroyed, or copied by anyone who cares to try. It's like cities, towns, and villages connected by roads. You transport whatever is on those roads at your own risk. Businesses began to see the need for a safer alternative as they did business with remote partners and employees in remote locations. Thus, the *Virtual Private Network* (VPN) was invented.

VPNs use encryption to protect the traffic between any two points. It's like building a tunnel with special access controls between those cities, towns, and villages. The tunnels aren't available to everyone, and to the people up above, they are invisible. Before you can enter the tunnel, you must prove your identity, your packages must be of certain types, and the delivery address must be verifiable. If that isn't secure enough for you, a VPN also has the ability to disguise the packages through encryption, too. That way, if someone manages to gain unauthorized access by fooling the access guards or by digging another tunnel that intersects with your tunnel, the intruder won't know which packages to steal because he can't tell one from another.

VPNs have been around for enough years now to consider them a standard security mechanism. On the other hand, the way vendors create their VPN hardware and software is not necessarily interoperable. If you are communicating with someone who doesn't have the same sort of setup, it may take a few days or weeks of juggling cables and commands to get it working correctly. In general, VPNs are considered fairly reliable as far as security mechanisms go. Sure, there are hacks, but you really don't hear about too many of them. Either they are not happening often, or companies are just not telling.

VPNs are capable of encrypting two different ways: *transport* and *tunneling*. The transport encryption sets up a secure, encrypted link across the Internet wires, and it encrypts the data (payload) you are sending to the other end. This is the equivalent of the delivery truck carrying a package via the underground passageway. (I'm not using the word *tunnel* here because I don't want to confuse you!) The encryption is invisible to the user — other than passwords, passphrases, or a special card to plug into the computer, the user doesn't have to press a button that says "encrypt" or "decrypt." All the data in transit is protected from sight. The only drawback to transport encryption is the fact that the headers on the data are sent in the clear. In effect, that's like disguising the package and then putting a label on it that says what's inside. Maybe not the smartest thing to do considering that intruders may occasionally gain access.

The other form of VPN encryption, tunneling, not only sets up a secure, encrypted link between two points, but it also encrypts the headers of the data packets. That's better. Not only do you have a disguised package, but the address and the contents listed in the package's label are in code so it's not easily recognizable. As I mention earlier, the VPN standards aren't necessarily standard, so you'll have to see what protocols the vendor is using. The vendor will have tons of transfer protocols to choose from, but the tunneling protocols are fairly limited. Just to give you an introduction, here are the tunneling protocols:

- ✔ GRE = Generic Routing Encapsulation
- ✔ IPsec = Secure Internet Protocol
- ✔ L2F = Layer 2 Forwarding
- ✔ PPTP = Point To Point Tunneling Protocol
- ✔ L2TP = Layer 2 Tunneling Protocol (PPTP + L2F)

If you set up a VPN for your customers, business partners, and employees, they can gain some comfort in the fact that their data isn't traveling in the clear. One point to remember, though: Many road warriors have automated the process of logging in to their VPN and have a shortcut on the desktop. On top of that, a laptop is not properly protected with proper access controls — turn it on, and it's yours. In that instance, a stolen laptop can easily be used to log on to a VPN, and you'd never know it unless the employee alerts you. In addition to access controls for laptops, you may also want to consider disk encryption to protect the data stored on the laptop. Just something to keep in mind.

VPNs are relatively easy to set up now, and you can usually find experienced staff to install and manage them. As I mention earlier, sometimes it takes a little effort to get two different VPNs talking to one another, but that doesn't last forever. Many vendors are including VPN capabilities in their routers so the system is practically "plug and play." Just remember to change the default settings such as the administrator password. VPNs are great at protecting the data in transport, but they do not encrypt the data on your drives — that data is still in the clear.

Wireless (In)security

If you haven't heard about wireless networking yet, you need to get out a little more often. Nothing has created such excitement as the introduction of "portable computers" in the '80s. Now we not only have portable computers (our laptops, of course), but you can sit in a café, in a park, or in your back yard and connect to the Internet. No wires. No hassles. Just free and easy surfing the Web. Well, for every upside there has to be a downside, right? That's certainly true for wireless networking. By default, anyone within radio wave distance can use your Internet connection and probably can hop on to your network as well. Shortly after wireless networking made its appearance, hackers created very small software programs that search the airwaves for unprotected wireless networks. And believe me when I tell you that there are tens of thousands of unprotected wireless business networks in America alone.

The act of snooping for wireless networks is called *war driving,* so called because you can do it while you drive around town in your car (with a laptop inside). Teams of people have a war to see who can gain access to the most networks. (It also refers back to an old practice of "war dialing," in which a hacker used a special modem that continually dialed telephone numbers in sequence in order to find modem tones to find networks.) Lists of open wireless networks can be found on the Internet, and in some cities the war drivers mark the sidewalks with chalk to indicate where the network is located and what you need to do to log on *(war chalking).* That's why I called this section wireless "insecurity." Wireless access points and wireless network cards are so easy to install that I doubt it would confuse a three-year-old. Even your grandmother can do it!

Wireless networks do have some security capabilities, and one of them currently in use is *WEP* (Wired Equivalent Privacy). Don't stake your life on WEP, though, because it's only an equivalent of security; it isn't real security. WEP encrypts the packets going out over the air. It doesn't encrypt them particularly well, though, and much of the information about the network is sent in the clear. There are many hacker programs available that can crack the basic configurations of WEP, too. AirSnort and WEPCrack are two popular programs. Of course I should also mention that WEP is much better than using nothing!

Given the number of business networks that appear on the war-driving Web sites, not many people have gotten the hint to at least turn on WEP, and even fewer know anything about securing WEP properly. I discuss this in depth for you in Chapter 13.

Because WEP employs fairly weak encryption, you can add to the security by adding a VPN and an authentication process. This will greatly enhance your security, but you should never give a wireless network totally trusted status. In the near future there are supposed to be more secure versions of the wireless protocol appearing, but they haven't quite made it yet. You can buy totally secure, NSA-approved wireless access points from Harris at about $5,000 each, but I doubt that many organizations will want to lay down that sort of money. The NSA has tested the encryption on the Harris wireless networks and found them to be safe. Well, probably not safe from the NSA, but you probably won't have any problem with war drivers.

Do You Need to Authenticate Users?

If you aren't concerned with who is using your network and its resources, then you probably don't care to implement any form of authentication. If, on the other hand, you want to know who's on and control where they go, then you'll have to at least list your users, give them logon accounts, and assign them passwords.

Authenticating your network users is one of the big bugaboos of network security. Currently the majority of networks around the world only require a valid User Name (UserID, Logon Name) and password to give a person access to files, directories, databases, and all other forms of network goodies. That's all well and good, but it really does nothing to ensure that the person who is logging on is really the person he's supposed to be. It turns out it's quite difficult to verify users' identities from a remote location. When you have thousands of users on your network, you can't realistically spend time verifying users by phone call or video links.

There are a number of very good authentication systems that utilize encryption. The encryption is used for a number a reasons, but mainly it is used to create and pass digital certificates and to encrypt the transmission of data between people and/or computers. I've included much more about cryptographic authentication systems in Chapter 10.

Who are your users?

Do you really know if your customer, Bob Jones, is really who he says he is? Yeah, you probably got a request from your client to create an account in his name and add him to the access list, but unless you've actually spoken to and met Bob Jones, do you really know who he is? Another point, when Bob Jones logs on to your network, can you really be sure it's him? Maybe he gave his logon and password to a co-worker to use. Maybe a hacker guessed the password and is using that account. You have no way of knowing whether or not the users currently on your network are who you think they are unless you take pains to authenticate them accurately.

The problem with most network logons, e-mail, and Web transactions is that there is a certain amount of *plausible deniability* involved. That is, the person who supposedly logged on, sent the e-mail, or bought something on the Web can deny he or she ever did it. And this is completely legal. The reason for this is that you can't verify, without a shadow of a doubt, that the person on the other end of the action is really who he or she appears to be.

Say that Mary Jones sent a libelous e-mail about you to everyone in the company. Mary is called into the office by the CEO and asked to explain her actions. She can deny she sent the e-mail, and the company would have to prove otherwise (presumption of innocence, you see). Mary could say that she walked away from her desk to go to the restroom and she forgot to lock her computer before she left. It's possible that one of her co-workers sat down at her desk while she was away and used her e-mail program to send the message to everyone. Don't laugh — it's happened.

The only way you could prove that Mary sent the e-mail would be if you had a strong authentication system. Strong authentication basically means submitting at least two out of three forms of identification: something you have, something you know, and something you are. It's not unlike paying for your groceries by check. In addition to your signature on the check, the cashier will also request another form of ID, like a driver's license. You've submitted something you have (driver's license) and something you are (your unique signature).

Encrypted tokens, certificates, signing keys, and biometrics are just some of the additional forms of identification you can submit in addition to your UserID and password for network access. I discuss some of these and more, coming up next.

Authentication tokens

Authentication tokens come in many forms and are designed to hold information about the owner's identity that is verified via special servers. In addition, the tokens are handed out in person, so there is verifiable evidence that the token was given to the correct person. Tokens usually employ a high degree of security, like encryption of the data, and most will destroy the data if the token is tampered with.

Proximity cards

Prox cards, as they are sometimes called, have small radio transmitters in them that send coded signals to specially built receivers. The receivers are programmed to accept only certain persons or restricted access codes. Each prox card transmits a unique code for each person. A log is created of the time and place of access. A prox card itself can't be a strong authenticator because it can easily be given to someone else. However, when combined with a PIN, you achieve two out of three factors for strong authentication. These systems are usually the most inexpensive to implement, but that doesn't mean they are cheap!

Contact cards

These tokens are like credit cards with a magnetic strip on one side. The data on the magnetic strip is encrypted when it's created. You slide the card through a special reader and the data is transmitted to a special database or authentication server. Again, these are most secure when used in conjunction with a PIN or password.

Challenge/response generators

Remember the old war movies where the guard on duty challenged the stranger wanting to enter the restricted area? The conversations usually went something like this:

Guard: Halt! Who goes there?

Stranger: A friend.

Guard: What's the secret password?

Stranger: The Yankees are playing the White Sox.

Guard: Thanks, you can enter.

That little scenario is referred to as *challenge/response* because the guard challenges the stranger to come up with the correct response. Challenge/response generators are the same idea but updated for the cyber age. The user has a card that resembles a calculator or small PDA. When the user logs on to the network, a special server recognizes the UserID and sends a challenge in the form of a number, word, or phrase to the user's computer screen. The user enters that challenge into the challenge/response generator, and it uses a special algorithm to come up with the correct response. Finally, the user types the response on his computer keyboard and the system gives him access.

This is a pretty good form of authentication because it uses both the UserID and password (something you know) and the challenge/response generator (something you have) that is interactive rather than passive. To increase the security and authentication, most challenge/response generators are also protected by a PIN. That gives the system two instances of something you know and one instance of something you have.

One-time password generators

We're just generating up a storm here! (You can groan now.) Very similar to the challenge/response system I've just described are the one-time password generators (also known as *OTP*). As with the previous system, you need to have special servers for this process and the servers must sync with the OTP generators to create the password. This type of system has proven quite successful.

The user enters a secret passphrase into the OTP generator, which transfers the data to the server. The server takes the passphrase, seeds it, and then goes through multiple iterations of secure hashes. The result is a code that is changed into human-readable form and sent back to the OTP generator. The user simply types the password, and he's in. This system also allows the user to log on to multiple stations, each time with a unique, one-time password.

Smartcards

Smartcards have often been touted as the hottest new technology, but the lack of standards has really put a damper into the product taking off like bottle rockets. Their use in the United States is slowly rising, but they've become very common in Europe for use as transit cards, health information for providers, and credit information. Americans seem afraid to have that much sensitive information stored on a little chip on a piece of plastic the size of a credit card.

For authentication, smartcards are great because they can carry any and all types of information: digital signatures, encryption keys, personal data, and even biometric information. The trouble is that there are six different standards for the type of chips used and the type of information each chip can store. Interoperability becomes a problem. But, if you're using a single vendor for your smart card needs and it's only used in-house, it could be the answer for you.

There is a lot that these various types of smart cards are capable of handling in regards to authentication. Some of the smart cards have cryptographic processors in them to be able to create new encryption keys on the fly. These cards can sometimes store digital certificates and digital signatures as well as biometric information, like a fingerprint. The next couple of paragraphs fill you in on some of the jargon used with these cards because it can all quickly become very confusing. After reading the sections below, you should be able to speak with a smart card vendor and know what he is talking about.

Memory cards

These types of smart cards can store only static information and cannot work as a computer processor. There are different data types and different degrees of security, depending on which type of memory chip is used. There are three main types of memory cards: *standard*, *protected*, and *stored value*.

- **Standard** cards are like unlocked floppy disks — they store data that can be overwritten and so should not be considered terribly secure.

- **Protected** smart cards can write-protect the data and can restrict access with a password.

- **Stored value** cards are the best of the memory cards. They have security mechanisms that are hard-coded into the chip. These usually don't store data files; rather, they store values such as encryption keys, hashes, or digital certificates. These cards also have "counters" in them that can limit them to a finite number of uses. When the counter reaches the end, you can either have the card recharged or simply throw it away. They're great for infrequent users because it doesn't matter if the user loses one, and you can set a limit to the number of times a guest can access the network.

Microprocessor multifunction cards

These cards are like their own little computers on one little bit of circuitry. They have their own operating system, file allocation, and access controls. It's amazing how computers went from the size of entire rooms in the 1970s to the size of a pinhead at present. These are the best cards to use when the security token is needed for a number of functions. Not only can this card store symmetric and asymmetric key pairs, but it can also house multiple digital certificates and the cryptographic software needed for special functions and interactions.

Java tokens

Java tokens come in smart card forms and buttons the size of a flat battery. Their coolness factor is very high, partially because they are programmed with the Java programming language and because they are almost exclusively used to perform cryptographic functions. The cards are known as *JavaCards,* and the buttons are commonly referred to as *iButtons*. The iButtons can be inserted into rings, dog tags, watchbands, and any number of wearable holders.

The JavaCards are usually interoperable with other smart card systems that follow the PKCS #11/Cryptoki standards. Cryptoki (pronounced *crypto key*) is an API *(Application Program Interface)* for devices that hold cryptographic information and perform cryptographic functions. Because the iButtons require specially shaped readers, they can't be used with smart card reader systems.

The iButton contains a microprocessor similar to the one you might find on a smart card. It is capable of storing cryptographic functions as well as any form of cryptographic key you can imagine (digital signatures, symmetric keys, asymmetric keys, message digests, and so on). It has the ability to perform 1,024-bit public key operations, too. In addition to storing crypto functions and keys, it can store personal data such as driver's license information and medical information. The iButton has a tamper-proof case and if anyone tries to pry it open, all information will be destroyed.

Biometrics

How many movies have you seen where the good guys place their hands on a scanner to gain entry to the lab? You've probably also seen eye-scanners, voice authenticators, and fingerprint scanners on TV and in movies. But for some reason, most Americans see the use of these products as the downfall for liberty and freedom. All a biometric device does is measure a certain characteristic of the human body. The machine does not store the actual fingerprint, voiceprint, or iris scan. It stores a mathematical equivalent of the characteristic. When you submit your body part to a scan, it converts what it sees to math and then compares that mathematical figure to the one stored in the database. No one can actually steal your fingerprint because it doesn't look like a fingerprint.

Nonetheless, biometrics are expected to provide a higher level of security than other forms of authentication because the biometric trait (your finger, eye, or voice) can't be easily lost, stolen, or duplicated. A biometric provides undeniable authentication. Of course there are arguments that a fingerprint can be copied and a voice recording can fool the device, but how often is this likely to happen? In reality, hackers go for the soft, easy targets like bad passwords and security holes in operating systems. Why would they focus their attention on getting *one* form of authorization when they can get literally hundreds with a password cracker? Unless you are a secret squirrel working for an unknown spy agency, I doubt that anyone would go to the trouble trying to crack your biometric trait.

To enable biometrics, you must first scan the part of the body that is going to be used for identification. When that is done, a template for that person's body part is created. The template contains the mathematical equivalent of the scan as well as some parameters for future acceptance. These parameters can be set from very loose to very strict. When the body part is offered for identification, it is compared to the template — there will never be an exact match, so the parameters in the template are consulted. If the template offers a loose interpretation of the scan, you might allow access to someone with attributes similar to the owner. If the parameters in the template are too strict, then even the real owner of the attributes might never pass again. The trick is to create a happy medium. In that way, you keep out possible imposters and you don't make the actual owner scan over and over again to get a positive match.

Do You Need to Ensure Confidentiality and Integrity?

When your company has spent tons of money in research and development (R&D) of a new product, you want to guarantee that the data stays on your system and that no changes have been made to the latest build. The same is true for sensitive proposals, financial data, and anything else considered a trade secret. Many companies understand the need to use firewalls, intrusion detection systems, access controls, and so on to protect the data from theft, but few are considering masking or hiding the data through the use of cryptography.

Additionally, personal data needs to be protected so its theft can't be used for identity theft or other nefarious purposes. The Department of Homeland Security is concerned about terrorists stealing personal data and assuming the identity of bona fide American citizens because these people are unlikely to be caught on visa violations.

There's one more thing you should consider: How valuable is your data if you can't ensure that it hasn't been changed and contains erroneous information or malicious code? It won't do your company's reputation much good if the data you sell is not dependable.

Protecting Personal Data

This goes beyond protecting the private, personal information of individuals just because the government has told you that you must. Protecting the privacy of your customers and clients is a good thing, but it shouldn't take an act of Congress to make you incorporate that type of security into your total security solution. There are times when you may need to protect a person's identity to protect that person from real or imagined harm.

If you are required by law to protect personal data, saving it in encrypted form will pass the government's due diligence test if it's ever stolen. That is, if you use encryption, the government will likely rule that you did all you possibly could to protect the data. In addition to making the data look like scrambled eggs in digital form, it can also be used as a form of access control if you give only the keys and/or passphrases to open the data to certain people. If someone other than the authorized group opens the data, then you can be certain that there is a security problem inside the company.

Think of people in witness protection programs. All of their data has to be locked up tight so the bad guys don't figure out who they've become and where they've moved to. Data encrypted with a good algorithm and a very long key would be next to impossible for the bad guys to break. Again, unauthorized people would not be able to decrypt the data. The same holds true for people who give aid in countries torn by civil war, political uprisings, or other forms of unrest. Attorneys wouldn't want their defense strategies read by opponents, and political candidates for office wouldn't want their opposition to know their campaign strategies.

What about the software you spent so much research and development money on? You wouldn't want your source code to suddenly appear on the Internet. Likewise, you need to guarantee that your customers get what they paid for. There have been cases where software was shipped containing back doors to security, Trojan programs, and viruses. If the software had a message digest or checksum, then you can discover if the code had been changed from the original.

There are thousands more situations where companies need to protect the confidentiality and integrity of the data they store, transmit, and/or sell. Encryption is an easy way to accomplish both tasks. A file full of encrypted gobbledygook is indecipherable. Its confidentiality is protected because the contents of the file can't be read, and its integrity can be guaranteed because it would do no one any good to make changes to an indecipherable mess.

File encryption can save storage space because some systems compress and encrypt data. It remains accessible to those with the keys and/or passphrases, but it's almost worthless to steal. There is no time limit to storing encrypted data, so you can rely upon it for the long term. Even if you do a bad thing like put your database on the same server as your Web server, a hacker can't use the security holes in the Web server to come away with anything useful.

Encrypted e-mail is also included here because after you encrypt a message, it stays that way. Hacking the e-mail server won't decrypt encrypted messages. If you remember to encrypt e-mail attachments as well (and that should be standard practice), that data is protected, too.

There are literally thousands of companies that offer long and short term encrypted storage solutions. They vary in cost depending on the amount of storage you need and the type of encryption you want to include. This is not necessarily the time to go with the lowest bidder because you want to make sure that you have the ability to recover lost encryption keys. Not all companies or products offer that capability.

What's It Gonna Cost?

I'd love to be able to give you a chart, spreadsheet, or even a rough idea of what your solutions are going to cost you. Unfortunately, asking how much encryption is going to cost is a lot like asking how much a car is going to cost. The answer is, "It depends." It depends on what you need, what you decide to implement, how much support and training you need, and what systems you are currently using. It wouldn't do you any good for me to recommend a solution for UNIX systems if your network is totally Windows-based. Likewise for Macs or special network transports like ATM.

You'll need to do your homework on the Internet for the solutions that suit you best. Some you'll be able to install and run yourselves, and others will require a team of specialists to get it up and running. Again, it all depends.

One thing to keep in mind, however, is interoperability. You need to be able to continue to operate with other offices, your customers, and even employees on the road. Ask yourself if you plan to change systems anytime in the near future. Talk to your customers to see what they are running and what their needs are. As I mentioned before, cryptography is a two-way street and you can't do it alone. You need to have your partners in-step and in agreement with your decisions so your ultimate roll-out will be as smooth as possible.

Chapter 4

Locks and Keys

· ·

In This Chapter

▶ Creating memorable passphrases

▶ Keeping your passphrase safe

▶ Generating keys and keeping them safe

▶ Taking a first look at cryptiquette

· ·

*T*he freezing desert wind slices through Ali Baba's thin clothing, chilling his bones. His teeth are chattering and his mind is going numb with pain from the icy cold, but no matter how hard he pushes and pounds on the enormous stone at the entrance to the treasure cave of the Forty Thieves, it will not move. Of course, this was exactly how the Forty Thieves wanted an attacker to end up when attempting to defeat the security of their treasure cave: frozen, miserable and — most importantly — *still outside their cave!* But why is Ali Baba standing out in the cold? Simple: The massive stone portal will open only if the magic phrase is spoken. Do you remember the magic phrase?

The magic phrase is the key to opening the Forty Thieves's cave, and in modern terms, that phrase is known as a *passphrase*. A passphrase is more than a password because, obviously, it consists of more than one word. In the world of cryptography, the passphrase or passphrases you choose to use will be very, very important.

Your passphrase is the main protection mechanism for your key (or keys). As you will soon discover, a combination of a poor passphrase and short key length are deadly when it comes to encryption. Your passphrase is subject to hacking just as regular passwords are. There are special programs available on the Internet used for the sole purpose of intercepting and cracking passwords. If you have chosen a short, easy passphrase full of words regularly found in a dictionary, then your passphrase can be cracked in little or no time. If a hacker obtains your passphrase, it's as good as no security at all because he will be able to use your passphrase to gain access to your encryption and decryption keys. And if a hacker can get your keys, he can read your encrypted messages and files. Therefore, it only makes sense to create a good passphrase to protect your files.

Likewise, if your encryption keys are very short — say, less than 140 bits — there is a possibility that a hacker could crack your keys and use them, whether or not you have a good passphrase. Again, there are programs available on the Internet that are used to try to crack encryption keys, and you don't need to be a rocket scientist to be able to use them. That's why all security experts will tell you that you need a combination of both a good passphrase and long keys. It's like using both the lock on your door knob as well as the deadbolt to secure your front door. When you use both of them, there is a better chance that a burglar won't be able to gain access to your home.

In this chapter, I discuss the importance of passphrases and keys and how to create, remember, and safely store them.

The Magic Passphrase

A passphrase is a combination of *password* and *phrase* and consists of more than one word and/or special characters. Because it is more complex than a simple password, it is harder to guess or crack, and it adds an extra level of security to the all-important encryption keys. The sequence of characters you create to make a passphrase to gain access to a security system is one of the first decisions you'll make as a user of the system. It is also the weakest link in nearly all computer systems. As humans, we make bad decisions when it comes to passphrases, and no matter how secure the computer system, a bad passphrase can cause huge problems.

You also have to protect your passphrase and be careful not to lose it (or forget it). Without your passphrase, you won't be able to use your encryption software; you won't be able to encrypt your files; you won't be able to send encrypted e-mail; and you won't be able to apply your digital signature to important documents. Your passphrase is the combination lock that protects the encryption keys that make it possible for you to encrypt data. If you lose or forget your passphrase, you have to destroy all of your old keys and create new ones. And you have to update computers, servers, back-up files, and people of the fact that your old keys are no good and present your new keys. It's as bad as having your wallet stolen and having to replace your driver's license and all of your credit cards. It's more than just a royal pain — your identity and your reputation could be at stake.

In using encryption software, you create a passphrase to protect each of your keys. This is the first line in the defense of your keys and you should be very careful of what you choose as your passphrase and what you do to protect it.

The weakest link

Several factors determine the strength of your passphrase:

- The length (number of characters)
- Its entropy (randomness)
- The safety measures used to protect the passphrase from unauthorized use

Truly random passphrases, such as those generated by machines, are extremely secure, but they are also generally so "unfriendly" that people cannot remember them. It's doubtful that you'd want to remember

> #F8$5-9d(HNd]^[J?P=Oj&x~%dDZk_sH3b.<Pi>od*F@Q

every time you wanted to get into your cave, but it's a much better passphrase for keeping strangers out than "Open Sesame!" (Ooops! I told you Ali Baba's passphrase!)

Of course you'll need to make your passphrase as long as possible. Many people complain that a long passphrase is too hard to remember. To that I say, "Bull-pucky!" If we can remember more than one 10-digit phone number, then it's not all that more difficult to remember a 15-character passphrase. The trick is to assign some memory tricks to your passphrases. When I first started using memory tricks for my passphrases, I increased the size of them to between 10 and 15 characters. Now all of my passphrases are more than 25 characters long. I may mistype them occasionally, but I never forget them.

Cryptographers use the term *entropy* to describe the randomness of a passphrase. Using completely random characters in a passphrase meets the entropy requirements, but you can also quickly make the passphrase too hard to remember. It's important to use as many of the keys on a keyboard as you can, which means upper and lowercase characters, numbers, and punctuation. If you used at least 10 random characters in your passphrase, the time needed to mount a brute-force attack on it is approximately 3.8×10^8 years.

Even if your passphrase is very long and complex, you have to make sure that your passphrase is adequately protected. I don't mean just protecting it by saving it as a text file and placing that file on a floppy, either. While saving your passphrase on some sort of remote storage device is an excellent plan, you should also be aware of who is around when you are typing in your passphrase. Is there a possibility that another person could peek over your shoulder and watch what you type? (This is called *shoulder surfing*.) Is the floppy that you used to store your passphrase left out in the open? Could someone use that floppy when you weren't around? It doesn't matter how long and random your passphrase is if it can be obtained by someone else.

Mental algorithms

My favorite method for creating and remembering a passphrase is to use a line from a favorite poem, or a lyric from a favorite song, as a mental algorithm for remembering the more obscure passphrase itself. For example:

"You must remember this, a kiss is just a kiss"

could produce the passphrase:

"U mst rem3mbr THS a k155 1sjusta k155"

The passphrase above is 37 characters long (spaces are also considered characters) and is very resistant to a *dictionary attack* or even a *brute force* attack. Why? Well, for one, the attacker would have to know your favorite song, and two, it's difficult for an attacker to guess your mental algorithm.

A *dictionary attack* on a passphrase means to use a cracking program that includes words in a standard dictionary in the program. All the words in the dictionary are compared to the words in your passphrase and, when matches are found, your passphrase is cracked.

A *brute force attack* on a passphrase also uses a special cracking program but instead of using a dictionary, the program tries to crack the passphrase letter by letter rather than trying to crack each word. A brute force attack takes a long time and uses a lot of computing power, but can be very effective in cracking complicated passphrases.

To a cryptographer, each user's passphrase is a vulnerable "point of failure" in the security system of protecting keys. In fact, it is often considered the *Single Point of Failure* (SPOF). A human creates his passphrase and must always remember it to gain access. Because even the smartest people can sometimes forget things, passphrases are also a security management issue. Forgotten passphrases, especially those that represent the only means to recovering encrypted data, can result in permanent data loss. Things get even more complicated when keys are divided amongst several people (I cover that in Chapter 7) and each person has to successfully enter their passphrase for the key to be used.

In order to have the strongest passphrase you can remember, it's extremely important to have some mnemonic techniques or self-made rules to aid your memory. Mnemonics are just simple memory devices to help you remember something. For example, when I was learning how to play the guitar, I could never remember the tuning arrangement of the strings until my music teacher told me to remember this:

Every Army Denounces God Before Encounter

If you take the first letter of every word, you get E, A, D, G, B, E, which are the guitar string tunings from top to bottom. There's also another one that I'm sure we all remember from grade school: In 1492, Columbus Sailed the Ocean Blue. You can use these types of mnemonics as passphrases as long as you misspell words, change where the capital letters occur, and use numbers and special characters, too.

Another type of mnemonic is to use some nonsense words that either remind you of the real word or sound slightly like the real word. I could never remember the name of all the "icky-stans" — the former Russian republics of Central Asia that became independent in 1991 — Turkmenistan, Uzbekistan, Kazakhstan, Kyrgyzstan and Tajikistan. I came up with the following words to help me remember some of them:

- Turkey Many Stand
- Ooze Becky Stands
- Count Zack's Stand
- Curdle Stan
- Dejected Stan

Again, these are all helpful in creating good passphrases. As in my previous examples, you'll want to mix up the characters a bit and maybe even make the sentences or phrases longer. These make an effective start on passphrases because they follow a *theme*. A theme could be lyrics to your favorite songs, names of your favorite sports cars and the year they were introduced, or even planets, stars, and constellations. Phrases from religious books are good, too. You can use the Bible, the Quran, the Torah, a book of Buddhist chants, or whatever books you have at your disposal. If you can remember it, it's a good theme.

If you're not good at remembering themes or phrases, you can also create a mathematical algorithm for creating good passphrases. For example, start with a date you can remember (but *not* your birth date). Change the numbers in the date to the corresponding letter of the alphabet. For example, the date 05-20-1989 would become E-T-AIHI. That's a good start because it appears to be fairly random. Now use the SHIFT key to transpose that date into special characters and 05-20-1989 becomes)%_@)_!(*(. Your passphrase could then appear as: e-T-aihi)%_@)_!(*(. I doubt that any password cracking software would be able to break that passphrase very quickly.

You can also get *password generators* online for free or at a nominal cost. Many of them will create long passphrases that are almost pronounceable so you are better able to remember them. Many of them also offer safe storage of passwords.

Safety first!

Because you have obviously purchased this book or checked it out from a library or something similar, I'm sure you have dealt with the issue of good passphrases before and are not looking for the standard do's and don'ts. Almost any book on computer security emphasizes the fact that good, strong, long passphrases are a must. But how many of them have given you really good advice on creating good passphrases and told you about the safety and storage of your passphrases? Not many, I bet.

When you are typing your passphrase, be aware of your surroundings. Is there anyone behind you or near enough to be able to see what you are typing? Some encryption programs (like PGP for example) provide you with a "secure" dialog box to enter your passphrase. In this secure dialog box the characters that you type will appear slightly distorted on the screen to make it difficult for others to shoulder-surf your passphrase. If your encryption programs at work have been custom coded for the company's use, the programmers should be able to include that feature for safety's sake.

And, of course, there is the problem with how to write down your passphrase and hide it so others can't find it. The obvious no-no is to write it down on a sticky note and put it up somewhere around your work station. But not to despair — there are literally hundreds of ways to write down your passphrase and hide it and still keep it safe from prying eyes.

Wallet-sized notes

A well-respected cryptographer has his own method of creating and keeping his passphrases safe. He creates his own algorithm (recipe) for creating passphrases, and he writes it down and keeps it in his wallet. He uses this recipe to create a passphrase each time he needs one and any time he forgets a passphrase, he can pull out the slip of paper in his wallet, and follow the recipe. Moreover, if ever his wallet were lost or stolen, no one would be able to figure out what this old, dirty, oft-folded piece of paper would mean.

Here's an example of what a passphrase algorithm, or recipe, might look like:

- ✔ Uppercase year
- ✔ Space mOm's initials space
- ✔ Current month misspelled
- ✔ Space favorite song misspelled space
- ✔ End ?!?

Now, if you were to find a piece of paper with this list, it would not make much sense to you, but to me, it creates a passphrase like this:

```
@))# cEd nov3mbr taMboor1ne ?!?
```

Now I'll break it down so you can understand it:

- 2003 typed in characters instead of numbers is "@))#"

- Hit the space key, type Mom's initials in the same format as the recipe: lowercase, uppercase, lowercase. Then hit the space key again. This becomes "cEd" with spaces on either side.

- Misspell the current month. This is a variable so all of your passphrases won't be the same. (Obviously a maximum of 12 with this recipe.) Only I know how I plan to misspell each month and I have to remember which passphrases use which month. In this case, the month is November and I've spelled it "nov3mbr."

- Hit the space key, enter the first word of my favorite song — misspelled, of course — and then hit the space key again. My favorite song is "Tambourine Man," and I've spelled the first word as "taMboor1ne". (Although the recipe does not say "only the first word of the song," I know that's what I mean.)

- Use the characters "?!?" to end the passphrase.

I know this seems very complicated, but the point of the matter is that you need to create a recipe that YOU understand. I understand the one I made and there are a lot of unwritten — but understood by me — rules of the recipe. This is one of those cases in which the explanation is worse than the technique itself. Just for kicks, create a recipe that only you can understand and try using it to create passphrases for a couple Web sites. When you look at your recipe later on, it should make sense to you.

Bookmarking

This method is slightly more involved, but it has saved my bacon more than once. First of all, write down your passphrase on a piece of paper. I know that EVERYONE tells you to NEVER write down your passphrase, but in this case, I'm giving you written permission to do so. You don't have to write out the passphrase in its entirety; just enough to help you remember what it is. You can write down a hint rather than the passphrase, if you're more comfortable with that.

After you've written down your passphrase, stick it in a book that always sits in your bookcase or office cabinet. Now pull out your card file, create a card for whatever this passphrase is used for — like "e-mail" or "budget" — and write down the page number on the card, too. Your card will simply have a word and a number on it, which doesn't give much away to anyone who happens to be nosing around.

Now if you ever forget the passphrase for your e-mail or the budget, look for that card in your file. The card will have a page number on it. Pull out the book you used to hide the passphrase. (You DO remember which book you used, don't you?) Turn to the page number indicated on the card, and you will find your passphrase written down.

The reason this is safe enough to use is that the cards in the card file won't make any sense to anyone but you. The other factor is that if anyone were to find a passphrase hidden in your book, they won't know what the passphrase is for. This is not the most secure method of creating and storing passphrases, but it's a lot better than no security at all.

Offline storage

This is similar to the wallet-sized notes system, but you store the passphrase in a plain text file on a USB storage drive (sometimes called *keychain drives* or *thumb drives*). Type your passphrase, approximation of your passphrase, or a passphrase hint in a text editor and save it. Don't name the file "passphrase for VPN" or anything obvious like that; give the file a non-obvious name. I use really boring and uninteresting names like "latin_plants." Store that file on your USB drive, and keep the drive on your keychain or in your purse. It's still within reach if you need to use it, and USB drives are accessible almost as soon as you plug them in. In some cases you can even password-protect these drives, which makes the storage system even more secure.

Better safe than sorry

I don't usually suggest this for individuals, but if you are an executive or an important member of the IT team, your passphrases may be needed in an emergency. If you were hospitalized for a long period of time, were on a boat in the middle of the Pacific, or were basically unavailable, it's conceivable that a situation could arise where your company's business would suffer if your passphrase wasn't available. Not to be morbid, but this is something that you may want to consider putting in your will or in a bank's safe-deposit box if your financial information was encrypted. Your survivors would need to be able to get the passphrase to access your protected information.

In short, this method involves writing down your passphrase in full. Noting what it is used for, sealing it in a safety envelope (one you can't see into), signing and dating the sealed edges, and storing the envelope in the company's safe or a bank safe-deposit box. Wherever the envelope is stored, there should be a limited number of people who have access to it. I have made this standard practice in every company I have worked for, and it's saved the day more than once. I've had situations where a system administrator quit without notice and the practice of storing passphrases in the company safe allowed us to access the administrator's accounts and files. No nervous breakdowns needed.

Passphrase attacks

In case you are skeptical of the ability of password crackers to actually do as they say they can, consider this statistic issued by CERT (Computer Emergency Response Team at Carnegie Mellon University):

"In 1998, an intruder collected a list of 186,126 accounts and encrypted passwords. At the time the password file collection was discovered, the intruder had successfully guessed 47,642 of these passwords by using a password-cracking tool."

It's not hard to get passwords — even encrypted passwords. You can sniff them off the wire from network traffic, you can nose around in hard drive directories and files, and some companies leave them on unprotected databases.

Dictionary attacks use precompiled dictionaries of known words, often in dozens of languages (so that mixing in foreign words doesn't help you much) and are normally very successful against a majority of passwords and even some short passphrases. Much more sophisticated dictionary algorithms are needed to apply dictionary attacks on passphrases of any length beyond three words. The best defense is to never use anything close to a real word — because you might find it in the dictionary — in any portion of your passphrase.

Brute force attacks are obviously slower because they approach the password or passphrase on a character-by-character basis, but with powerful computers, they can be used against very complex passphrases. They examine each character of a letter and try to find an encrypted format that will match. As soon as one character is cracked, they go on to the next one. It may take many days or months to catch passphrases this way but, if the attacker is after a bank or credit card company, it may well be worth the effort.

Don't forget to flush!

Most systems store passphrases on the hard drive of the desktop computer. In order to increase security, most systems even encrypt the passphrase. But Windows and Macs have acquired a bad reputation of not adequately encrypting their passphrases or of storing them in obvious locations in the file directories. UNIX machines have been a bit better than this, but there are still ways of obtaining passwords from memory.

All computers store keystrokes in a variety of areas: swap files, caches, and SRAM, for example. There is a chance that attackers can cause your computer to dump its memory to a file in the hopes of obtaining a password. Even if you shut down your computer and reboot, not all of these temporary storage areas are overwritten. It's a weakness of computer security, and there's not really much you can do about it. You can erase temp files and folders and flush your caches, but that's about all you, as a user, are able to do.

The best advice is not to store any passphrases on your desktop computers. Save them to an external storage device such as a floppy disk, CD, or a keychain or thumb USB drive. In the case of the passphrases you use to log on to the network, there's not much you can do about that personally. Your network administrators should be able to increase the encryption of network logons and change the file storage to non-obvious directories.

The Key Concept

With all this talk about passphrases, I bet you thought I forgot about the keys. The keys are what are used to start the encryption process to lock a file and also to unlock (ore reverse) the process to decrypt the data. Contrary to popular belief, there is no part of the passphrase in a key; the passphrase is just a lock that *you* create to protect and access the key.

So, just what exactly *is* a key? Simply put, it's a number in binary form that is stored as a text file. You can open your key files and copy them to other files or, in the case of PGP, paste them into an e-mail message to send to someone else. Here is a portion of my PGP public key (a private key is never, ever published or otherwise made public):

```
mQGiBD6wIvsRBADxHMROiJJBin68dtvztxWMu+nIaSFGUn8m5iroeWMP4GvmZ
d3tl5k6FXuqi8jglzDtKZZLOWbYpM5IeZ9tTRyzjcLZCWorkM5UdF1XooDOOh
lVSjDcJgykqquOUnLoI/I5htYye5bPtzKHdOIhuC7Kq9oA/b+QYATaBMmnavP
IOwCg/9fY+OkJ/5GYxgp7UfLkXP/ShnEEAJQ1JFi4X5eqWQTlnHznUFNNM8y4
vpiaL1C2fLBH3orYXmzr8N/4MylSOPJhCMWCgeTOFAfMBC4+6jWfiWFt8Q6Pv
XGgAZD41/TpX8MURNNQCvGH3zeCjzjl/yTyaJG8a+AlMcK58DzKSlBwgegyod
yBiPbatWluqAEFJItDwZWaBACyLVO9r+jKMdvO3RuryUNgIbCG3MO3vBBoxrA
a4tzLobOxLUW5ewTJG9NfLKJOLL6h5Unx21Bb5/CvfYbLfXdbHdwcVGbuIOAs
KvfOMjgQZwRZQz5jcqgrGQYi
```

That's not my entire key, but it's enough to give you an idea of what one looks like, isn't it? It certainly doesn't look like a number, but to your computer and the PGP program, it is.

But just because this is a key does not mean that I can use it for other encryption programs. The key above can be used only with PGP. Likewise, an AES key can only be used to encrypt and decrypt data with the AES algorithm and a 3DES key can only be used to encrypt and decrypt data with the 3DES algorithm. Keys are generally not interchangeable between applications.

Key generation

Keys are generated by a program within the encryption program. If you are creating your own encryption program (and many programmers do), there is a specific formula for creating a key, which is really just another algorithm. That algorithm creates a stream of pseudo-random data that starts when the user tells the program what size key to create and for which algorithm.

After you tell the program that you want a 128-bit AES key, for example, the key generator goes to work in creating a number. In order not to start from the number 0 every time, something called an *initialization vector* plays roulette in effect, and starts the count-off with a number. The *pseudo-random number generator* (PRNG) starts from that number and keeps going "eenie-meenie-miney-moe" until it picks a long random number. After the number is created, the key generator goes through some more processes to make sure that the number is valid, has not been used before, and will not be used again. We're not finished yet, though. The last, but not least, step is to add some more random data to mix with the number that the PRNG created.

The additional number that is mixed with the key number is called a *seed*. In effect, that number is used to help "grow" a better number. The seed number is created by gathering random data from things that are happening to your computer — mouse movements, cursor location, print commands, disk read and write speeds, and so on. All of that data is gathered at the same time and is thrown into a pool of random data for future use by the key generator algorithm.

If you turn your computer off, all the random data that has been gathered by the computer is dumped. There is a slight possibility that, if you generated a key right after a computer was rebooted, there wouldn't be enough random data to create a good seed for an encryption key. Most key generators solve this problem by dumping gathered data to a file before the system is shut down. In that way there is already a pool to start with. It's always a good idea, though, to generate a key on a computer that has been continuously running for a long time.

One of the major problems with poor encryption programs is that they use a very poor PRNG. If you are coding your own program, never use the random number generator that comes with programming languages or the one included in operating systems. They don't gather enough random data from your computer to meet the entropy tests. For a list of software for random number generators, go to the WWW Virtual Library on random number generators at `http://crypto.mat.sbg.ac.at/links/rando.html`.

Back in the old days . . .

I'll digress just a moment here to tell you how things *used* to be back in the old days — like sometime in the late '80s or early '90s. Back then, most key-creating programs relied upon the user's input to help generate the key. The program would ask you to move your mouse or type at random on the keyboard until the key generator had enough random data to seed a key. The problem with that was that it often took a minute or two of mouse movements and keystrokes to complete the process. Most users got bored and would end up tapping on the same keys over and over or just move their mouse in a circle, which resulted in flawed random data. Luckily, we don't have to rely on that process any more.

Protecting your keys

As I mention earlier, a good passphrase is one method of protecting your keys, but almost as important is the need to store your keys in a non-obvious location. If you are on a network with a full PKI *(Public Key Infrastructure)* system, there's probably not much you can do about that as the system administrators will have set up key servers, back-up keys, and recovery keys (if they're good, that is!). But what do you do if you're using your own system? There are five good, safe methods of keeping your keys safe:

1. Don't save your keys on your desktop computer (unless your company requires you to).

2. If you must store your keys on your desktop computer, see if you can change the name of the folder or locate the keys in a different directory. (You'll have to check with your IT staff about this.)

3. Always save copies of your keys to a removable drive such as a USB keychain drive, CD, or floppy disk.

4. Keep the USB drive, CD, or floppy with your keys on your person.

5. If you cannot keep your key storage media on you, put it in a safe place such as a safe, a bank safe-deposit box, or a locking cabinet.

Back before there were USB drives, I always kept a copy of my keys on a floppy disk. I also had to keep the disk at work in case I needed it in a hurry. We had one locking file cabinet for three people to use. My solution? I slipped the floppy disk on to the bottom of the file drawer instead of in a hanging folder. The folders easily slid back and forth above the disk. What was funny was that my co-workers always assumed that I was putting the disk *in* a folder and they drove themselves crazy trying to find it. This method may not be the safest in the world, but it sure beats saving the floppy in a desk drawer!

There are a number of complicated methods of safely storing keys that are mentioned in Part II on PKI. This is because that type of storage is often a component (or policy) of a PKI system. If you need information on sharing keys, key escrow, or other key protection systems, please check there.

What to do with your old keys

One question I often hear from people is, "I have an old key on a server and I've forgotten the passphrase. Is there any way I can delete the key?" I'm sorry to have to tell them that they are out of luck. Without the original passphrase to the key, you can't delete it from any public server. Although this is a royal pain, it was meant as a form of security to prevent unauthorized persons from messing with your keys.

If you do have the passphrase to your old key, you can revoke it. How you do this depends on the type of system you used to create the key in the first place. In PGP, there is a very clear command to revoke your key. You can also assign someone else (or other authority) to revoke the key when you give the word. Many Certificate Authorities work in this manner. The other method of getting rid of old keys is to set an expiration date. If you do not reinstate the key before the expiration date, the key expires and becomes useless.

It's a small bone of contention with me that PGP and other systems, by default, have a key expiration date of "Never." I think it should be the other way around and that the default should be a one-year expiration date from the date of creation. But I'm not in charge of such things, and they obviously didn't ask me for advice.

Some cryptiquette

I have to thank my good friend, Dave Del Torto, (also known as DDT) for the term *cryptiquette*. He is one of the original cypherpunks and his soap box for years has been the proper creation, storing, sharing, and maintenance of keys. There is more cryptiquette information elsewhere in this book and on the Cheat Sheet in the front, but here are a few items to start you off:

1. Always set an expiration date for your key when you create it.

2. If you lose a key or the passphrase, please advise others of your new key and update your key on all servers where it is stored.

3. If someone sends you a public key, never publish it to a public server without the owner's permission.

4. Always save your passphrase somehow, somewhere.

5. Always make backups of your keys and put them somewhere safe.

That's your teaser for now. Look for other cryptiquette rules elsewhere in this book!

Part II
Public Key Infrastructure

The 5th Wave   By Rich Tennant

FREELANCER NED WILLIS CONSULTS WITH A MEMBER OF HIS TECHNICAL STAFF

"...and that is pretty much all there is to PKI."

In this part . . .

People are really confused about Public Key Infrastructure, also known as PKI. They focus on the words "public" and "key" but they forget to include the last word, "infrastructure." That's the important part. Infrastructure has been used most commonly to refer to the roads, bridges, rail lines, electric power cables, water lines, and similar public works that are required for an industrial economy to function. In a network, an infrastructure is the servers, desktop computers, operating systems, application software, routers, hubs, network operating systems — the interconnectivity between all the machines. It's what allows the Internet to work.

In this part, I tell you all the things you need to build a public key infrastructure. Yes, it's bigger than a bread box and you'll need lots of different pieces to put it all together. I define and describe those pieces and how they work together, and I'm sure that by the time you finish this section, you'll be able to figure out what you need and what you don't need to build a robust public key system.

Chapter 5

The PKI Primer

The dream of PKI (Public Key Infrastructure) is that it was supposed to be the answer to all our digital dreams. It was supposed to give us all irrefutable digital IDs and make it possible to utilize a "single-sign-on" feature to be able to log on to one network and have all others recognize that sign-on. It was also supposed to allow us to access other networks, resources, and data with ease; all the while protecting all information with encryption. The reality is somewhat different.

One of the big problems with access to all networks is that of trust. A UserID and password is a vehicle for controlling access but it doesn't really do anything about verifying that the User is who he or she claims to be. That's how hackers get into networks — they often use a legitimate UserID and password to log on. It's like having drivers' licenses without a picture — anyone who presents a credential has to be given the benefit of the doubt because there is no secondary method of checking the ID.

Digital Certificates and public/private encryption keys are one method used by computer security staff to help to give the network an added level of ID to check. The basis of trust is higher because it is assumed that the person presenting digital certificates and encryption keys are more likely to be that person. Why is there an extra level of trust in this case? Because of all the hoops a person has to jump through in order to obtain these digital credentials. If these digital credentials have been processed properly, one or more persons has attested to the identification of the owner. If the identity ever comes into question, you can go back up the chain to see who issued the certificates and what identification process was used prior to issuing the digital certificates.

PKI uses Digital Certificates and encrypted public keys to authenticate users, encrypt files and directories owned by the user, and, in the process, ensures data integrity and the non-repudiation of users. PKI uses encryption to create Digital Certificates which are gathered, distributed, and maintained by an intricate infrastructure of servers and software. An infrastructure in the civil sense includes roads, traffic lights, directional signs, the distribution of electricity to users, phone lines, clean water and water processing plants, and offices of workers to help organize the use and distribution of everything. An infrastructure doesn't necessarily need to be complex, but it does need to operate efficiently. PKI can be as complicated but there are several vendors who will sell you complete systems. With the exception of PGP, there are no "single-box, all-in-one" PKI solutions and even PGP has limited PKI uses.

This chapter is what PKI is and what PKI isn't. I don't discuss the actual encryption technologies at work here because the digital certificates and encryption algorithms are covered in other chapters. So, if you or someone in your organization has caught the PKI bug, it's important to understand the issues and the commitment necessary to implement a full PKI solution.

What Is PKI?

As I've mentioned, the major part of PKI is the infrastructure itself. The infrastructure is built to create, organize, store, distribute, and maintain Public Keys — which are the PK in PKI. In this case you're dealing with Digital Certificates which are just another name — or another form — of public keys and private keys. But, instead of a person creating those keys himself (as you do with PGP), a person goes to a *Certificate Authority* (or *CA*) to have the keys created.

The CA is a computer system that requires human interaction to issue digital certificates. Basically, you request a digital certificate from your computer which interacts with the CA computer. The CA "operator" then needs to see some sort of personal identification (such as a drivers license) before the operator tells the CA computer that it's okay to issue you a certificate. The certificate is then sent from the CA computer to your computer.

Before I get too deep into the explanations here, let me outline the infrastructure for you. This infrastructure consists of special servers and software — some of it you own and operate and others are outside your domain. Without further ado, here's what you are dealing with:

> ✔ **Certificate Authority (CA)** — Usually an outside entity such as Verisign, CyberTrust, or RSA. These are sometimes referred to as *Trusted Authorities* because, for PKI to work, you have to be able to place your trust in an outside third party to issue Digital Certificates.

- ✔ **Digital Certificates** — Essentially two files: private key and the public key. These are originally issued by the CA and, if you need to verify a Digital Certificate, that is who you go to for verification. Digital Certificates are usually kept on your computer and may also kept on key servers within an organization.

- ✔ **Desktop computers and servers** — Frequently need to have a special application or PKI "client" for the user to be able to encrypt and decrypt data.

- ✔ **LDAP or X.500 Directories** — Databases that collect and distribute keys internally. Often you'll have one directory for internal use and another for remote users or outside business partners.

- ✔ **Registration Authority (RA)** — Internal version of a CA. If a large organization has many offices and/or divisions, they will often let the RA handle requests for Digital Certificates, verify identities, and then forward that information to the CA to actually issue the Digital Certificates.

That, in a nutshell, is a PKI system. As you can surmise, it takes a lot of coordination to plan a PKI solution, obtain the necessary hardware and software, install the system network-wide, and start using it. Of course you can buy a total solution from a vendor that includes the servers, software, instructions, and support. If you have a small to medium-size business, this might be the more cost-effective way to go. It all depends on what you need the PKI for and whether or not you expect your needs to grow.

So many companies and top executives have jumped on the PKI bandwagon without a good understanding of what, exactly, they will be using it for. They've heard that it's the latest thing and it will solve lots of problems, but they haven't stopped to identify their problems or what they hope PKI will solve. Make that a priority at your company — plan before you leap!

PKI solutions vary from vendor to vendor on how they are sct-up and operated. A main part of this involves the encryption technology used and the different forms of digital certificates. Because of this, not all PKI systems will understand one another. For example, if your company wants to be able to communicate via PKI with another company or a client, you need to make sure that your system and theirs will be compatible. If you plan to use the PKI system internally only, then that is not such a major concern.

Certificate Authorities (CAs)

This is the Grand Poobah of PKIs. Without a CA you can't issue Digital Certificates, which contain the public/private encryption keys that a person (or a company) uses to encrypt and decrypt data. The security of a Digital Certificate is tied to the CA; if you don't know or don't trust the CA, you probably shouldn't trust Digital Certificates issued by that CA.

Digital Certificates are available in different levels of trust; depending upon the amount of identity verification done by the Certificate Authority. The first level of trust is normally used to identify an individual rather than a company. To positively identify an individual, the CA usually asks for a driver's license and/or a notarized letter as proof of identity. Another, higher, level of trust available in a Digital Certificate involves a background and credit check and lots of other hoops to jump through. Because these certificates are usually reserved for persons or e-commerce sites responsible for a high level of trust, they can also be based on biometrics such as a fingerprint or iris scan.

If you have a small office or Web site, you can get away with using a third-party CA, such as the ones I mention. Be careful who you choose to be your CA, though. The CA should have been in business for a reasonable amount of time, have a solid reputation, and likely to be recognized by others as a trusted party. If your CA is "Bob's Discount Certificate Authority" you may find that other individuals or companies won't want to trust your Digital Certificate because the CA that issued it is either unknown (and thus, "untrusted") or because the CA has a dubious reputation.

Large companies who will only be using digital certificates internally often set themselves up as the CA because they trust themselves and they know who to extend that trust to. An internal CA won't hold the same level of trust with outside users, but because it's intended to be used only internally (within the organization, its partners, and employees), trust doesn't usually become an issue.

Digital Certificates

Digital Certificates are used to verify the identity of a person or business via the CA. For a person, a Digital Certificate can also be used to identify access rights and responsibility roles. Some Digital Certificates are limited to use only for encrypting (and decrypting) e-mail while others may allow access to sensitive files. They can also be issued to specific computers to identify their roles, such as desktops, laptops, firewalls, and routers. When the Digital Certificate is issued, its uses and limitations are spelled out within the certificate itself. Figure 5-1 is an example of the area within a Digital Certificate that spells out what it can be used for.

Digital Certificates are files stored on your computer that contain the public keys that an individual uses to encrypt and decrypt data. You need to have PKI-aware or PKI-compliant software programs to be able to use your Digital Certificates. One software program almost everyone has that is able to use and recognize Digital Certificates is your Web browser. In the Internet options or preferences area of your browser, you can find a listing of all the certificates that are stored in your browser. Figure 5-2 shows you where the certificates are stored in the Mozilla Web browser.

Figure 5-1:
The purposes for which this digital certificate can be used.

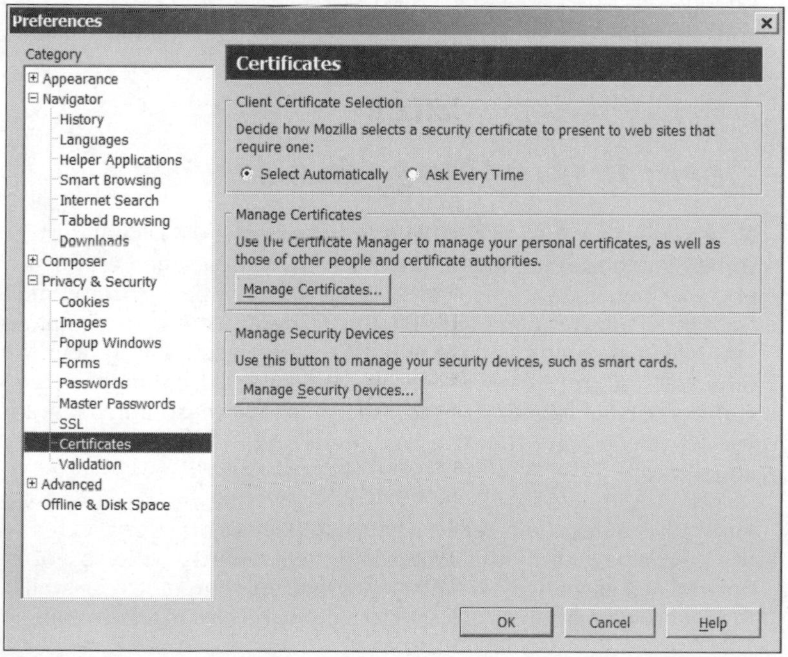

Figure 5-2:
The Digital Certificate options in the Mozilla Web browser are found in the Preferences menu.

In fact, that's one of the main usages of PKI today: authenticate users and servers over the Web for e-commerce transactions. Digital Certificates are also used to encrypt email and data and ensure that remote users (home workers, road warriors, partners, clients, customers, etc.) have a secure connection with which to communicate. PKI can't do all that alone, so many companies have set up VPNs for the secure, encrypted connections, and PKI for the authentication and data encryption. That's not a bad combination and it normally works very well.

One of the biggest problems with Digital Certificates is making sure you have the right one. Is Betty Smith the same person who goes by Liz Smith at the office? Is she the same person who has a Digital Certificate under the name Elizabeth Smith on her home computer and uses the certificate to send encrypted email? When you look for the certificate for Bob Jones, you see that there are no less than 20 Bob Joneses and all of them have different e-mail addresses. Which one is your Bob Jones using? Are some of these certificates old ones that your Bob Jones forgot to revoke? It's important that you get the correct Digital Certificate because you are placing trust in these people based on their certificates.

PGP key certificates come with what is referred to as a fingerprint. This *fingerprint* is a series of alpha-numeric characters (or occasionally various words) which are unique to each public key attached to the certificate. Figure 5-3 shows my PGP key with the fingerprint clearly marked in a separate area towards the bottom of the dialog box. If someone wants to make sure that they have the right key for me, they can call me or send an email and ask me to verify my fingerprint.

Desktops, laptops, and servers

Now that we've opened the Pandora's Box of who a Digital Certificate belongs to, we can look at the inanimate objects that are issued certificates: computers. You have to place your trust in various computers from time to time, so Digital Certificates can help to not only identify computers, but also to give you information on the level of trust the certificate gives them. Web browsers often use the certificates stored in the browser program to verify Web servers used in e-commerce transactions. The reasoning behind this is that you want to be sure that you are connecting to the real online shop and not an imitator.

Firewalls, routers, and servers can also have Digital Certificates to help identify them and identify their roles and their security policies. For example, a firewall can exchange certificates with other companies' firewalls and servers for secure communications and to establish rules for their connection.

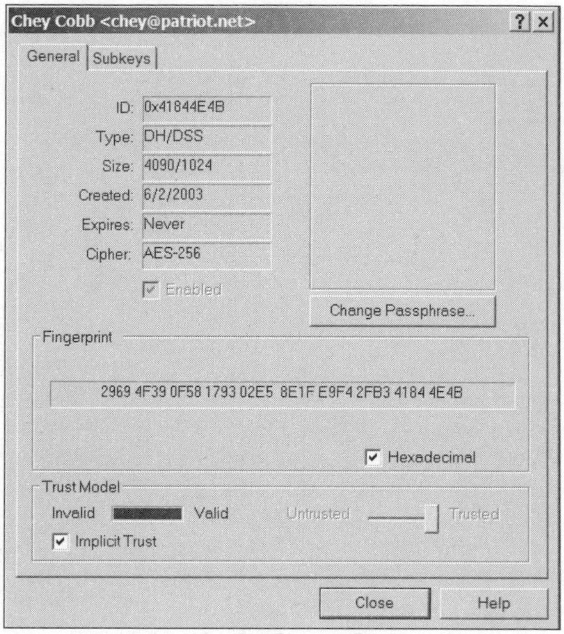

Figure 5-3:
The PGP properties dialog box which shows the fingerprint associated with the public key.

Although the Digital Certificates used to identify servers and other computers are really no different than the ones used to identify individuals, you still need to make sure that the certificate is the correct one. Our Web browsers automatically check the properties of the certificates and tell us when there is a problem by popping up a dialog box that tells you that something is not right. Many people just ignore these dialog boxes and click "OK" but they really should check the certificate properties and find out why the certificate isn't working. For this you will need to call the owner of the certificate and ask them what is wrong (you will probably be referred to the technical assistance personnel). Figure 5-4 shows a certificate that cannot be verified.

How various software programs deal with certificates varies quite a bit from program to program. For example, MS Outlook and Qualcomm Eudora are both email applications. You would think that they would both handle Digital Certificates the same way, but they don't. This is due to the way the program was written and is not the fault of the certificates themselves. All certificates are basically the same and contain the same types of information. However it is the software programmers who make the difference — not every programmer writes a program to deal with Digital Certificates in the same manner. That's where incompatibilities happen.

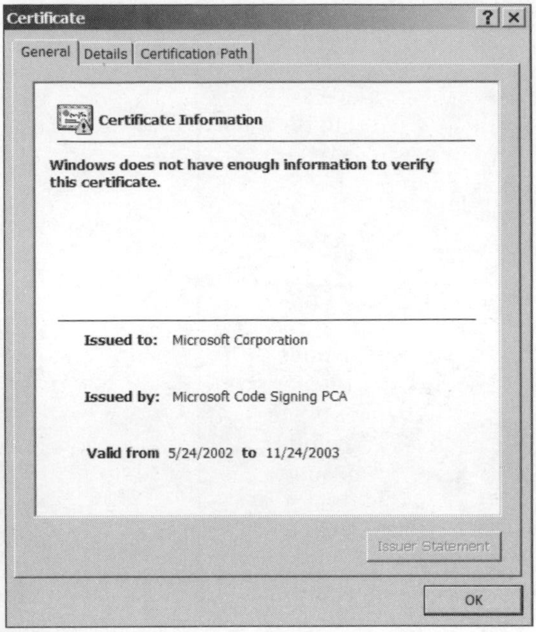

Figure 5-4:
Checking
the
properties
of an invalid
digital
certificate.

Key servers

Because CA servers are used to issue Digital Certificates and to verify their authenticity, there must be some other method used to store and distribute keys. And there is — they are called *key servers.* These servers become the equivalent of air traffic controllers because they make sure the right keys are in the right areas and they keep track of what all the keys are doing. As air traffic controllers identify planes and then make sure all the airplanes are in the right place at the right time, key servers do almost the same thing with keys. In order to do this appropriately and efficiently, key servers need to contain the correct information about all the keys that are floating around in cyberspace.

Key servers are the one of the most problematic portions of a PKI system. They hold all the Digital Certificates' public keys and distribute them to computers that request them. The servers contain information on who can ask for which keys, which keys are allowed to do what, and, just as importantly, which keys are invalid and should no longer be used. The hard part is making sure that all the key servers have this information. Keeping the key servers up to date is a big chore, especially when this task is being handled manually by the support staff.

If a person in a company changes jobs, it's very likely that his responsibilities will also change. Those changes need to be made to his Digital Certificate and his key. If a person leaves a company, then his or her Digital Certificate and key need to be revoked. Sub-contractors who work onsite need to have certificates and keys that will only work for a limited period of time and then expire automatically. The possible scenarios for changes in keys is endless but all these changes need to be made so the PKI system will work appropriately. Not only do the changes need to be made on the key servers, but the desktop computers and laptops need to query the key servers on a regular basis and ask for updates.

Registration Authorities (RAs)

Registration Authorities (RAs) are strange birds in the PKI system. They are roughly equivalent to a CA, but are one level down in a trust hierarchy. In some governmental PKI systems one office is deemed the CA and agencies and subordinate offices have their own RAs. The RAs screen the applications for Digital Certificates, do the background checks or identification checks, and then submit the paperwork to the CA to issue the Digital Certificate. The reasoning behind the use of RAs is to help reduce the workload on CAs.

In some situations, the RAs can issue sort of a temporary Digital Certificate so the applicant can begin using his or her Digital Certificate immediately. Normally these "temporary" Digital Certificates are limited as to what they can be used for. These Digital Certificates are not fully trusted until they are eventually signed and approved by the CA.

I've been to multinational companies that set up all of their overseas offices with RAs and the CAs are located in the U.S. Once a month or so, all of the overseas offices forward the certificates issued by the RAs so that the CAs can review them, sign them, and send them back. Only certificates that have been digitally signed by CAs are highly trusted.

Uses for PKI Systems

The dream of PKI was to issue a Digital Certificate to everyone which they would store on a smart cart, electronic token, floppy disk, or similar device. When a person wanted to conduct a bank transaction, she would insert her certificate token into a reader and would be automatically identified. When she was finished with her banking, she could board a bus and place her token on the reader which would verify that she has a monthly transportation card. Then, when she got home, she could log on to her favorite online shopping site and run her token through the reader. That would give the shopping site her name, address, store account number, and credit card number. So why isn't this type of PKI a reality? Compatibility is the big issue. Not all computer networks and software applications work the same way. It would require enormous cooperation amongst vendors and network owners to change their systems in order for them to be completely compatible with everyone else's.

Because there are so many different operating systems, different versions of operating systems, and different software programs and versions, this would be an enormous and expensive undertaking.

The other problem with a world-wide compatible PKI system is that of ownership. No one involved would be able to agree upon the setup of a central authority to be the CA. Some claim this would be a governmental responsibility while others feel that it should be run more like a public utility. The issue is trust. Who would you ultimately trust with all the Digital Certificates issued in the world? And who would fund such a project?

Therefore, PKI is mainly used for secure transactions between companies or governmental agencies. An e-commerce Web site that uses SSL for encryption is a portion of PKI system. Encrypted e-mail is also another transaction that may be a part of a PKI system. Some companies or agencies may want all staff to digitally sign any documents they've created. Because a digital signature is derived from a Digital Certificate and its key, this is also part of a PKI system. There are so many possible scenarios and solutions it's almost impossible to list them all. However, PKI in the workplace is usually tied to three things:

1. Identifying system users

2. Using Digital Certificates to describe access permissions

3. Using Digital Certificates to encrypt email and other data

If you're a small company and can't afford an expensive PKI system; especially if you just want to do a few things, you're much better off using PGP. PGP is a type of PKI solution without all the overhead. Instead of depending upon Certificate Authorities and key servers, you rely upon a circle of trusted colleagues and acquaintances to verify your identity and you use free public key servers to distribute your public keys. It works well for small organizations, but it can get really complicated for large ones. I've heard through the grapevine that PGP Corporation (www.pgp.com) is close to releasing a full PKI solution in a box. I'll be interested to see how it works in real life.

PKI can be used to indicate a company's commitment to maintaining a secure infrastructure. Note that PKI is not used to *replace* any security policies or procedures, but it can be used to strengthen implementation. Because Digital Certificates can be used to control access to computers, networks, and documents, it can help keep unauthorized personnel out. If all documents are digitally signed by their creators, then you can also control the integrity of your data and also tie ultimate responsibility to the data's creator. It's difficult for someone to say they didn't write a particular memo if their digital signature is on it.

Governments are beginning to require that PKI be used for secure transactions in certain industries and with certain types of data. There are many state governments and foreign government agencies that require that a PKI system be in place before you can do business with them. These government entities want to make sure they can identify users, control their access, and encrypt communications. In some situations, legislation has been written to make PKI a legal requirement.

Here are the URLs for some of the United States regulations concerning the use of PKI:

- ✔ **CA** — www.ss.ca.gov/digsig/regulations.htm
- ✔ **NC** — www.secretary.state.nc.us/ecomm/ecrules.htm
- ✔ **TX** — www.dir.state.tx.us/standards/srrpub13.htm
- ✔ **WA** — www.secstate.wa.gov/ea/ea.aspx?m=undefined

Because there is a call amongst people to initiate electronic voting of some kind, I wouldn't be surprised to see PKI being examined as a possible solution. Because it is used for authentication and encryption, that could solve the problems of identifying the users and encrypting their votes. There would need to be much stricter standards for PKI than there are now to use it for electronic voting, but if it makes sense on the money side, you can be sure that some states will at least consider it.

Common PKI Problems

I can't go into all the wonderful things about PKI without discussing some of the downsides. Most of these problems stem from the fact that there is no "standard" PKI implementation and compatibility issues. Other problems have to do with user awareness. Most people would not know that they are dealing with a PKI system if it crept up and bit them on the nose. Users are not familiar with how to interact with these systems which are generally not very user-friendly.

Here are some of the basic problems with PKI systems:

- ✔ Not all applications accept the same Digital Certificates.
- ✔ Not all applications are built to accept Digital Certificates at all.
- ✔ Digital Certificates can be forged.
- ✔ People generally don't know how to tell the difference between a good (trusted) certificate and one they shouldn't trust.
- ✔ The user interface for Digital Certificates is poor.
- ✔ If the Certificate Authority's security is poor, you can't trust their certificates.
- ✔ It's difficult to tell which Digital Certificate belongs to which person; especially if the person has a common name.

- ✔ When a Digital Certificate is no longer valid (revoked), not all key servers are updated with this information.

- ✔ If you lose your passphrase for your Digital Certificate, it's difficult or impossible to either use your keys again or remove them from the key servers.

- ✔ If you lose your keys (hard drive crash or lost floppy disk), you can't always recover the lost keys.

- ✔ Setting up and maintaining a PKI system is very labor intensive and complex. It is not something that just anyone can do.

Actually, I could add another 15 or 20 problems to the list, but they would all be variations of the themes mentioned above. Although several vendors offer complete PKI solutions, they don't necessarily promise that their solution will work with other companies' solutions. So, if your company goes with Vendor A to install a system and your biggest client goes with Vendor X, there's no guarantee that your two systems will be able to talk to one another securely.

Given all the problems stated, I must explain that many of the problems come from improperly configured PKI systems. When a PKI system is 100% correct in its setup, most of these problems are resolved. The fact remains, however, that we humans are prone to making mistakes with computers, so PKI systems often have mistakes in their configuration. Your best bet is to deal with professionals and ask them to explain how your setup resolves or removes some of the major problems that I've stated.

After you've initiated a PKI system you must remember to tell your staff how to use it properly. If they don't know how it works, they won't understand the problems. Getting your users to interact with the system appropriately will also go a long way in resolving some of the PKI drawbacks.

Chapter 6

PKI Bits and Pieces

*T*here are many detailed books in bookstores and libraries about the intricacies of PKI. Within the PKI structure are Certificate Authorities, Root Certificates, Registration Authorities, and Certificate Servers. At first glance this can be an overwhelming list of nonsense to the uninitiated. My intent with this chapter is to describe in more detail some of the concepts I introduced in the previous chapter in order to give you a slightly deeper level of understanding of PKI systems. You'll need this information in order to have an intelligent conversation with any of the many PKI vendors. It's also important to remember that these vendors don't all have the same definition of a "total" PKI solution. In some cases you'll still have to buy extra software and hardware, while some vendors really do give you an all-inclusive package. So, if a PKI solution strikes you as being a viable solution for you, get a checklist of what exactly the vendor includes in their cost.

For this chapter, I concentrate on the innards of a PKI system — those things that make everything else work. That means the certificates, the computers that store and issue the certificates, and some of the configuration issues. Again, this is not meant to be a full tutorial, but it will give you a better foundation from which to begin.

Creating your own PKI system gives you more control over the system and how it works. You can begin with bits and pieces and build up as you need. Alternatively, you can go with a "total solution" from a single vendor. The total solution route has its advantages in the fact that you will get assistance from the vendor in setting up and fine-tuning your system, and you'll be able to get training and support from them, too. Whichever route you take, I highly recommend that you try to stay with one vendor. That way you can be more confident that all additions will integrate well.

In order to be able to trust the veracity of your PKI system, your entire network will need to be secured — that includes physical access as well as network access. The reason for this is that you don't want an intruder to get into your system and steal or copy encryption keys. You also want to ensure that the people who have been given Digital Certificates are the only ones who have access to the network. Otherwise, you won't be able to trust who has owner-ship of the Digital Certificates. Security does not have to be expensive, but it does require a commitment because it's not a one-time deal; it's an ongoing process.

Why would you want a PKI system, you ask? The most common reason companies install a PKI system is so the staff can encrypt and/or digitally sign documents. This keeps the documents safe, limits who can change them, and gives you something called *nonrepudiation*. Nonrepudiation is a way to guarantee that the creator of a document cannot later deny having created it. It also means that you can prove who sent and received messages. Which leads to another reason for using a PKI system — you can encrypt and/or digitally sign e-mails. This has great benefit when you are sending and receiving sensitive or proprietary data. PKI can also be used for access control and authentication as well. The Digital Certificates are linked to specific individuals (or computers), and you can configure Digital Certificates so that the individual can only use them for certain tasks. All in all, PKI is a quite sophisticated system.

So, let's take a look at some of the important parts of a PKI system, what they do, and how they might work for you.

Certificate Authorities

You can think of a Certificate Authority (CA) as the king. He is the ultimate authority and a figure of great trust. He is in charge of making identity papers for all his subjects. He signs these papers and stamps them with the Royal Stamp. Along with the identity papers he lists what responsibilities and privi-leges the bearer has. Because the king has issued and signed these papers, all subjects of the PKI kingdom trust these papers.

In order to set up a working PKI, you have to go to the king of the PKI king-dom and ask for one of these identity papers. This identity paper identifies you to the PKI kingdom and also spells out what tasks you are allowed to do. When the king is satisfied that your identity has been verified, he signs that paper for you. By magic, two keys have appeared in your pockets that are linked to the identity paper. The king keeps a copy of the paper for future ref-erence. This paper is your Digital Certificate. Each Digital Certificate contains the following information:

- **Certificate Version** — The X.509 version number (that is, 1, 2, or 3).

- **Serial Number** — A certificate serial number that uniquely distinguishes this certificate from all other certificates issued by the same king (CA).

- **Signature Algorithm Identifier** — Information about the algorithm used by the king.

- **Issuer Name** — The name of the king (certificate's issuing CA).

- **Validity Period** — The activation and expiration date of the certificate.

- **Public Key** — The public key.

- **Subject Distinguished Name** — A name specifying the certificate's owner.

- **Subject Alternate Name Email** — The owner's e-mail address.

- **Subject Alternate Name URI** — The owner's Web site URI/URL.

All PKI kingdoms have agreed on the format of Digital Certificates, so they all have the same types of data in the same format. That means they are able to exchange digital signatures between kingdoms (companies or organizations) and that all kingdoms will accept the identity of the bearer and the description of the certificate's uses.

One more thing: The king doesn't really give out Digital Certificates out of the goodness of his heart. He doesn't have this huge altruistic streak that makes him want to make online transactions more secure. No, this is a business to him and, like all businesses, he charges for his services. And he charges a lot. So, if you need a lot of certificates from the king (CA), it could get very expensive!

So in the real world, this all translates as follows:

- You request is sent to a Certificate Authority like Entrust, Verisign, GeoTrust, Baltimore, Thawte, and so on. The request includes verifiable personal information about you like a driver's license number or a passport number.

- The CA issues you a Digital Certificate after you have completed the application. During the application process, your computer has generated both the public and private keys that are linked to the Digital Certificate.

- In order to get your certificate signed by the CA, you send in notarized paperwork to the CA's office. After they verify your identity, they sign the certificate. This is called a *root signed* certificate.

- Now you can use that certificate to encrypt and/or digitally sign e-mail and to encrypt and/or digitally sign documents.

The above is a very simplified example of how the system works. It can get much more complex when Digital Certificates are used in the corporate world. Businesses can get their own Digital Certificates or they can have their own internal CAs. Certificates can be issued to either computers or individuals, too. But if you just want a Digital Certificate to be able to use S/MIME encryption with your e-mail program, you can contact one of the companies I mention and get one for yourself. Individual certificates are sold to individuals for a moderate fee.

Pretenders to the throne

If you own a Web site or conduct some form of e-commerce and you want to conduct business online, you will need to have Digital Certificates issued by a CA. If you want to set up a PKI system for your company, you will also have to have Digital Certificates. If you don't want to deal with any of the public third-party CAs, you can set up your own kingdom and crown yourself as king! Install Certificate Authority software (or use the CA software included with most major Web server software), and you can issue your own Digital Certificates.

You can check out free software such as OpenSSL or SSLeay which have CA services. Microsoft has included CA services in their server software for a number of years now.

Many small businesses operate their Web sites and e-commerce sites this way or have set up their own internal PKI systems with their own CAs. In effect, you become your own *trusted root* and can sign all the certificates that you issue certificates to your desktop PCs and servers and to individuals.

Setting up your own CA takes a moderate amount of skill and the ability to sit at a server for quite a long period in order to complete the configuration and testing process. It's not terribly difficult but it isn't easy-peasy, either. There are a lot of windows, dialog boxes, forms to fill out, and tons of questions to answer. It requires good concentration and patience more than anything else. For that reason, I recommend that you at least read through the step-by-step instructions first. Almost all CA software products and their installation information can be found online. You may want to print out the document and read it over when you've got the time to take it all in.

Registration Authorities

Sometimes the PKI kingdom and the king are overwhelmed or tired of having to process all the certificate paperwork all of the time. It's time then to delegate responsibility to someone else. Enter the Registration Authority (RA). It's like the prince of the PKI kingdom and he can do things under the king's authority.

The prince is a lower-level authority than the king, and in many respects can be seen as subservient to the king. The king tells the prince what authority he has and what duties he can undertake. In most situations, the prince acts as a middleman between the person requesting a Digital Certificate and the king. That's because the king can sometimes be overwhelmed with requests coming from many different entities and the prince can help take a load off. Often the prince will process applications for identity papers (Digital Certificates) and sometimes give temporary papers until he can verify the person's identity and then he forwards the identity papers to the king for him to sign.

If you have a small organization or a small e-commerce business, you probably won't need an RA. As I indicate above, the RA is a type of support vehicle for a CA that gets overwhelmed with requests. You'll most often find RA in large organizations that have many offices. Each office can have its own RA with the CA located at the headquarters building. The RAs can store up their requests for signed Digital Certificates and then forward them to the CA to handle all in one batch. An RA has its own digital signature (which identifies it as an RA) that is issued by the CA and gives the RA authority and permission to issue Digital Certificates. The RA's Digital Certificate is signed by the CA to show that it is authentic. When an RA issues certificates, it creates a chain of records indicating the issuance and signing process. Not so amazingly, this downward delegation is called *chaining certificates*. If you were to examine the details of a Digital Certificate issued by an RA, you would see a hierarchical relationship and the certificates at the top of the hierarchy signify a higher level of trust and authority than those at the bottom of the hierarchy.

Certificate Policies (CP)

In order for any authority to work correctly — a CA or an RA — you need to tell the authority what rules to follow in issuing, storing, revoking, and expiring certificates. Without rules there is no order and the certificates that are issued are flawed. I would advise any company setting up their own CA not to accept the default settings to the CP configuration file. It takes a fair amount of serious consideration to correctly set up a CP, but the effort will be truly worth it because you won't have to keep going back to correct your mistakes. If you make mistakes when you issue Digital Certificates, you'll have to revoke all of those certificates and reissue new ones. Believe me — that's a real pain!

So, what are some of the policies that a CP covers? Have a look here — and remember that these are just *some* of the policies you need to have answers for:

- ✓ Where are the records and logs of the CA to be stored?
- ✓ Who is in charge of critical functions of the CA?
- ✓ Are the keys to be backed up?

- Where are the backed up keys stored and for how long?
- Will you be allowing key recovery?
- Do the keys have a limited validity?
- What is the standard validity period for any key?
- Can the CA delegate to RAs?
- Will the CA issue Digital Certificates for authorization to use applications or resources?
- Will the CA issue Digital Certificates for encryption?
- Are there any applications or resources that should be refused Digital Certificates?
- When a certificate is issued by a CA, is there an initialization period where the certificate must be used within a finite period of time or be subject to revocation?
- And so on, and so on, and so on . . .

All persons involved in maintaining the CA should be aware of the policies and there should be a written version and a digital backup of the policies in case the authority server needs to be rebuilt.

Digital Certificates and Keys

So how do the keys get generated when you request a Digital Certificate? At some point in the application process, the Certificate Authority software sends a command to the computer that is being used to request the certificate. That command basically says, "Generate the public and private keys with X algorithm and create a fingerprint with X message digest." The CA software also gives the requesting computer the random number information to start generating the keys. The public key is then attached or linked to the actual certificate itself, and the private key is stored separately — usually on the hard drive of the requesting computer. The keys are protected from unauthorized use with the passphrase that you gave the CA during the applications process.

Some Digital Certificate keys are only used for authorization (such as, "This is John Smith and he is allowed to update the database server."). Other Digital Certificates use the public and private encryption keys for encrypting email (as with S/MIME described in Chapter 8). When you send someone your Digital Certificate, you are also sending them your public key.

Digital Certificates are issued to computers as well as individuals. When they are issued to computers (such as the Digital Certificates that come installed in your Web browser), they are used for computer-to-computer communications. These communications might be something like identifying themselves to one another and when to start an encryption session. It all happens very quickly, and the user doesn't even realize that credentials and communications are being exchanged.

Very often Digital Certificates are used to identify individuals who wish to log on to a network or to use specific resources and applications on the network. The Digital Certificate can tell the server at a glance who you are and what you are allowed to do. And, a record of all transactions are kept. If you deny that you logged on to Server XYZ and downloaded the new budget figures, the log will show whether or not you are telling the truth. That's because no two certificates will have the same keys and other identifying attributes.

Managing Digital Certificates and the associated keys requires policies and procedures to deal with issuance, storage, recovery, modification, and so on. That, in a nutshell, is really what the infrastructure in Public Key Infrastructure is all about. Almost anyone can set up a server to issue Digital Certificates and keys, but it takes a whole lot more to effectively build and manage a system that can handle the complexities and the traffic load without completely falling apart.

The management of the certificates and keys can be handled by the CA, but that's a lot to ask of one machine, especially if you do a lot of business with certificates and keys. Sometimes it's better to offload the management to a database server — and that's the subject of the next few paragraphs.

D'basing Your Certificates

Sometimes a PKI system is so busy that it makes sense to take some of the load off the CA and move it to another server. In this case, because certificates and keys have uniquely identifiable fields, it makes sense to move them to a database. SQL Server and Oracle servers are able to handle this job, but there are also free utilities to make this change easier.

What I'm talking about are LDAP servers. LDAP is actually a protocol to make use of X.500 directories and Digital Certificate are X.509 objects. The acronym stands for *Lightweight Directory Access Protocol* and its's a relatively simple protocol for updating and searching directories running over TCP/IP.

The LDAP contains such information as certificates, tags in the certificates, matching key storage locations, and matching key labels. When a person requests the public key from someone else, the request goes to the CA which then uses the combination of the user name and matching tags to locate the certificate on the LDAP server. The LDAP server checks the validity period of the certificate to see if the certificate is valid and then retrieves it.

You normally won't need a separate database for your certificates unless you have a very large and busy PKI system. In most small business environments, the CA is able to handle the certificate requests without bogging down.

Certificate Revocation

Most certificates are given a lifespan when created, but there are times that you might want to revoke a certificate to keep it from being used. For example, a person might lose his keys or change positions within the company, or an e-commerce site using SSL may merge with another company. In these situations, and many more, a certificate should be revoked. But, this is much easier said than done.

Do you remember the days when merchants had little booklets of bad credit card numbers? (Yes, much simpler and more trusting days.) A certificate revocation is much like that. It uses a *Certificate Revocation List (CRL)* which is a list of certificate serial numbers signed by the CA. When someone attempts to validate the certificate, the CA can look up the serial number to see if it is good and form a response. However, this is yet another job that CAs find very time consuming and it slows down the process of issuing certificates and the other jobs that a CA is responsible for. The usual answer is to put the CRL on an LDAP server.

This, though, brings up other problems. How often should the CRL server send updates to the CA? Should it even send them to the CA or should the authentication process work some other way? Ideally persons, applications, and other computers ought to be able to query the CRL via the LDAP which then queries the CA. These are some of the issues you'll have to contend with when you are dealing with Digital Certificates. It's not a hard job when you have a limited number of certificates, but when the numbers of certificates reaches into the tens of thousands, it becomes quite a large task.

There is something you can do to reduce the burden of updating CRLs — and this is something you can do when certificates are initially issued. There is a field in the certificate in which you can set an expiration date. When that date comes around, the certificate automatically becomes unusable for new transactions. Of course, you'd still have the job of issuing a new certificate to replace the expired one (like getting a new credit card when your old one reaches its expiration date). Reissuing a new certificate in this case is a lot easier and less labor intensive than revoking one and updating the CRL. As I mentioned before, it's not such a big deal when you are dealing with a limited number of certificates, but setting expiration dates should be standard procedure when you are dealing with large numbers of certificates.

Picking the PKCS

I know I've sort of hit you out of the blue with this, but this is the first chance I've had to work this subject into a chapter. Of course you're wondering what the heck I'm talking about! PKCS stands for *Public Key Cryptography Standards* and it's sort of a catch-all for all the standards not covered by public key algorithms, key exchange protocols, and Digital Certificate standards. They were developed by the big guns in cryptography — RSA Data Security. When different vendors started creating their own programs to handle public key encryption, they found that a lot of incompatibilities were popping up that they hadn't expected. Now, with PKCS, the vendors can state up front which PKCS standards they follow. That way you can compare products to see if they will play well together.

When you are applying for a Digital Certificate, you are likely to see some statement in the application about PKCS. All it means is that if the CA server understands how to read PKCS format, then it will understand your certificate request. PKCS #10 describes the standards for certificate requests.

I'll give you some short and sweet explanations as to what the different standards are and what they mean. The first thing I'm sure you'll notice is that even though the last standard is #15, there are really only thirteen listed. That's because #2 and #4 were later rolled into PKCS #1.

PKCS #1: RSA Encryption Standard

It only makes sense that if RSA is describing all the cryptographic standards that they should make their own product #1. Makes sense to me, anyways.

The PKCS#1 describes a method called *rsaEncryption* that is used for encrypting data using RSA's public/private keys algorithm. This standard actually gets very technically detailed about how Digital Certificates should be handled and how this standard should work with a number of the other standards.

PKCS #3: Diffie-Hellman Key Agreement Standard

PKCS #3 describes a method for implementing Diffie-Hellman key agreement. It standardizes how the Diffie-Hellman agreement can have two people share a key that is known only by them and no one else. After the key has been shared, the two people can begin encrypting their communications.

PKCS #5: Password-Based Cryptography Standard

PKCS #5 describes how to encrypt a fixed length string of a private key with a secret key derived from a password. Recommendations are made in this standard on how to implement what is usually referred to as *PBE* or Password Based Encryption.

PKCS #6: Extended-Certificate Syntax Standard

An Extended-Certificate is an X.509 Digital Certificate and a set of attributes that have been signed by the CA. The "extended" bit refers to extra information like an e-mail address, which is not normally included in certificates. It's assumed that extra information or attributes will be included in certificates at some point in time.

PKCS #7: Cryptographic Message Syntax Standard

This standard describes how you can put digital signatures into digital envelopes and then be able to put one digital envelope inside of another. This is normally used as a security mechanism in S/MIME. It also describes how the message can be time-stamped and authenticated.

This standard also makes S/MIME encrypted e-mail compatible with another e-mail encryption standard called *PEM* (Privacy Enhanced Mail). This is so an e-mail program that uses S/MIME can exchange messages with an e-mail program that uses only PEM.

PKCS #8: Private-Key Information Syntax Standard

PKCS #8 describes how information should be included in an encrypted private key and how the key should be formatted. Some of that information will be about which algorithm was used to create the key in the first place. There's also some information as to how the private key should be encrypted.

PKCS #9: Selected Attribute Types

PKCS #9 is basically a long list that describes certain attribute types for use in PKCS #6, PKCS #7, and PKCS #8. You'll notice that #6, #7, and #8 all deal with syntax, so PKCS #9 gets more specific about what the syntax is, how it is to be used, and where it is to be used.

(For those of you who never had to deal with DOS or UNIX command-line syntax, you may have no idea what the word *syntax* means. The simple answer is that it means getting the right words in the right places. If you get the words wrong, the computer doesn't understand what you're saying.)

PKCS #10: Certification Request Syntax Standard

Oh no! Another syntax standard!

PKCS#10 describes the syntax for the requests for certification. Certification in this standard means the request for a Digital Certificate. The request is sent to a Certificate Authority, so this makes sure that the CA can understand what you're asking for.

In addition, there's information in this standard on how the CA asks for the paperwork it needs to totally verify your identity. There's also a way that a challenge password should be handled for the protection of the certificate.

PKCS #11: Cryptographic Token Interface Standard

The PKCS#11 standard describes a programming interface named *Cryptoki* (pronounced "crypto key") for handling cryptographic operations with hardware tokens, smartcards, and USB smartkeys. There are a lot of popular applications that use PKCS#11 to provide smartcard support for their SSL and S/MIME transactions.

PKCS #12: Personal Information Exchange Syntax Standard

This standard specifies a format for storing and transporting a user's private keys, certificates, and so on. This information needs to be shared with applications, and this standard makes it easier for programs and systems to read this information.

PKCS #13: Elliptic Curve Cryptography Standard

Elliptic curve cryptography has only recently started being used for encryption. The theory has been around for quite a while but vendors and cryptographers hadn't tested it to the max so they haven't been using it.

Because elliptic curve cryptography is still in its infancy, this standard is still being developed and isn't finished yet.

PKCS #14: Pseudo-Random Number Generation Standard

This standard is still under development, too. At present there are a number of different methods of creating a generator for a pseudo-random number, but there's no one outstanding method that is on its way to becoming a standard.

PKCS #15: Cryptographic Token Information Format Standard

PKCS #11 described how applications should interface with tokens and smartcards and so on, but PKCS #15 is to establish a standard so people can use one token (or smartcard) with any program or system. At present, you need to have special software to be able to read a token, and these software programs don't all work the same way. The result is that tokens are not interchangeable. This standard is trying to change that.

Chapter 7

All Keyed Up!

I've rewritten this chapter a hundred times already because keys are so important and a central issue to all cryptography. I want to make sure I've got everything covered. It's also very hard not to create too many puns about "key issues" and "key complaints" and so on. I'm sure you all would be groaning in pain if I allowed myself all the cliché phrases. So, I'll spare you as much as I can.

If I could have had anything to do with it, I would *not* have chosen the word *key* to describe anything having to do with cryptography. I think I would have called it a *door knob* or anything else that doesn't have multiple meanings. But, the word *key* is a standard and it doesn't look like it will be going away any time soon, even though it's the most confusing concept for beginners to grasp and the hardest item to control in a crypto system. Given that, you'd think they could have given it a better name.

I know I've gone over some stuff on keys already, and there will be more on keys in later chapters. However, because keys are central to the cryptography theme, I thought I'd use this chapter to throw everything about keys together so you'll have one place to refer to whenever you have a question or just aren't sure about something. Hopefully you'll find this entertaining, interesting, and educational.

So, What Exactly IS a Key?

First off, I'll tell you what a key is NOT.

- ✔ A key is not larger than a breadbox (not usually, anyway)
- ✔ A key is not an encryption algorithm
- ✔ A passphrase is not a key
- ✔ A key is not shaped like a key
- ✔ A key is not a token (but it can be stored on a token)
- ✔ A key is not interchangeable between algorithms
- ✔ A key is not an indication of trust

These are just some of the many misconceptions and misunderstandings about keys that I hear every day. Most of the confusion comes from the fact that we — the people who are computer technology experts — fling the word around so casually and indiscriminately, that we confuse the very people we are trying to educate. So, for the purposes of this chapter, I'll use my description of a key — *the computer file that you use with your cryptographic program to start the encryption or decryption process.*

A key does not encrypt or decrypt anything — the algorithm does that. The information in the key is used to encrypt/decrypt, but it is not the algorithm itself.

Making a Key

If you have a program like PGP, you make your own key or keys. If you order your keys through a bank-like company called a Certificate Authority, they tell your computer to make the keys which are then stored on your computer. A certificate authority will also send you a file called a *Digital Certificate*. The digital certificate is not a key itself; it guarantees that you are the owner of the keys.

There are also many authentication systems and *PKI* (Public Key Infrastructure) systems that constantly make keys for secure connections. Some of these keys, called *session keys,* are disposable keys that are thrown away at the end of the transmission. Keys are cheap and easy to make. When you are making SSL connections on secure Web sites, you don't even realize that a key is being made — or that your browser already has keys installed in it. Keys are everywhere.

There's nothing really magical to making a key — the cryptographic program actually does all the work. But, before the program makes a key, you have to give it certain parameters to follow: what type of algorithm it should use, how many bits the key should be composed of, and any expiration date you may want to assign. Before the cryptographic program begins generating the key, it will usually ask you for a passphrase. The passphrase has no bearing on whether or not the key will be strong enough to use. The passphrase is only a protection mechanism to make sure you are the only person to use the key. It's kind of like having a PIN for an ATM card. The PIN is the protection and the ATM card is the key.

Whether the key is a good one depends a lot on the parameters you (or the cryptographic program) give for its generation. I go into that in more detail throughout this chapter.

If your encryption program has an option that says something like "generate keys faster," please disable or turn off that function. Your computer will be able to generate better keys without that function. It may take a little longer for the key to be made, but it's worth it in the long run.

A key is a computer file. If you were to open that file with a general purpose viewer to see its contents, it probably wouldn't make any sense to you at all. It would just look like random characters. But, it doesn't have to make sense to you — it only needs to make sense to the cryptographic program and the algorithm being used. The file is usually stored on your hard drive and this is not really the best place for it to be because people can steal or copy keys left on a hard drive.

The Long and Short of It

I'm sure you've heard this before, but you need to make your keys as long as possible. Why? Longer keys are generally much harder to crack. Look at it this way, of the house keys shown in Figure 7-1, which do you think would be safer to use?

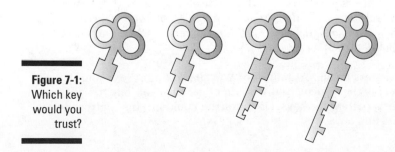

Figure 7-1:
Which key would you trust?

I'm sure you decided that the key on the far right is the safest because it's longer and has more teeth than the first one on the left. A long, complicated house key usually indicates that the lock is quite complex and would be hard to pick. In addition to the length, the randomness of the placement of the teeth and the random peaks and valleys of the teeth also contribute to the strength of the lock and key. If you're a burglar, the type, size, and length of the key to the lock are important considerations. If you feel the lock will take too long to pick, you won't try and you'll go on to other prospects.

The same reasoning goes into picking the key size for your key. It doesn't matter that everyone says a 126-bit key is strong enough — in truth that may not really be the case. It all depends on the algorithm you are using and the lifespan of the key. It's okay for data that has a short life-span (meaning it's not really sensitive or important after about a week) to have a short key length, but for long-term encryption such as for files and sensitive messages, you should make the key as long as reasonably possible. While it's true that the longest keys may make the encryption and decryption process a little longer, it's the protection you're after and not the length of time you have to wait.

There are formulas I could show you that indicate how long it would take to crack a key of a certain length. But, those formulas are constantly changed because hackers and crackers find newer, better, faster ways to crack keys. I would rather you just remember that longer is better.

If you have a nice, long key with a short passphrase, you're defeating part of the protection. The same goes with combining a very short key with a long passphrase — it's not as secure as it could be. For best results, use a long passphrase and a long key. That's what the professionals do!

Randomness in Keys Is Good

I mentioned the randomness of the size and placement of the teeth in a house key. Randomness is also an important issue when it comes to the generation of a key. The encryption program you use also has both the encryption algorithm and an algorithm that makes sure that the composition of the key is random. Randomness in keys is called *entropy* and the algorithms used to make the keys random are called *Random Number Generators (RNG)* or a *Pseudo-Random Number Generators (PRNG)*. I cover the RNGs and PRNGs in more detail in Chapter 2.

Why is randomness an important issue? Well, if all keys were assembled or generated exactly the same way, it wouldn't take a hacker long to figure out that there was a pattern for keys. Of course he could use that pattern to his advantage and find a way to easily crack keys.

Storing Your Keys Safely

As I mention several times throughout this book, it's not a good idea to keep your keys stored on the hard drive of your desktop computer or your laptop. It's too easy for someone to gain access to those machines and copy or steal your keys. Of course, that person would also have to figure out your passphrase to be able to use the key, but do you consider that good enough security? If I took your ATM card, are you sure I wouldn't be able to figure out your PIN and steal your money?

Unlike your ATM card, if you lose your key, it cannot be replaced! (Well . . . there are key escrow and key recovery schemes, but generally you're out of luck if you misplace your key, have a hard drive crash, or have your key stolen.)

Sometimes keys have to be stored on your hard drive for applications and services to be able to access them. If this is your case, you'll just have to accept that fact, but make sure your computers are secure otherwise. You can check with your IT department or Security Officer to see how the keys on your desktop and laptop are being protected.

If your cryptographic program has an option for saving keys elsewhere, it's in your best interest to do that every time you generate a key or import a public key for someone else. Programs such as PGP have "Export" commands to move your keys and you can also manually cut and paste the keys to another storage media. (There are many different key formats and key copy commands, so I can't give you a how-to list here.)

When you are using public/private key encryption, you'll probably have a list of public keys somewhere on your desktop or laptop computer. It's also a great idea to have a back-up of these keys somewhere because you've obviously spent some time and effort in gathering them. The list of public keys is sometimes referred to as a *key ring*. Just like losing your set of physical keys, if you lose this key ring it's not only a real nuisance, you won't be able to encrypt or decrypt messages to and from these people until you get their keys again. If your private key was lost (oh no!), you'll have to revoke the lost keys, generate a new set, and then notify all your friends and colleagues. And, you won't be able to decrypt any messages that come through with the old key in the meantime.

The best method of safely storing your private keys and public keys is to move them to copy them to some type of external storage media that isn't always connected to your computer. Floppy disks, CDs, and the new USB drives are good choices. It's OK to leave your public keys on your computer, but you should definitely move your private keys on to some sort of remote storage. When you need your keys, all you have to do is plug in the disk or drive and use them.

When moving or copying your keys to another location, don't name the file or folder something obvious like "My Encryption Keys." That's just common-sense security.

Keys for Different Purposes

And here you thought keys were just used to start encryption and decryption! Not to burst your bubble, but keys are used for many, many different purposes now. This has nothing to do with the algorithm, key length, or passphrase; it's about what the key is going to be used for. I refer to these as different *classes* of keys. A lot of this has to do with PKI and, to be honest, most of the time you don't have to interact with anything to use these keys — the programs or applications use different protocols to make sure the appropriate keys are made and used.

Here's a quick breakdown of the various classes of keys:

✔ **Signing keys** — These keys are used to create digital signatures.

✔ **Authentication keys** — These keys are often used to authenticate computers to computers or users to computers. SSL keys are used to authenticate computers to computers, for example. You'll also find authentication keys used in PKI systems to authenticate users to systems.

✔ **Data encryption** — These are the keys you are probably most familiar with because they are used to encrypt files or messages that will be kept for a long time.

✔ **Session keys** (short-term) — These keys normally used to encrypt a secure channel across the network (or Internet) for a short period of time. These keys are thrown away at the end of the session.

✔ **Key encrypting keys** — These keys are also known by the acronym, *KEK*. If your application needs to send a key to the other end, but doesn't want to send it in the clear, that key is often "wrapped" or encrypted with another key called a KEK.

✔ **Root key** — This is a master key of sorts used for signing all keys that originate from an authoritative source: a company or a trusted third party such as a Certificate Authority.

Keys and Algorithms

Just as a key for a Ford truck won't work with your front door lock, keys made for algorithms are made for that algorithm alone. A key made for the 3DES algorithm will only be able to encrypt and decrypt with the 3DES algorithm; it can't encrypt or decrypt with Twofish, for example. You usually don't have to worry about that, though, because your encryption program knows which algorithms it has made and will look for the correct keys. If the correct keys are not present, it will tell you so. Then it's time to call the IT department for help.

Most cryptographic programs are able to choose different algorithms to work with. Sometime you choose which algorithm to use and other times the programmers or vendors have set up the rules and parameters for you. In that case, the appropriate keys will be made and exchanged and you rarely have to worry about this.

One Key; Two Keys . . .

There are encryption algorithms that only generate one key and others that generate two keys. The keys made by the single-key algorithms are called *symmetric keys*. That doesn't mean that each key is shaped the same, or that one side looks the same as the other, it simply means that the same key is used to encrypt data and decrypt data. Both keys are made of the exact same data. Sometimes you'll see this referred to as a *secret* key, but I'll call it a *symmetric key* for now just to help keep things straight.

Some encryption algorithms generate two keys, and that's called *asymmetric algorithms* with *asymmetric keys*. What this means is that two keys are generated; one key is kept by the user and the other key is shared with anyone the user wants to have it. The keys are different from one another and don't seem to have any connection to one another. However, hidden in the keys is some special stuff that indicates they have some mathematic properties in common. This "special stuff" is not obvious, either. These keys are also known as *public/private keys*. The *public* key is one you give to other people. The *private* key is the one you keep to yourself and never share with anyone. I explain how that works in a minute.

One thing I want you to note is that sometimes people mistakenly call their *private key* a *secret key*. As you can see, this creates a lot of confusion because the single key created by a symmetric algorithm is also known as a *secret key*. I can't stop people from making incorrect references, otherwise I'd wave my magic wand and make everyone do things right. (Chey for President?) What you can do is question a person's use of the phrase "secret key" by asking them if they mean a single key, or one of a key pair. If they really mean one of the keys of a key pair, then they really mean "private key."

So, here's how you start using public and private keys:

1. The algorithm is told to generate the keys. (If you are using PGP or similar, it will ask for your passphrase at this point.)

2. Your computer stores the two files: a private key and a public key.

3. You can copy or move your private key to a safe place like a floppy or USB drive.

4. If you want others to have immediate, unlimited access to your public key, you send your public key to a public key server. (There are hundreds of public key servers — a very popular one is `www.keyserver.net/en`.)

5. If you want to limit who has your public key, you send it to those people in an e-mail message (or similar).

6. Now you're ready to start encrypting and decrypting messages. You can't do this with a wave of your hand, though; you need special programs capable of handling encryption and decryption. E-mail programs generally all have this capability.

I'm sorry that I can't give you a step-by-step guide on all the different public/private keys and encryption programs with instructions on how to use your keys. That entails a book in itself! But, I do give step-by-step lessons in Chapter 8 on how to use public/private keys with Outlook Express and Eudora. In that chapter I use Digital Certificate public/private keys and PGP public/private keys because they are the most common.

I can't give you all those individual steps, but I can give you a good idea on how the concept works. For that I'm going to revert to some graphics to tell my story.

Public/private keys

These keys are "linked" to each other by some special math operations done by the encryption algorithm. I'm being overly simplistic here, but imagine you have one key and you break it down the middle: One part is your public key and the other part is your private key (see Figure 7-2).

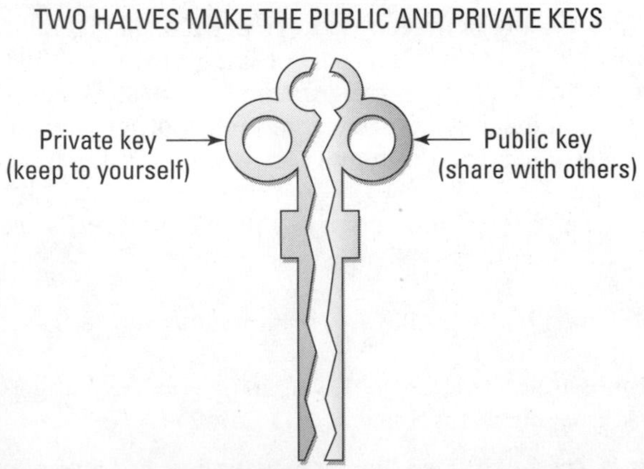

TWO HALVES MAKE THE PUBLIC AND PRIVATE KEYS

Private key → ← Public key
(keep to yourself) (share with others)

Figure 7-2:
Two halves
make the
public and
private keys.

Please note that I have said this is overly simplistic, because it is. In reality, you could never look at one key and be able to figure out what the other key is like. In my example, the two sides obviously fit together, but that's only to help you understand the concept.

I'm going to have Boris and Natasha exchange some e-mails using their public and private keys. They have already exchanged their public keys with one another and, of course, they have their own private keys. Next I describe how the process works.

The magic encryption machine

As this is just an exercise in comprehension, I'm going to tell you that the encryption machine is actually a "magic shredding and de-shredding machine." This machine has two key locks in the front of it; one is for the private key and the other is for the public key (see Figure 7-3).

Boris puts his message in the magic encryption shredding machine, inserts his private key in one lock, inserts Natasha's public key in the other lock, and turns both keys. This action makes a separate, encryption key. You don't see this key or even realize it exists. It does the actual encryption and the result is a special confetti — the encrypted message. (The temporary key information is actually included in this confetti, but you don't see it or notice it.)

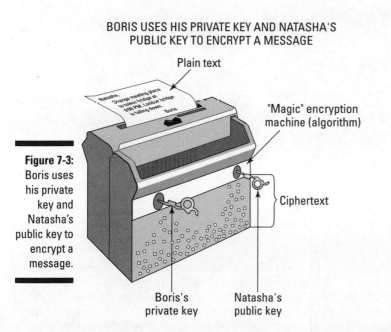

BORIS USES HIS PRIVATE KEY AND NATASHA'S
PUBLIC KEY TO ENCRYPT A MESSAGE

Plain text

"Magic" encryption
machine (algorithm)

Ciphertext

Figure 7-3:
Boris uses
his private
key and
Natasha's
public key to
encrypt a
message.

Boris's
private key

Natasha's
public key

Boris then packs up this special confetti in an e-mail message and sends it to Natasha. He doesn't need to tell her about the keys, because she'll use a similar process to decrypt the message.

The magic decryption machine

Now that Boris has e-mailed Natasha his encrypted message, she's now confronted with a pile of nonsense (that's what an encrypted message looks like). To decrypt the message, she has to use her "magic" machine to get the plaintext version of what Boris wrote.

As shown in Figure 7-4, Natasha puts her private key in place and then puts Boris's public key in its place. (Remember that Boris had already mailed her his public key and she owns her own private key.) When those two keys are in place, she's asked for her passphrase and the temporary key information "pops" out of the confetti and quickly starts the decryption process. Then the plaintext message magically appears! This happens very, very quickly, too.

NATASHA DECRYPTS BORIS'S MESSAGE

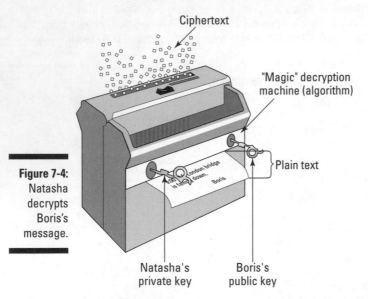

Figure 7-4:
Natasha decrypts Boris's message.

The actual process is almost as simple as shown here in my pictures! When you are using e-mail in particular, it knows about your private key and asks you where you've kept it (if you are not storing it on your hard drive). I will also ask you to locate the public key for the person who is receiving your message. Usually, public keys have the person's name or e-mail address associated with them and you can search public key servers with that information.

Finding private and public keys works a bit differently with high-end corporate PKI systems but, for the most part, finding the keys is usually automated and you don't have to worry about it.

Symmetric keys (again)

The process of encrypting and decrypting data with a symmetric (secret) key is almost exactly the same as the examples I've shown to you in the public/private key figures. The real difference is that there is only one key used to encrypt and decrypt.

Using one key presents a bit of a problem. If you are using the same key to encrypt a message as you are to decrypt it, how does Boris get that key to Natasha without someone else finding it first? Sending it by e-mail is just plain dumb — unencrypted e-mail can be read by anyone who wants to try. And, it's not hard to do. So, that method is out. Boris could send the secret key by snail mail or express mail of some sort, but there's still a slight chance that the package could be intercepted.

There is one solution that many people have proposed and that's breaking up the key into pieces and giving them to a number of people. When the key needs to be used, all the people who have the pieces have to go to the computer and enter their parts. If one part or piece is missing, the key won't work. But, that doesn't work too well in the real world. What if you have shared pieces of the key with three people and one of those people is on vacation when you need to use the entire key? Or, what if you go into work at 6 a.m. on Sunday morning to catch up on some work and an important encrypted message comes in? Do you think the three people you need would be willing to come in to the office on their day off, just so you can read a message? I'd be willing to bet the chances of them agreeing to come in fit somewhere with a snowball and Hades.

That, in a nutshell, sharing the secret key with others has always been the weakest part of symmetric key encryption. Cryptographers have muddled over this problem for decades. If you are using a system that relies solely on symmetric keys, you have to make sure that they method in which symmetric keys are shared is safe and secure. You wouldn't want someone to intercept the symmetric key during its "sharing" process!

Trusting Those Keys

Remember this: Just because Boris has a key, it doesn't necessarily mean you should trust him! Having a key does not imply trust. It simply means that the person who owns it can encrypt and decrypt data. Even a valid key does not mean that it actually belongs to the person whose name is on it. Sounds like a real conundrum, doesn't it?

The fact of the matter is that anyone can make a PGP key and assign any name (or even no name) to the key. You have no way of knowing that Boris actually owns that key unless you make contact with him somehow. Phoning him up and asking him to verify the PGP fingerprint is one way of verifying his key. Contacting someone you know who also knows Boris is another method. But, can you really trust Boris with the information you're going to send him? That's totally up to you to decide. (PGP allows you to assign levels of trust to kcys.)

Keys that come with Digital Certificates are a slightly different matter. When you get a Digital Certificate, you generally work with a well-known public company (called *Trusted Third Parties*) that charges you money for the certificate and the keys. The reason they charge you money is that they spend some effort trying to get you to prove who you are. For example, they could ask for your driver's license, passport, bank records, incorporation papers, or similar information and then they do a check on these documents. More companies do this than individuals, but the fact remains that you can go back to the Certificate Authority (the company that issued the Digital Certificate and the keys) and ask about how they verified the identity that goes with the certificate.

When dealing with keys that come from Digital Certificates, you still have no assurance that the person or company that owns the keys is trustworthy. Just because someone has a Digital Certificate or PGP keys doesn't necessarily mean that person is a good person. Anyone can get encryption keys. That person could be a con man or he could be a priest. It's still up to you to know who you are dealing with.

Key Servers

One method used to distribute keys (any type of key) is to use a key server. You can set one up for corporate use or you can buy a PKI system from one of the many vendors. Basically, you're dealing with a database with set fields to hold information about the keys and you use access lists to control who can get which keys. It sounds easy, but it can quickly become a quagmire, depending on how many keys you are storing and sharing and what the keys are used for. (See "Keys for Different Purposes," above.)

One main drawback to key servers is that they can become a single point of failure. That is, if the server is attacked or an electronic part goes "zap," no one can get any keys and the whole system falls apart. It's also a beefy target for unscrupulous types who have one repository for all the keys. If you have all the keys, you quite likely can read just about anything you want. (Although the passphrases would have to be cracked, too.) That means they must be extremely robust servers (with the elusive 99.9 percent uptime) and extremely well protected with security mechanisms, too.

You can set up fail-over systems with redundant key servers, but they must monitor one another constantly for changes and complete updates as soon as possible. If the redundant key server is out of sync with the main key server, it can still work, but there will be some problems.

Keeping keys up to date

Imagine that your building is protected with just one door (improbably, but just go along with me for a minute). Let's say that you have ten people who need to have copies of the keys so they can come into work after hours. You can expect that at least one person will lose a key. But what if that key was so important that you couldn't chance a lost copy floating around. You'd have to change the lock, make new keys, and gather all the old keys from the ten people. A real pain, right? Well, imagine that at least one of those people loses their office key once a month. Now that's a royal pain and it would get to be very expensive, too.

That can happen with encryption keys, too. Some keys are so important that they have a limited distribution but you can always count on the fact that at least one person is either going to lose the key or forget the passphrase to the key. To be really safe, you'd have to revoke the existing keys, generate new ones, distribute the new keys, and probably change some applications to accept the new keys, too. That's one of the jobs that is expected of a key server — to manage the keys.

On a normal day, even regular (not-as-sensitive) keys get lost or the passphrase forgotten. Therefore, the key server needs to have the information about the revoked key and the information about the new key — and the key server needs to get that information to all the users. How do you do that? If all the users' desktop and laptop computers are constantly querying the key server for updates, the key server wouldn't have much time to do anything else. Yes, this is a problem and it has no simple answer. It's just something you have to decide how to handle yourselves.

In addition to lost keys, you'll have keys that have expired and need to be reinstated, you'll have new keys for new employees, you'll have old keys for staff who have left the company, you'll have keys for part-timers or contract personnel, and you'll have keys for staff who have been promoted. Their key's permissions need to be changed. So, you can see why key servers are a great idea in theory, but a lot of work in practice.

Just a note — PGP key servers, because they are open to the public, rely totally upon the owner of the key to update his information. That's one reason you should contact the owner of a PGP key to make sure the one you have is current.

Policies for keys

Whether you are going to have a key server or not, you really owe it to yourself to come up with your policies (rules) for the use and maintenance of keys before you even set one up. You won't think of everything ahead of time, but it sure saves doing everything by the seat of your pants as you build and implement a key server.

What am I talking about? I'm talking about things like:

- Who has access to the key server?
- Who is in charge of keeping the server working?
- How do you handle emergencies with the server?
- Who on the staff can use keys to digitally sign data?
- Who is allowed to use keys to encrypt data?
- What data should be digitally signed and what data should be encrypted?
- Who has the authority to issue keys?
- What are the requirements to obtaining a key?
- How do you handle key revocation and updating of desktops and laptops?

And so on, and so on, and so on. There are numerous sites on the Internet that can help you with these decisions. After you make these decisions, you need to write them down to make them policy. A note of caution, however — make your policies realistic. If they are not realistic, they won't do you any good. For example, you can't say that the CEO is in charge of deciding who gets keys — that's an administrative job, and I'm sure the CEO would get really sick of being interrupted every time someone needs a new key!

Key escrow and key recovery

These terms are often confused as meaning the same thing, but they're not. *Key escrow* is the actual storing of the key and the passphrase somewhere, somehow so that it can be pulled out of storage and used when needed. *Key recovery* is the process of storing a key in broken pieces and having the ability to recombine the pieces when needed.

Key escrow is something the government has wanted to be able to handle themselves for many years now. The agencies want this ability so they can easily read encrypted messages of those they suspect are involved in some sort of illegal activity — like drug running, counterfeiting, terrorism, and so on. Civil libertarians have successfully defeated the government's attempts to do this many times. It's an invasion of privacy thing. And, we'd never know if and when the government agencies were abusing the power.

Key escrow for organizations is something you should consider, but the difficulty is how to implement it. I've heard of administrators putting each individual key on individual floppies and then putting each individual passphrase on individual floppies, too. Those floppies are then stored in a safe with limited access. At first it sounds reasonable. Then you start to think of all the times the administrator would need to access the safe and get a floppy when changes are made to a key or the person who owns the key leaves the company. What a chore! And how do you make sure that all the people who have access to the safe don't go snooping themselves? You'd never know if a floppy had been copied.

There's also the problem of erasing the key from a floppy. Forensically, you should never trust anything except a factory-fresh floppy disk. Even if you erase and reformat the disk a dozen times, someone who has the skill and the tools can still read the information on the disk. You'd have to literally shred all the old floppies to make sure the key didn't fall into the wrong hands.

You certainly don't want to escrow all the keys on a server. That would be like a diamond shop with no locks on the door. Believe me, if a hacker heard that you were storing all your keys and passphrases on one server (or even many), the hacker would find a way to get in and steal that data. It's just too tempting to pass up.

The better method is key recovery. Key recovery is like splitting keys into pieces, which I mentioned earlier, but this time you use many servers instead of people to handle the pieces of the keys. And, yes, there are programs that can help you with this process.

So, you break the keys into a number of pieces and you store the pieces in random locations. Tied in with these pieces are security questions. When a key needs to be recovered, the owner has to answer a number of random security questions before the application will reconstitute the key. The best way to do it is to have something like seven security questions and the owner has to answer five of the seven questions correctly to be able to get the key put back together.

This sort of key recovery has a lot of appeal because it can be done without the involvement of one of the IT staff or the manager of the keys. I've heard rumors that a new version of the "enterprise" version of PGP is going to come with this feature built in. Sounds pretty cool to me.

Of course, there are security problems with key recovery as well, but there aren't as many problems as there are with a key escrow system. Whichever you eventually use, remember that the servers need very limited access (both physical and logical) and there ought to be a number of security mechanisms in place.

Part III

Putting Encryption Technologies to Work for You

The 5th Wave

By Rich Tennant

Dear Margaret,
What I have to say to you is very personal...

In this part . . .

In this part I look at some of the most common encryption technologies you are likely to find in the workplace. And if they are not in your workplace, maybe they should be.

This part goes in depth into e-mail encryption and takes a look at some of the other types of data you should be encrypting. Don't forget that you need to protect all that private information you gather on your e-commerce customers. There are many new state and federal regulations that require that certain types of data be encrypted.

And don't forget authentication, either. It's well and good to encrypt your data, but you also have to make sure that you really know who you are working with on the other end of the Internet.

Chapter 8

Securing E-Mail from Prying Eyes

· ·

In This Chapter

▶ Learning the basics of e-mail encryption

▶ Discovering the standards of S/MIME and PGP

▶ Deciding on Digital Certificates or public/private PGP keys

▶ Setting up e-mail programs to use S/MIME and PGP

▶ Obtaining Digital Certificates

▶ Generating your PGP keys

▶ Sending and receiving encrypted messages

▶ Storing your Digital Certificates and PGP keys with confidence

▶ Trying other encryption programs and plug-ins

· ·

*I*n 1998, an online bookstore called Alibris was caught intercepting e-mail that their clients had been sending to their competitor, Amazon.com. In court, Alibris contended that they had done no harm and had gained no economic advantage, so there was no crime, really. The court didn't accept this argument and charged Alibris $250,000.00 for snooping into other people's e-mails.

In recent years, courts have decreed that the company-supplied e-mail belongs to the company and not the employee. Therefore, all e-mail sent on the company's system belongs to the company and is subject to review at any time by the company's technicians and/or management. Because of this ruling, some companies have directed their technical staff to snoop in e-mails to try to detect fraud and abuse. The courts have upheld the rights of companies to do this, but now companies have another problem at hand — how do they monitor e-mail while still complying with new privacy laws?

There's an oft-quoted rule of thumb regarding company e-mail that I'll relate here: Never say anything in an e-mail that could get you in trouble if everyone in the company could read it. That's good advice because management now has the right to snoop in your e-mail.

If you share a home computer with others in your family, you may not want everyone in the family to be able to read all of your e-mails. But, your e-mail program probably saves all your outgoing e-mail in a "sent mail" folder anyway. Do you think it would be all that difficult for your family members to sneak a look at those e-mails? Whether or not they have the right to do this is not a question I think would stand up in court.

Surprisingly, most e-mail clients (e-mail programs) have the ability to use some sort of encryption to secure e-mail from prying eyes, but most users are not aware of this capability. In this chapter I look at the two easiest and most popular forms of e-mail encryption and show you how to set your system up to use them.

E-Mail Encryption Basics

When e-mail programs were first created, no one ever conceived of the fact that eventually some security measures would have to be added to keep people from reading others' mail. The early Internet users were a very naïve group — they tended to believe in the honesty and integrity of people and envisioned the Internet as a self-policing community. Sigh. How wrong they were.

Eventually, the people who created the e-mail protocols and the e-mail programs realized that they had to go back to the drawing board to try to retrofit some form of security.

Before they ever got to the security aspects, they first had to create a way for e-mail to interpret data other than straight text in the e-mail messages. Early e-mail programs could not handle attachments or fancy formatting in messages. The vendors of e-mail programs got together and created *MIME* — Multipurpose Internet Mail Extensions. MIME allowed e-mail programs to send and receive data other than text — pictures, audio, HTML, and so on. And, it didn't matter whether everyone was using the same e-mail programs because MIME became the standard for translating different types of file formats into something the e-mail programs could understand.

S/MIME

I had to start out with MIME to lay the groundwork for the next transition in e-mail. When problems with e-mail security raised their ugly heads, the vendors of e-mail programs realized that they would have to figure out a way for everyone to be able to send *secure* e-mail. That is, e-mail in some sort of coded or encrypted form. It only made sense that this new feature be standardized, so they created *S/MIME* — Secure Multipurpose Internet Mail

Extensions. Standards being as they are, I don't have to remind you that the assorted vendors have interpreted the standards to suit their needs. That means that S/MIME (or MIME, for that matter) doesn't always work perfectly between different e-mail programs. But, it works well enough to at least give it a try.

Not too long ago there weren't many security options for computer users, and it was even illegal for individuals to own any form of strong encryption device. Encryption was considered "munition" by the government along with chemical and biological weapons, tanks, heavy artillery, and military aircraft. This is a throwback to WWII and the Cold War when all governments were developing new ways to keep secrets from one another.

Export of encryption software is still controlled because hostile forces could exchange encrypted files and messages and the government wouldn't be able to figure out what they were saying. Luckily for us, the government has recently relaxed their attitude about encryption and the average user doesn't have a thing to worry about.

In addition to the standard of S/MIME, another standard came to be in a rather unusual way. I'm talking about *PGP*, or Pretty Good Privacy.

PGP

The PGP program is a competing standard with S/MIME and was created in 1991 in response to the government's request to put "back doors" into encryption programs so that the government could read encrypted files and messages that they suspected of containing criminal information. This raised the hackles of privacy rights advocates and programmers alike. Phil Zimmermann created PGP and distributed it throughout the world on the Internet. It quickly became so popular that it was accepted as a standard worldwide. The government charged him for the crime of exporting munitions. The whole battle took on a cult following and, at times, even bordered the surreal, but eventually the government dropped charges against Zimmermann and relaxed their stance on the exportation of encryption.

The PGP program is now available both as commercial software (with support) and as freeware. The source code of the program has been extensively examined by experts the world over and has been deemed safe and strong. Many e-mail programs now include PGP plug-ins that create buttons on the toolbar for ease of use.

PGP has some problems coordinating its actions with S/MIME, but these problems are trivial and can usually be handled with some configuration changes done by power users or network administrator.

Digital Certificates or PGP Public/Private Key Pairs?

This is where most people give up the ghost on using encryption products. They know that keys are involved, but they don't know exactly what they are, how they arc created, or what to do with them. They can understand the concept of keys, but when they run into the words *Digital Certificate,* they tend to run screaming from the room. It's the terminology that is at fault here; not the user. To make it easier for you, it's important for you to understand that Digital Certificates and PGP public/private key pairs are essentially the same thing! There are only two main differences:

- Digital Certificates are issued by a central authority who verifies your identity
- Digital Certificates are public/private key pairs
- PGP public/private key pairs are made by individuals
- PGP public/private key pairs are not centrally controlled

It really is that simple. Both Digital Certificates and PGP public/private key pairs are used the same way to digitally sign files and messages and they are both used to encrypt files and messages. The real significance is that a Digital Certificate has a third party behind it to attest to your identity. When PGP public/private keys are used, it is up to the recipient to verify the identity of the sender.

What's the diff?

I'll try to give you some analogies that will help make sense of this for you. Say you need to prove your identity to someone. There are two ways you could go about it:

1. You could go to a notary public, have that person review your forms of identification, write a letter saying, "You are you," and notarize it. The notary then tears the letter in half and keeps one part in a safe and gives you the other half. This is your Digital Certificate. You use your Digital Certificate to sign files and messages and/or encrypt them. If anyone ever doubts the half-letter you show as proof of identity, they can go back to the notary public to verify that it is you.

2. You write a letter saying, "I am me." You tear it in half. You keep half and you post the other half on the bulletin board at your local grocery store. These two halves are your public and private keys. You use your half-letter to sign and/or encrypt files and messages. You encourage people who know you to go to the bulletin board and sign the half-letter you put

up there. If anyone doubts the half-letter you show as proof of identity, they can go to the grocery store, view your letter, and see how many people have signed your letter showing that they trust it's the real deal. If they don't trust the signatures, they can contact those people to verify that they signed your half-letter.

When should you use which?

Now, please understand that the above examples are extremely simplified explanations. The real deals are a bit more complicated, but you really only need to understand the basics to be able to use them. It's sort of like operating a car — you don't need to know how the combustion engine works to be able to drive your car, but you sure need to understand whether your car runs on regular gas or diesel fuel!

As with most technologies, there are pros and cons to both digital signatures and PGP keys, which I described above. Which one is better? That really depends on your requirements and your budget. Here are some things to keep in mind when making your decision:

- Example 1 (above) usually relies upon a highly organized structure and infrastructure and anything this complex isn't likely to be free. On the other hand, the robust rules of the system can almost certainly assure you that a Digital Certificate and its owner are a true link. Digital Certificates are almost exclusively used with S/MIME and proprietary PKI systems like RSA.

- With Example 2, you have no way of knowing whether everyone who signed the half-letter on the bulletin board really knows that person. Maybe it was signed by a bunch of kids as a prank. You'd have to start contacting some of those signers to see if they really know you and will attest to the fact that they did sign the half-letter. But, Example 2 is free and much easier to set up than Example 1. PGP keys are used with the PGP program that (usually) integrates with your e-mail program.

Sign or encrypt or both?

This bit gets confusing for most people, too. I'll try to make it a little simpler for you:

- You **sign** a file or message when you just want to prove that the document comes from you and to ensure that it has not been changed in transit.

- You **encrypt** a file or message when you want to hide or mask it.

- You **sign** *and* **encrypt** a file or message when you want to hide the message *and* prove it came from you and prove that it was not changed in transit.

It all depends on the level of secrecy and veracity you want to have. Whether you use S/MIME, PGP, or a vendor's proprietary system, the program will give you the options of one or the other or both. To make it easier for users to decide, your company should have a standard policy that describes which method you use under certain circumstances.

Cryptiquette Rule #1: If someone sends you an encrypted message, always reply with an encrypted message. Obviously, the original sender wanted to maintain a sense of secrecy, so you should respect that and make your responses secret, too.

Remember that passphrase!

To use your Digital Certificate or PGP keys for signing and/or encrypting, you enter your passphrase. Your passphrase is like logging on to the program that does the encrypting and decrypting, and it's your method of protecting your digital signature or keys from being stolen or used by others. Therefore, your passphrase should be more than a single word but not something terribly obvious, either. How about a passphrase like this to give you an idea:

```
crYptO mos def B KOOl. True dat!
```

(Translation: Cryptography is most definitely cool. That's true!)

Notice that the passphrase mixes upper- and lowercase letters, substitutes some numbers for letters, and includes punctuation marks. That, and the fact that some words are misspelled, makes it a fairly good passphrase. It's unlikely that someone could guess it and cracking it would take a lot of time. Now, to be completely sure that you will never lose your passphrase (because that would mean you couldn't use either your Digital Certificate or your PGP keys ever again), save the phrase to a plaintext file, name it something unusual like "Mama's recipes," and save it on a floppy disk. Then put the disk away somewhere safe, but not so obscure that you'll never find it again. You should also lock the floppy to keep it from being overwritten or formatted by mistake. But, you know the drill — this floppy is your savior, so take good care of it and don't lose it.

Using S/MIME

S/MIME capabilities are built into most popular e-mail programs because it is a standard for signing and encrypting e-mail. S/MIME uses Digital Certificates for both signing and encrypting. Your Digital Certificate is a "container" for your *public* key to accomplish these tasks. The *private* key portion of the Digital Certificate is encrypted and kept on a different system. Exactly where this private key is stored depends on whether you are using a public service — such as RSA, Verisign, or Thawte. If your company has their own, self-contained PKI system, it's likely that the private key is kept on one of those servers.

Just as an FYI: Thawte's Digital Certificates for personal use are free, while the other companies charge a fee. Each certificate is good for one year and must be renewed annually.

Setting up S/MIME in Outlook Express

Believe it or not, it's easier to set up S/MIME with MS Outlook Express than it is with the full-featured e-mail program, Outlook. Perhaps that's because Outlook Express is closely linked to the MS Internet Explorer Web browser, and Web browsers are already set up to store Digital Certificates. In the examples below I've used Outlook Express 6.0 on Windows XP Pro. Your screens and dialog boxes may look slightly different than those shown here, but you can always use your e-mail program's Help feature to find version-specific information.

Setting up S/MIME in a corporate environment is very different from setting it up yourself on your own computer. However, I like to give you the feel of things so you can get a good sense of what is going on. If you don't want to set up S/MIME in Outlook Express at this time, you can skip this section and come back to it later.

I'll warn you in advance — this setup involves many steps, so give yourself plenty of time. It's not something you can start, leave for a while, and then come back to later. You have to do it all in one go, or not at all. Give yourself at least 45 minutes to complete the tasks. You'll also have to have a buddy go through the same thing so you can exchange encrypted e-mails. Or, if you have more than one e-mail account, you can set it up so that each account has its own Digital Certificate and you can send test messages to yourself via the various accounts.

Ready? Set? Go!

First of all, I'll need you to open Outlook Express — not plain old vanilla Outlook, but Outlook Express. Figure 8-1 shows the different icons for the two programs:

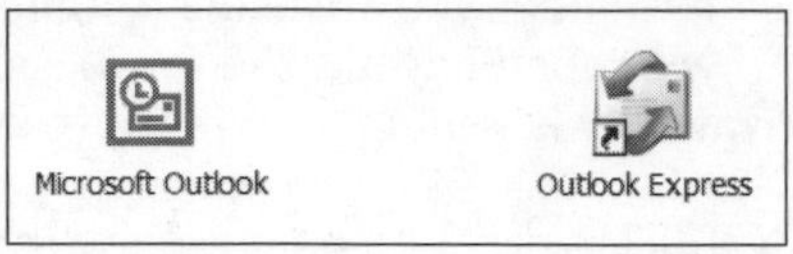

Figure 8-1:
Icons for
Microsoft
Outlook and
Microsoft
Outlook
Express.

With Outlook Express open, choose Tools⇨Options. When you have the Options window open, click the tab that says Security. Your window should look similar to the one in Figure 8-2.

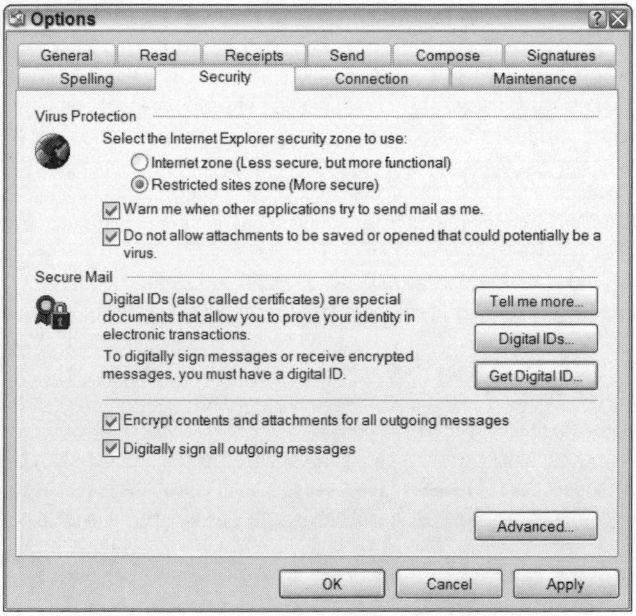

Figure 8-2:
Tools⇨
Options⇨
Security Tab
in Outlook
Express.

Please make sure that all the radio buttons in your window match the example above. When you have all those set, click the Advanced button. There are a few more settings to change before you go on to get your Digital Certificate. In the Advanced Security Settings dialog box, I want you to check the same boxes as are shown in Figure 8-3.

Getting your Digital Certificate

After you click OK in the Advanced Security Settings dialog box, you'll be back to the Security tab in the Options window. Notice that there is one button on the page that says Get Digital ID. This opens your Web browser (if it isn't already running) and directs you to a Microsoft Web site that gives you a number of different companies from which you can obtain a digital ID. It's an accepted practice for most companies to charge for digital IDs, but I'm going to recommend that you go to a company called Thawte — their Digital Certificates for personal use are free!

Figure 8-3:
Select these
Advanced
settings to
make sure
your mail is
sent
encrypted.

Waaaaaay down at the bottom of the Microsoft Web page is a link for Thawte. Click that, and it will take you to the page at Thawte for applying for a personal Digital Certificate. If you have trouble with the link, try typing this URL instead: **www.thawte.com/html/COMMUNITY/personal/index.html**. When you get to that page, go again to waaaaaay down to the bottom of the page. In the last paragraph on the Thawte page, you should see a small, Act Now hyperlink. (Obviously they didn't want to appear to be obnoxious.) Click that link and it will take you to the beginning of the registration process. It should open up a smaller window that looks like Figure 8-4.

Now the next bit takes a while to complete. As you navigate through the various pages of registration information, the site will be asking you for personal information; some of it very sensitive, like Social Security Number, Driver's License Number, or Passport Number. Now Thawte doesn't verify that any of these numbers you enter are correct at this point, but do make sure you are using some sort of valid information. Note: Since companies who issue Digital Certificates use personal information to verify who you are, they also have an obligation to protect all this personal information. Their reputations depend upon the fact that they are very careful with your data to make sure it doesn't fall into the wrong hands. That's why these companies are also referred to as *Trusted Third Parties*.

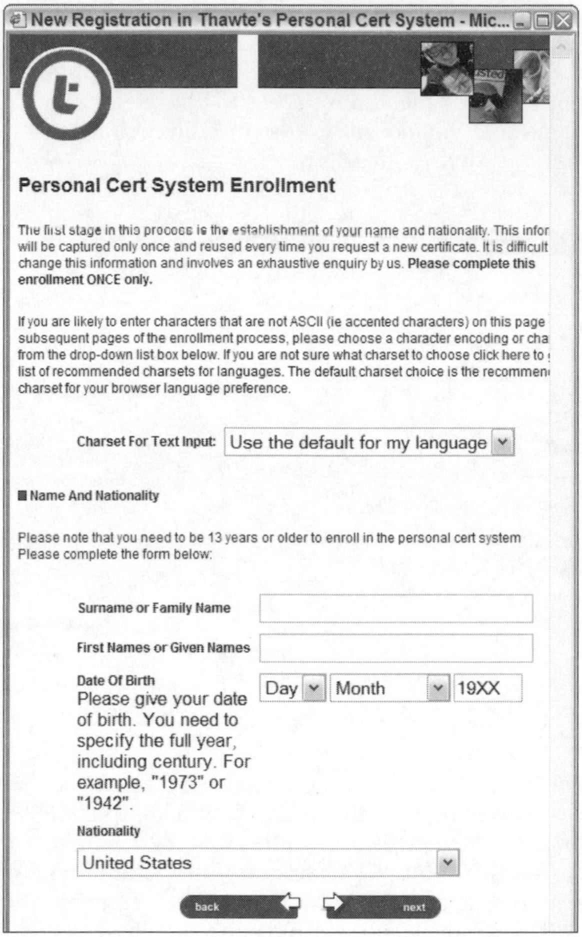

Figure 8-4:
The first
page of the
application
process for
Thawte
personal
Digital
Certificates.

This certificate is for experimenting with anyway, and I don't expect you to hang onto it forever. But, you are applying for a valid Digital Certificate and you will be able to use it with other programs that have the capability of handling them. Remember to enter a real e-mail address, too! Thawte will be sending messages to you and, if you've used a bogus e-mail address, you'll never get through the registration process.

As you continue answering the questions for your certificate, you'll eventually be asked for your passphrase. Think about this beforehand and pick something reasonable and not something like "12345678." Then, just to be safe, create a TXT file, type in that passphrase, and store that file on a floppy disk. Put it away for safekeeping. That way, if you ever forget your passphrase, you'll know where to go to find it. Again, don't name the file something obvious, like "passphrase.txt," and don't hide the disk in an obvious location. But, enough of the reminders for now.

Thawte has the ability to recover your key if you lose it. It does this by asking you a series of questions to identify yourself. You'll be given the opportunity to choose your questions and answers during the process of requesting your certificate. Be sure to write down your questions and answers so that you can refer back to them, but hide them in a secure location or store them in another text file on a floppy.

At this point you'll have to pause and wait for Thawte to send you an e-mail to confirm your e-mail address. (You'll be getting another one from them later on.) After you get that e-mail, follow their directions and copy and paste the information where they tell you to on the corresponding Web page. Thawte will come back immediately with confirmation of your e-mail address.

Next in the series of questions, you'll be asked about some settings again. You can accept the default if you want, but I suggest that you set the security level to High (the default is Medium). If you set the security to High, you'll be asked for a password to protect your certificate. Don't let that confuse you. *Do not* use the same password or passphrase you gave earlier; use something different. What they are asking for now is a password to provide some sort of access control to your certificate.

In order to properly protect your certificates, set the security to High when applying for a Digital Certificate and set your Web browser's security setting to High, too. Use a different password to protect your certificates than the one you used when you created your certificate request.

You're almost done now! The Thawte Web page will create a key for you and will send you another e-mail to congratulate you and tell you about their trust authority process. But, because I'm just doing this for fun, you don't want to hear about that now! You want to know how the dickens you get your certificate. The certificate is not in Thawte's e-mail and there's no direction in the e-mail on where to go or how to get your certificate! There's not even any clear instruction on the Thawte Web site. (That was very naughty of them!) Well, one of the reasons you bought this book is because I'm going to tell you what to do next!

You have to give Thawte about 20-30 minutes to process your request for your certificate. After that time has passed, go to www.thawte.com/cgi/personal/cert/status.exe. If it asks for a UserID and password, use the e-mail address you used to register your certificate as your UserID, and use the password/passphrase you used to create the certificate as your password.

You should be at the personal certificates page now. On the left side of the screen you will need to choose View Certificate Status, which will pull up the certificate you've applied for. If you haven't waited long enough, the status will be *pending*. If the certificate has been approved, the status will be *issued*. Your screen should resemble Figure 8-5.

Figure 8-5:
Viewing
your
personal
certificates
at Thawte.

■ **personal certificates**

Below is a list of certificates you have requested, filtered if necessary. **You can select a certificate to view more status details.** You can change the filter on the list of certificates shown below by selecting the relevant certificate status from the dropdown box below and pressing "Filter". By default all the certificates you have ever requested are shown.

All Certificates Requested   ▼   filter

Type: Status: **Date:**

<u>MSIE</u>:   issued   Sun, 20 July, 2003, 01:53:53 GMT
         Request Another

Figure 8-5:
Viewing
your
personal
certificates
at Thawte.

Again, Thawte doesn't tell you what to do next, but I am here to save the day! See where it says "Type" on the Web page and underneath that it says "MSIE"? Click the MSIE link, and it takes you to another Web page. At the very bottom of this Web page is a short paragraph that says "Fetch and Install Certificate." Figure 8-6 shows you what I mean.

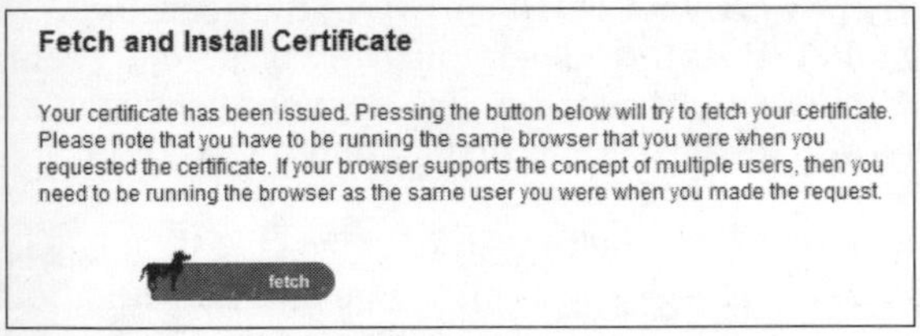

Figure 8-6:
Fetch and
Install
Certificate
from
Thawte's
Web site.

Fetch and Install Certificate

Your certificate has been issued. Pressing the button below will try to fetch your certificate. Please note that you have to be running the same browser that you were when you requested the certificate. If your browser supports the concept of multiple users, then you need to be running the browser as the same user you were when you made the request.

fetch

After you click the little button with the doggie, your certificate will be installed into Internet Explorer and Outlook Express. Now you'll be ready to go back to Outlook Express to finish up what you started.

Sending an encrypted e-mail

Now that you have your certificate and it's been automatically installed on your system, you won't have much to worry about after you finish configuring Outlook Express.

You'll need to go back to the Tools➪Options➪Security tab (it may still be open, just as you left it before getting your certificate). There's a button that says Digital IDs. Click that button and you go to another screen that shows your current certificates (digital IDs). You should see Thawte Freemail Member — Personal Freemail RSA 2000.8.30. (If you don't see it, you should go back to the Thawte site and try Fetch and Install again.)

Then, on the right side of the window, you'll see a button that says Advanced. Click on that. As with all the other clicking you've done, you'll see yet another window open. (You probably only have half a zillion windows open by the time you're finished with this operation!) This window has all kinds of options. Make sure that you check every single one of the options, as in Figure 8-7.

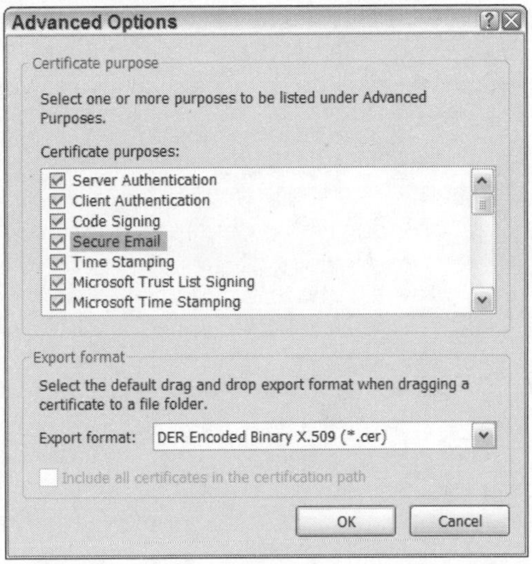

Figure 8-7:
Choose these Advanced options in Outlook Express to use encryption.

After you have checked all the boxes, click OK, and you're ready to send an encrypted message, a signed message, or a message that is both signed and encrypted. Remember:

- ✔ Signing a message proves you're the person who sent it.

- ✔ Encrypting a message scrambles it so others can't read it.

- ✔ Signing and encrypting a message proves that you're the person who sent it and scrambles it, too.

To send an encrypted message, you have to be sure that the other person (the recipient) has a certificate, too. Outlook Express automatically searches the public Digital Certificate servers to see if one exists for your recipient. (It searches by e-mail address.) If there is no certificate for your friend, the message will not encrypt. (If you decide to send a message to yourself using another e-mail address, you'll have to go through the application/registration process for the other e-mail address to get another Digital Certificate.)

So, here you go.

Compose a new message in Outlook Express and address it to a friend who has a Digital Certificate. When you are finished creating the message, but *before you send it*, choose Tools⇨Encrypt Using S/MIME (see Figure 8-8). After you have done that, you will see a small blue lock appear on the far right side of the message window, by the To: box. Then go ahead and click Send. Outlook Express will ask for your password only if you set the security setting to High when you created your certificate. (That password is the second one you gave, not the first one you gave to create the certificate. If you left the security setting at Medium, you will not be asked for a password.)

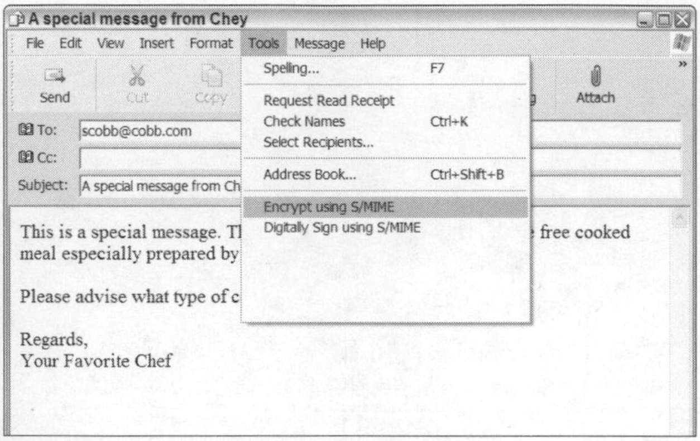

Figure 8-8:
Encrypting
your
message.

When composing an e-mail that you intend to encrypt, pay special attention to the Subject line. You wouldn't want to accidentally give everyone a clue to your secret message by entering something like "New Product Specifications and Pricing" in the subject heading! That's because everything in an e-mail is encrypted *except* the subject line.

Now your friend has received a super-secret message from you. If anyone other than your friend tries to open it, it will look roughly like this:

```
3QTn+zHWb7OKr7ihbxBHXcQgdbt+OROZT+nYK1yjV4OARKKYhuPDAnW188u1TzYa
A28n4e1dE82f57kRQHwGtmusfuMpHZJJ8ARYZf/Ba5SmHr2yr6Ycu4bkDjj5e4QU
P6I3KBdOzXeRm666BxrJZ2MOibUDkpEM5gfgZxOzFcQ6uqotpVKNEzjWiIG4zVdk
NfzjH1gKwZdQnzpHvnOgZGD+mxtjRdXZgP1VR9iizGqb1xeJORRMQKUHNHuiIOMV
JOus5ZfMJCxyKNmMjcJoTUhcwuGMiIf3holg8AkstYFykEeOZV9Zhz54YOCH3FTB
```

Of course this is just a pretend example. Most encrypted messages will have page upon page of text that looks like a chicken has played with a typewriter. However, when you friend gets the e-mail, he may note that there is a little blue lock attached to the sender's name (that's you!). When he clicks on it to open it, he may be faced with the dialog box shown in Figure 8-9.

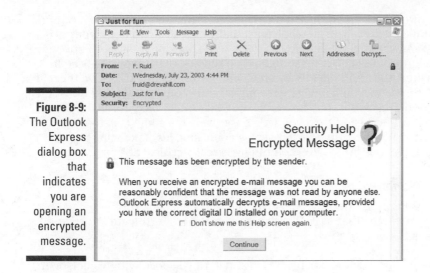

Figure 8-9:
The Outlook
Express
dialog box
that
indicates
you are
opening an
encrypted
message.

After he clicks Continue, the message automatically decrypts and he will be able to read it. Now you can both play with signed and encrypted e-mails and attachments.

You'll have to admit that after you got the Digital Certificates all set up, it was not difficult to send encrypted emails. However, if you were in a corporate environment, the IT department would be in charge of all this work. It's a lot of overhead on their end, but that makes it so much easier for everyone in the long run.

Backing up your Digital Certificates

Ugh! You knew I'd bring you back to the ugly present at some point, didn't you? Well, I have to take care of some housekeeping before I can go on to the next subject. That housekeeping involves backing up copies of your Digital Certificates. That way if you start using a different computer, or your hard drive dies, you can use your old certificates and you don't need to go through the arduous process of applying for new certificates.

The two most common problems that users experience with e-mail encryption are:

1. They forget their passphrase.
2. They lose their personal keys.

No matter how experienced. No matter how intelligent. No matter if they have been trained on encryption software or not. People *always* make the same two mistakes! Don't count yourself in those numbers!

Here's how to back up your Digital Certificate. Whether you realize it or not, the Digital Certificate you've received actually contains two keys: your private key and your public key. You're going to be backing them both up, but to separate floppy disks. The reason you'll be keeping them separate is so no one can steal them and effectively steal your online identity. To save these two different keys, you'll navigate through a series of windows and questions and you'll do this separately for each key. First you'll save your *public* key and your certificate and then you'll do essentially the same task to save your *private key* and the certificate. If it seems confusing, just take your time. We're just experimenting here, so nothing is really critical at this point.

Exporting your public key

In Outlook Express, choose Tools➪Options and then click the Security tab. Click on the button that says Digital IDs. Your Digital Certificate information appears in the next window.

Select your Digital Certificate by clicking on it. (If you accidentally click on it twice and open another window, just click Cancel to get out of that window.) After you have selected the certificate, notice that the Export button becomes operable. Click Export, which starts the Certificate Export Wizard. Click Next to get started.

The first thing the wizard asks you is if you are going to export the private key. At this point you're exporting the *public* key, so click the radio button next to No, Do Not Export the Private Key. What you will be "exporting" (actually just a fancy name for "saving somewhere else") this time is your Digital Certificate and its *public* key.

You'll notice in the next window that certificates can be exported in a number of different formats. For this exercise, accept the default, which is DER encoded binary X.509 (.cer). The other formats are sometimes required by different types of systems, but you don't need to worry about that now.

Click Next, and the wizard asks you for a file name. Be sure to give the path to the floppy disk (or whatever external media you are using) and name the file something like "bigdogs_pubcert.cer." (You can use the Browse button if you need to navigate to a special drive and/or folder.) Normally you would make the name something a little more obtuse, but we're just experimenting at this point. After you have your path and name all set, click Next again.

The next screen indicates that you are exporting your certificate information. Click Finish, and you're done with the first part.

Exporting your private key

To save your *private* key, you need to go through the same steps as above, except that you choose Yes, Export the Private Key when you get to the Certificate Export Wizard. You will be asked for a password to protect your key, which is the password you used when you set the security settings to

High. Enter that password, and continue with the Wizard until it asks you where to file it and what to name the file. Save the file as you did before, but use a different file name.

You can also back up copies of the Digital Certificates used by your friends. They are stored in the Address Book, along with all the other information you have on your friends. If you double-click on a person's name, you will pull up the Properties for that contact. There are a number of tabs in that window and the last one says Digital IDs. When you click on that tab, you'll be able to see the Digital Certificate associated with that e-mail address. From that window you can export the digital ID just as you did your own.

'Nuff said! Play around with it now and have fun. Until you're comfortable with what you're doing, only send files and data that are replaceable. You don't want to send someone the only copy of a file you have and then have the program play funny games with you! In any case, enjoy sending your secret messages.

Fun and Games with PGP

As they used to say in the Monty Python shows, "And now for something completely different." Yes, I'm switching gears on you. This is not just a ploy to keep you awake; it is in recognition of the fact that not everyone uses all Microsoft software. It's also in recognition of the fact that not everyone will have the time and inclination to go to the trouble of registering with a trusted third party to get Digital Certificates. This time around I'm going to be anarchistic and do things the people's way!

All joking aside, PGP has become extremely popular with regular people because there is no outside parties involved in the certification process. PGP is all about people trusting people. People create their own certificates — only this time they are called *keys* — and they are placed on public servers so anyone and everyone has access to the database of keys. Instead of storing Digital Certificates, you save all your PGP keys on a keyring.

Rather than using trusted third parties to verify the owners of keys, PGP relies upon the community of users to verify identities. In PGP related literature you'll often see it referred to as the "Web of Trust." I don't really like that term because "trust" is an intangible and can't really be quantified.

It goes like this. When you create a PGP public key and upload it to a public key server, there is no way for others to be sure that the key really belongs to you. The other users can call you to check out the properties of your key; that is one way to establish trust. Another way is to have people who know you (and supposedly trust you) vouch for your key by digitally signing it themselves. That may all seem a bit crazy now, but I promise that it will make more sense to you as I go along.

For this exercise I'm using Eudora 5.2 (paid version). It's an extremely popular program and I've used it since 1994. You can get a free version at Eudora's Web site, but you'll have to put up with banner ads and a loss of some features. I don't think the free version supports PGP plug-ins, but that doesn't mean you can't use PGP with it. You'll just have to use separate menus instead of built-in buttons on the Eudora menu bar.

I'm also using PGP 8.02 (paid version). You can get free versions of PGP from numerous sources, but they may lack certain features and they certainly won't have Eudora plug-ins. As before, my operating system is Windows XP Professional. Your screens may look slightly different than the ones I've included in this section.

Installing PGP (the paid version) is really quite straightforward and easy. I was surprised it went so fast. It shouldn't take you more than five minutes to install this program.

I'd also like to mention at this point that there are a number of free PGP programs available on the Internet. That's because the source code for PGP was made public many years ago and some people have created organizations to keep the free versions of PGP available for individual use. This is one way of promoting the use of cryptography. Two of the free versions you may want to consider are PGP International at www.pgpi.org/products/pgp/versions/freeware and GnuPG at www.gnupg.org. Both of these sites have free PGP programs available for various operating systems and platforms.

The commercial version of PGP does a lot more than just encrypt e-mail now. You can set up a partition on your hard drive that encrypts data placed into it, you can do a "secure" wipe of drives to almost totally eliminate all traces of files and programs (a good computer forensic technician can still recover some data from drives that have been wiped up to nine times), and you can even encrypt ICQ conversations to keep outsiders from listening in.

Setting up PGP

This is going to be a lot easier than setting up S/MIME and it takes less time, too. PGP supports many different e-mail programs. In fact, while you are going through the install routine, PGP will ask you which e-mail programs you will be using (as shown in Figure 8-10). This is your chance to try PGP with different e-mail clients.

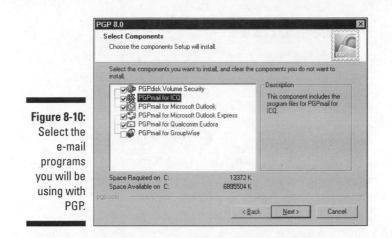

Figure 8-10:
Select the
e-mail
programs
you will be
using with
PGP.

Now, without a doubt, the most important part of PGP (and any encryption for that matter), is creating a good, strong, long key and an equally good, strong, long passphrase. The key is used in the encryption process and the passphrase is used to protect the key from unauthorized use by others. PGP has a key generation wizard with a really nifty component — it helps you gauge whether or not your passphrase is good, strong, and long enough (see Figure 8-11). As you type in your passphrase, there is a quality meter that gives you a graphic representation of your chosen passphrase. The trick here is to get the quality meter to fill all the way over to the right — that's your clue that your passphrase is good enough. I'm sure you are intelligent enough to come up with a phrase that you can remember and will be effective in protecting your keys.

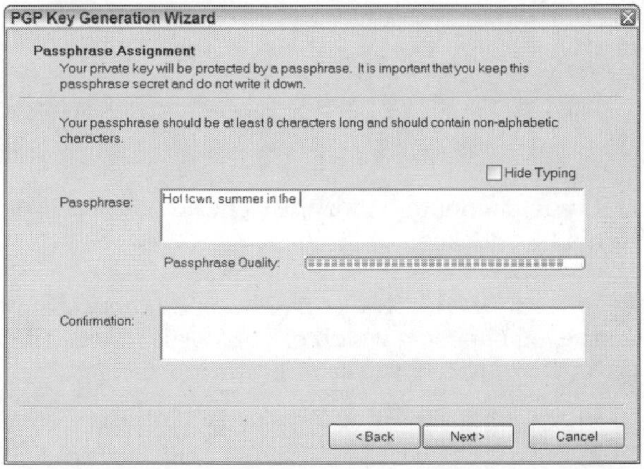

Figure 8-11:
Judging the
quality
of your
passphrase
in the
PGP Key
Generation
Wizard.

Deciding on the options

Before I get to the part where you start sending encrypted e-mails to friends and family, I need you to go through the Options for PGP. By setting the Options correctly you will ensure that not only will the program work properly, it will make it easier for you to use the program.

One of the pet peeves I have with PGP is that the installation program doesn't put a shortcut on the desktop. It's a small thing, I know, but after you install the program there's nothing to indicate that you have completed the installation correctly. The only clue you are given is a tiny yellow lock icon that appears in the taskbar. PGP itself is already running and clicking on the lock in the Task Bar will show you the PGP tools available for use.

Click on that icon now and choose Options from the menu (see Figure 8-12), which opens a new window with the now familiar tabs for accessing the various option items. I'm going to go through the different setting with suggestions for each.

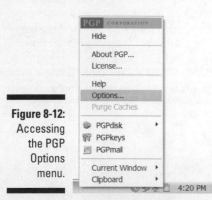

Figure 8-12:
Accessing
the PGP
Options
menu.

The first Option tab you encounter is for the General settings. I recommend the following options be checked:

- ✔ **Always Encrypt to a Default Key** — By choosing this setting you won't have to be bothered choosing which of your keys to use. (It can get very confusing when you have a lot of keys.)

- ✔ **Faster Key Generation** — Creating keys uses a lot of processing power! If you have a very long key it can sometimes take several minutes to generate a key. But, faster key generation can conceivably, and inadvertently, create a weak key — even if it is long. For this fact alone, I recommend *not* using this feature. It's better to take the extra minutes to create a really good key.

✔ **Show PGPtray Icon** — This makes sure that you have the icon in your taskbar. If you don't have this checked, it can be a chore finding where the PGP programs have hidden themselves.

✔ **Cache Passphrase for 30 Minutes** — The default is not to cache the passphrase, but I suggest setting this to 30 minutes or less. If you have a lot of encrypted messages to send in a short period of time, PGP will save the passphrase in memory during this period so you won't have to keep typing it in over and over again. Cool!

✔ **Share Passphrase Cache among Modules** — This means that the passphrase in memory can be accessed by all the different PGP operations. So, if you are switching between secure ICQ and e-mail, you won't have to type your passphrase every time you change modules.

The next tab (the Files tab) is for the directory and file paths for storage of your public and private keys (your "keyring"). It's probably best to change this and not accept the default. Why? Because every good hacker knows exactly where PGP keys are stored by default. I suggest you create a special directory and name it something other than "My PGP Keys." If you are storing your keys on an external drive, this is where you would change those settings.

After the File tab comes the E-mail tab. There are only a few suggested settings for this area and, without further ado, here they are:

✔ **Use PGP/MIME When Sending E-Mail** — By checking this setting it helps ensure that compatibility is maintained when you are sending encrypted e-mail to someone who has a different e-mail program than you do. On the other hand, if your recipient has a hard time decrypting the emails you've sent, there's a good chance that MIME is at fault. Uncheck this item and send the message to your friend again. It might just fix the problem. (I've noticed this happens when I send e-mail to friends who are using Apple's e-mail program.)

✔ **Automatically Decrypt/Verify When Opening Messages** — It may be a bit obvious, but having this option checked does speed things up!

✔ **Word Wrap Clear Signed Messages/Wrap at Column 75** — You may have noticed that occasionally the messages you get from others are a real mess. The line formatting seems to get all messed up. By choosing this setting and making the column width 75, it will make most of those messages behave and wrap normally on the screen.

After you have made those changes, you can skip the Hotkeys tab for now. You probably won't start needing those until you become a little more comfortable with the program. For now let's focus on the Servers tab (see Figure 8-13). This is where public PGP key servers are listed. You need these to be able to find the public keys for the people you are sending encrypted messages to.

By default, PGP has two public key servers already listed. In the picture shown below you'll notice that I have quite a few more listed than you will have. That's because PGP public key servers are a lot like phone books — not everyone will be listed in every phonebook and sometimes you need to look in specific key servers to find someone's key. There's a good list of public key servers at www.keyserver.net/en.

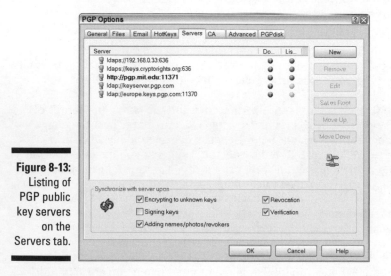

Figure 8-13:
Listing of
PGP public
key servers
on the
Servers tab.

Again I'll skip a tab; this time I'll skip the CA tab, which stands for Certificate Authorities. Because I'm not using certificates with PGP (although you certainly can if you want), there's no need to play around with that section now. The Advanced tab (see Figure 8-14) is probably the most important one of all the PGP options. This is where you tell the program which encryption algorithms to use and how to use them. Have a look at the next figure to see how I've set my program up. I'll explain why these settings are good ones.

First of all you'll notice that I've chosen Triple DES as my preferred algorithm. That's because Triple DES is widely accepted as good and strong. That may change in a few years if and when Triple DES is cracked, but for now it's considered the standard.

Below my preferred algorithm is a list of other algorithms that can be used for encryption. I've checked all but AES and Twofish. Although AES is the algorithm recommended by the government and is their new standard, I don't feel that AES has been adequately tested yet for me to be comfortable with it. I feel the same way about Twofish. I've read a lot of good stuff about it, but I haven't found enough testing data to convince me to use it. All the others; CAST, Triple DES, and IDEA are good standards to accept. Ultimately, the decision as to which algorithms to allow is up to you. But, use whatever algorithm you want. It doesn't hurt anything to pick them all.

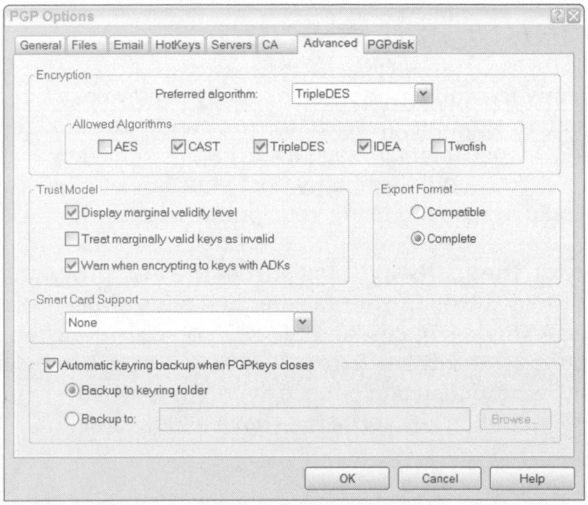

Figure 8-14:
Setting
up the
algorithm
choices
in the
Advanced
options.

The next section in this window has to deal with the "trust" you give to keys. I'm not going to go into all the intricacies of the trust model now — that's a whole subject in itself! It's enough for you to know that it's up to you to decide whether or not you trust the validity of anyone's keys. You want to make sure that you choose Warn When Encrypting to Keys with ADKs. An ADK (Additional Decryption Key) is a special key that is generally used by security officers in a corporate setting. This allows the security officers to read encrypted mail without alerting the sender or receiver. They may want to have this ability if they suspect something fishy is going on. You probably won't run into many instances where you'll receive this warning, but it's a nice thing to have. It lets you know if someone else could possibly read your encrypted messages.

In the Export Format section, I suggest that you click the radio button next to Complete. By choosing that option it will guarantee that all pertinent information about the key is included when you export your keys for backup or for other purposes. If you choose Compatible, there is a slight possibility that important key information won't be included.

Because I'm not going to be using smartcards in our practice exercise, you don't need to select that option. However, the next section on this screen concerns the Automatic Keyring Backup When PGPkeys Closes check box. It's much like having backup keys for your house, cars, garage, mailbox, and storage facilities. It's murder if you lose your keyring in either case so having a backup set is very important — important to maintaining your sanity if nothing else! Please select this option and have the backup stored in a particular folder or external drive or floppy.

That's all you have to do with the options. Now that you have those in order, it's time to send someone a message!

Playing with your keyring

Finally! You're ready to send a message. It's really pretty easy but be sure that you have someone to send the message to! You can have your friend send you his public key in an e-mail message or he can post his key on one of the public key servers. You should probably post your key on one of the servers, too, so your friend can respond using your public key.

You put your key on the server by using part of the PGP program called PGP keys. Click the PGP lock icon in your taskbar and slide along the menu and choose PGPkeys. A window opens, and the key you created when installing PGP will probably be the only key listed. Now select your key by clicking on it; then go to the Server menu and choose Send To. Another menu will appear that lists a couple of public key servers — have a look at Figure 8-15 to see what I mean.

Figure 8-15:
Sending your key to a PGP public key server.

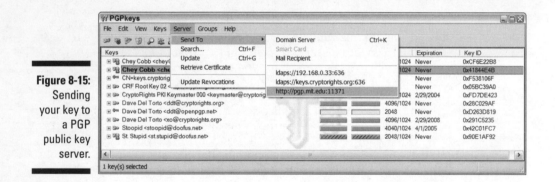

The servers shown on your installed version will not be the same as mine because I've added key servers where my friends and associates have their keys stored. When you have successfully uploaded your key to the server, PGP will give you a confirmation that the transfer was complete.

Now let's say that you have to find a key for a friend or business partner so you can send her an encrypted message. PGP makes it easy for you to search the key servers for that person's key and import their key to the storage area in PGP. In PGP vernacular the storage file for your keys is aptly named your *keyring*. Your keyring is the window that appears when you choose PGPkeys.

Open your keyring by clicking on the PGP icon in your taskbar and choosing PGPkeys. Highlight your name; then click Server and move down to Search. You'll be given a list of servers to check. If you like, you can search for my name and use my key to send a message to me. My key is at `http://pgp.mit.edu:11371`. Type **Chey Cobb** in the box next to where it says UserID and Contains (see Figure 8-16). Then click Search. Soon my public key will appear in the bottom box.

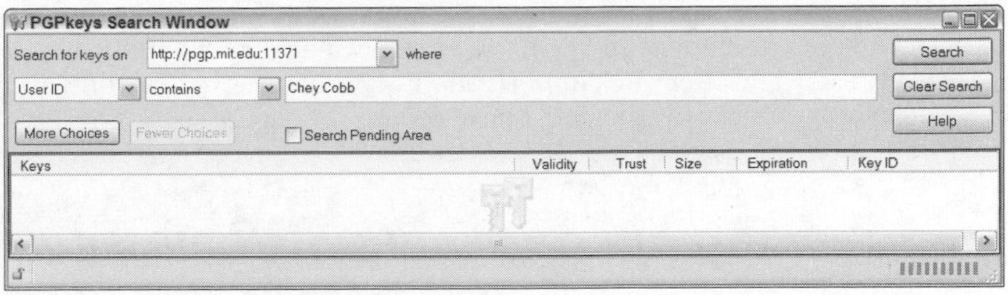

Figure 8-16:
Searching
for Chey's
key on the
MIT public
key server.

After you have my key in the search results window, you can easily import it to your keyring. Simply right-click on the key and choose Import to Local Keyring. That's all there is to it! When you go back to your PGPkeys window (your keyring), the key you selected will be sitting there, waiting for you to use.

But, let's say that you have a friend you want to correspond with and she hasn't uploaded her key to any of the public key servers. Easy-peasy! All she has to do is send you an e-mail with her key, as shown in Figure 8-17. Again, PGP makes this process really easy. All she has to do is to open her keyring and choose the key she wants to send to you. She should right-click on her key, move down the menu to Send To and then move her cursor over to Mail Recipient. That will create a new message in her e-mail program and automatically attach her key to the message. All she has to do then is to address the message to you and send it on its way.

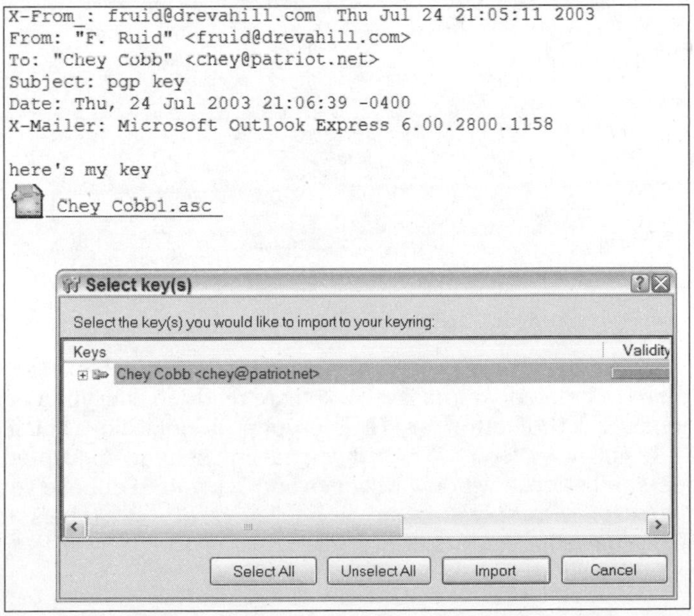

```
X-From_: fruid@drevahill.com  Thu Jul 24 21:05:11 2003
From: "F. Ruid" <fruid@drevahill.com>
To: "Chey Cobb" <chey@patriot.net>
Subject: pgp key
Date: Thu, 24 Jul 2003 21:06:39 -0400
X-Mailer: Microsoft Outlook Express 6.00.2800.1158

here's my key

    Chey Cobb1.asc
```

Figure 8-17:
Receiving a
PGP public
key as an
e-mail
attachment.

When you receive the message with the key as an attachment, double-click on the attachment and PGP will open a window showing the key. You select the key and then click Import, and PGP will store that key on your keyring. Now you're ready to send a message.

Sending and receiving PGP messages

Trumpet blare and drumroll, please. I'm about to engage in amazing feats of encryption!

Open your e-mail program. In my case I'm using Eudora, but Outlook and Outlook Express will work in a very similar way. Start a new message and you'll notice that there are some new buttons on the toolbar (see Figure 8-18). These buttons have been placed there by PGP to automate encrypting, signing, and decrypting messages. There are no commands to learn and no fiddly menus to sort through. With a click of a button, your messages are sent the way you want them to be sent. (Note: if the buttons are not there, use the command in your e-mail program to customize your button bar. You should be able to drag and drop the PGP buttons to your menu.)

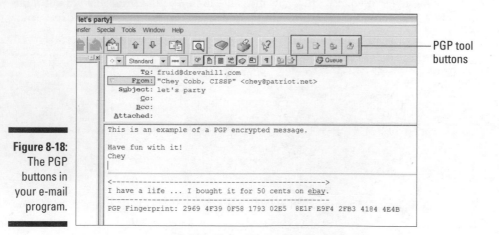

Figure 8-18: The PGP buttons in your e-mail program.

PGP tool buttons

After you have created your message, you are ready to encrypt it and send it to your friend. Click the button for PGP Encrypt — it looks like a small envelope with a little yellow lock on top of it. If you haven't sent an encrypted message to this person before, a window will open and ask you to choose your key and the recipient's key. Simply drag and drop the keys, one at a time, into the window, as shown in Figure 8-19.

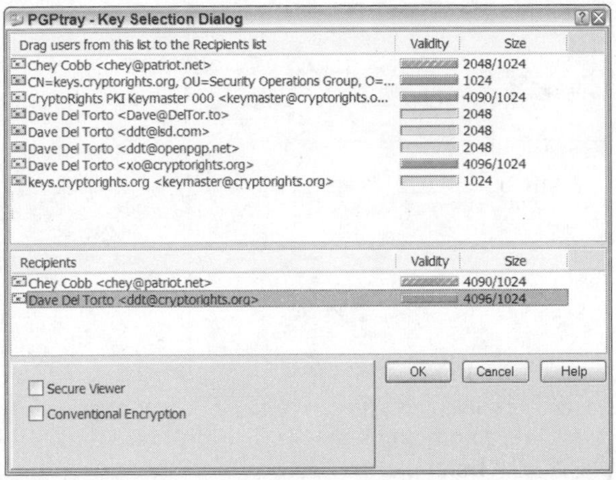

Figure 8-19:
Selecting
the keys to
use for
encrypting
an e-mail
message.

When you've done that, simply click OK, and the message immediately turns into gobbledygook right before your eyes. The encrypted message will be bracketed at the top and bottom by the following bits of text:

```
-----BEGIN PGP MESSAGE-----
-----END PGP MESSAGE-----
```

This lets the PGP program know where the encryption begins and ends. If these perimeters weren't at the top and bottom of the message, PGP would have a hard time, maybe even an impossible time, figuring out what to decrypt. But, you don't have to worry about that because a properly installed PGP program will automatically surround the message in this manner.

Now do whatever it is you need to do to send your message on its way.

When your friend receives her encrypted message, she'll find that some e-mail programs will automatically start the decryption process and with others she'll need to click the PGP Decrypt Verify button to start the process. Then her e-mail program will ask for her secret passphrase in order to decrypt it (see Figure 8-20).

It's a good idea to leave the Hide Typing check box selected to discourage shoulder-surfers from getting a look at your passphrase. However, if you need to see your keystrokes to make sure that you've entered the passphrase correctly, remove the checkmark from the check box and you will be able to see what you type.

If your friend has correctly entered her passphrase, the decrypted message will suddenly appear. Shazam! That is way too cool.

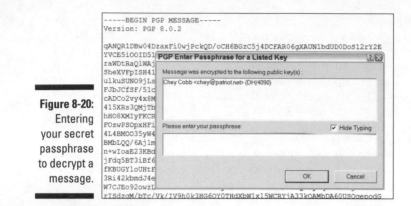

Figure 8-20:
Entering
your secret
passphrase
to decrypt a
message.

PGP in the enterprise

If your company is planning to use PGP company-wide, there is a commercial version available just for that use. The program makes it possible for the IT department to remotely install the PGP program on all desktops and configure the options for the e-mail programs. In addition to that, you get all you need to create your own key servers (instead of having to rely upon public key servers), and there is the capability to recover lost keys as well. For all intents and purposes, this is practically a complete PKI (public key infrastructure) solution all in one box.

At the time of this writing, PGP is preparing to launch a new product for use by corporations of any size and structure. I refer to it as "PKI in a Box" because that is what it sounds like to me. More features are automated and there is less work for the end-users to do when sending encrypted messages or storing encrypted files. I would have liked to include more particulars about it here, but the product is still being developed. Keep an eye out for it as it may be something that is affordable and effective.

Other Encryption Stuff to Try

In my research for this book, I discovered tons of different encryption programs, plug-ins, and other cool stuff. Unfortunately it was impossible for me to download, install, and test everything I saw. One cool thing is that many of these programs and plug-ins are free!

But, just because something is free and is supposed to be secure doesn't necessarily mean it's good to use. You have to be very careful on the Internet. Not everything is as it appears. Hackers have created Trojan programs that look like they'd be good to use but in reality their programs create back doors that allow them into your system or export data from your computer to theirs. For that reason alone you should proceed with caution when playing around with programs you are unfamiliar with. Don't be silly — ask questions.

Go online to find out what others think of these programs and what experiences they've had. In many cases others will post notices of malicious programs. Google is a good place to start your search. Click on Google's *Groups* tab and it will search various newsgroups for postings. Try using "encryption plug-ins" as your search string. I got over 4,500 hits when I tried that one and it was full of good advice from experienced users.

Just for fun, here's a site that I know has some good freeware for Windows programs: www.secureaction.com/download.shtml. One note of caution: Whenever you try a new encryption program it's best to install and test it on a test machine and not the one you rely upon for daily use. Why? Well, you don't know what incompatibilities might arise from the installation and you certainly don't want to start encrypting critical files if you're not sure how the program works. Believe me, I have had to console many business execs who thought they could reverse the actions of an encryption program. I had to tell most of them that their data was now the equivalent of corned beef hash and only the NSA would be able to recover the encrypted data. I really don't like to hear grown people cry, so do yourself a favor and test, test, test before you install unknown encryption programs on your production computers.

Now here's something I bet you never knew — the popular compression program PKZip, which has been around for a long time, is now capable of implementing strong encryption! For years PKZip has had the ability to encrypt files as well as compress them, but the encryption turned out to be horrible and files were extremely easy to crack. With release 6.0 PKZip has the ability to encrypt using RC2, RC4, DES, 3DES and AES encryption algorithms. You can encrypt using a password/passphrase or Digital Certificates. What's even better is that the program is very cheap. As of this writing, the personal version is only $29. That represents a whole lot of good security for very little investment.

So expand your horizons and try PKZip and other encryption programs. Not only will it give your system better security, it will also give you or your IT department a lot more rest — you won't be waking up in the middle of the night wondering if your files are safe!

Chapter 9

File and Storage Strategies

- -

In This Chapter

▶ Learning why you should encrypt data

▶ Looking at possible encrypted storage solutions

▶ Trying on the different algorithm types

▶ Figuring out what solutions will fit your needs

▶ Protecting the integrity of your data

▶ Having a go at policies and procedures

- -

As I have mentioned in previous chapters, most of the current encryption strategies involve "encryption on the fly" — that is, protecting the data as it's being transmitted from one system to another. Web browsers use SSL and digital certificates, e-mail uses S/MIME and PGP, and VPNs are protecting the connections between machines — little or nothing is done about keeping the data encrypted once it hits the storage media. Like I said before, this is like connecting two wicker baskets with a steel pipe. If you want the data badly enough, you won't bother with the steel pipe, you'll go straight for the holes in the baskets. And we all know there are tons of little security holes in those baskets (servers) that hackers regularly exploit.

It's not just hackers you have to protect yourself against, either. Employee misuse and abuse is a big problem. In the early days of computers in the work-place, we used to receive training on new machines and software. Nowadays we are all expected to teach ourselves — and this can lead to unintended misuse. It's not that all employees are out to get their employers; lots of people genuinely don't understand how their mistakes can affect others. Some employee misuse and abuse is intentional, though, and you need to protect your system against malicious intent.

Recently, the state of California passed a privacy protection law that requires companies to protect the private information of any California resident. This applies to all businesses; even if the business is not located in California. What does that mean? It means that all e-commerce Web sites that have

California residents as customers must protect the personal data of those customers. The California law does not require encryption, but it strongly suggests that encryption of that data would be considered adequate protection. Will other states follow California's lead? It remains to be seen at this point, but I do expect to see court challenges of this legislation.

In this chapter, I discuss why, when, and how to encrypt data at rest — that is, data sitting on a storage device. I'll look at some of the pros and cons of the various solutions and give you a fair look at some of the solutions you may want to consider.

Why Encrypt Your Data?

Before you decide to encrypt your data in storage, you need to ask yourself some questions. Answer truthfully, now:

- ✔ What is the usefulness of your data?
- ✔ Is your data valid?
- ✔ Can you verify the owners/creators of the data?
- ✔ What would it cost you to replace or repair the data?
- ✔ If your data started appearing in bus stops all over the city, would it bother you?
- ✔ If your data became front-page news, would it affect your business?

I like the bus stop question the best. That one usually stops people short and makes them think. I've had decision makers in both public and private industry tell me that their data didn't need protection, only to suddenly reverse their decision when they imagined hard copies of their data floating around the city unconstrained.

Encrypting your data is also a way to stop abuse and misuse because only the people who have the correct keys can open the data. Therefore, you can control who can see and change data. For example, you could set your system up so only the HR department and executives could open the files containing salary data and yearly budgets. Everyone else who tried to view this data would only see meaningless garbage instead of spreadsheets and memos.

By signing with digital signatures or fingerprinting your data with one-way hashes, you can ensure the validity of the data. You can find out if it has been changed, when the change was made, and who made the change. From those facts you can also find out if the change was authorized. This is important to protect critical software, too. When software has an associated hash, any change made to the program can be detected by a change in the hash. That can save you from using Trojanized software that has back doors and sniffers incorporated.

Then, too, many people underestimate the value of their data. They forget the man-hours or the man-months it took to create it. Although your data may be a conglomeration of public-domain information, its value is in how you massaged that data in order to turn it into a profit-making product. You may also have software that you have used for years, but it was created by someone long gone from your employment. If that software became unusable, what would it cost you to replace it? You'd have to hire programmers and you may never end up with the same usability.

And, what about the vast amounts of data that sits on the desktops and never makes it to backup media? Think of all the correspondence, facts and figures, proposals, and general business information that could be at risk of misuse or abuse. Many desktop machines are not automatically locked when the user walks away for a few moments. Almost anyone can sit down at an unlocked machine and fiddle with the data. Who would know? Not to mention the fact that it would appear that the changes were made by the data owner. The veracity of this data should surely be protected.

Here are some types of data that you may want to consider encrypting:

- Financial data (yours and your customers')
- Personnel files
- Executive correspondence
- Sales figures and projections
- Intelligence about your competition
- Market intelligence about your customers — past, present, and future
- All data on a laptop, because they are easily lost or stolen

Shame on me! I've used "encrypting" in a very loose sense here. What I really mean is that you may want to consider encryption technologies to either digitally sign your data, encrypt your data, create a hash, create a MAC, or a combination of these. They all use algorithms and keys, so I include them in the encryption basket of goodies.

You may have already protected your network with filtering routers, firewalls, DMZs, network address translation (NAT), intrusion detection systems (IDS), access controls, and physical security for the server rooms. But, have you ever tried to read the logs from firewalls? It's like trying to read *War and Peace* with no punctuation, no paragraph spacing, and very small text — not only that, imagine that it's all written in pidgin English. Not only are the logs difficult to read, it's even more difficult to figure out if any particular event was really a hack attempt or not. The same is true with intrusion detection, the tattle-tale of network security. Intrusion detection systems have the capability of over-loading you with so many alerts that your only recourse is to ignore them and pretend all those red flags are just the system crying wolf.

No system is hack-proof. Nor are they idiot-proof. People who can't get through the security mechanisms will find newer and better ways to circumvent the systems. And, when you consider all the "allowed" traffic that has to pass through the system, you'll realize that that legitimate traffic can carry piggy-backers. But, all this is moot if the data is strongly encrypted. Imagine the frustration of a determined hacker who has spent weeks crafting just the right exploit only to find out that he has stolen tens of megabytes of gob-bledygook. The hacker now has to decide whether to try to crack the encryption. More likely than not, the hacker will go on to easier targets. Most hackers are opportunists — remember that.

So, what if you've done your risk assessments and it comes down to the fact that there's nothing in your system that a hacker would really want. What about your employees? Many of the big credit card hacks and identity theft hacks were carried out by former employees who were holding a grudge against their former employers. If those companies had encrypted their data, the hackers still would have been able to get in, but the hackers would still need the valuable *key* needed to unlock the data.

I could go on all day quoting facts and figures, but now it's time to get down to brass tacks. Let's just say that you've decided to give encryption a try. Where do you start?

Encrypted Storage Roulette

Beware of the term *secure storage*. Many of the companies offering off-site, secure storage really only offer physical security. They have buildings with steel plates in the walls, electrified fences surrounding the property, access controls on all the doors, and a lot of rent-a-cops. This is a good strategy to keep in mind for disaster recovery, but you won't find many secure storage facilities that incorporate encryption into their security offerings.

On the other hand, there are some companies that offer secure, encrypted storage off-site. Many of them offer you a "virtual vault" that you can access online with a password. These are probably a good idea for home users, home businesses, and small businesses as they charge by the amount of data being stored. The advantage is that you can access the data from any Internet connection. For businesses looking at terabytes and petabytes worth of stor-age, they are best off developing their own solutions.

There are basically two different types of secure storage:

- Commercial Off The Shelf (COTS), preferably with one vendor for ease of interoperability.
- Built-It-Yourself. Buy all your components individually and manually build a system that meets your requirements.

What are the differences? Well, with the COTS solution you get what you pay for. Many of the COTS products work well if your network consists of all the same operating system, but if you have a "multi-ethnic" population of UNIX, Linux, Mac, Windows, and so on, you may run into interoperability problems. Many of these solutions for large storage requirements are not cheap, either. I've seen them at $30,000 and up. On the other hand, you get vendor support and installation assistance, too.

If you want a custom-built solution, you need some very savvy, talented people. This may seem extremely expensive but if you think about it, you'll need to have some talented people on hand to maintain whichever type of system you have anyway. If your staffs build a custom solution, you'll have support ready at all times. If you have a mix of operating systems and applications, these people should be able to create code to get around compatibility issues.

The subject is full of pros and cons and, unfortunately, one size does not fit all. That means you'll have to spell out your requirements with a look to future storage needs and prepare a wish list. Be prepared to compromise if none of the solutions meets all your requirements, but if you have prioritized your needs, you'll be prepared to decide which features or processes you can do without.

Symmetric versus asymmetric?

Here we get into the thick of the argument — which is better and which is more secure? There's no one answer as it all depends on the greater need — speed or security.

Symmetric key algorithms are very fast and therefore rarely cause a bottleneck in processing. They use a single key to encrypt and decrypt which is considered to be very secure. That is, very secure *if* you've properly protected the key. If you store the key with the data, bad move. That's sort of like keeping your house key under the door mat or on top of the door frame. It's the first place thieves look, and you've just made it very easy for someone to unlock your encrypted data. There are methods of securely storing and sharing that key that I discussed in Chapter 7.

Symmetric key algorithms have two sub-types: block ciphers and stream ciphers. Simply put, block ciphers cut the data up into same-sized chunks and encrypt a chunk, prepare another chunk, encrypt that, and so on. Stream ciphers don't bother to cut the data up into chunks; they encrypt data one byte after another.

Just in case you missed it in earlier chapters, here are some of the most commonly used symmetric ciphers:

- AES
- 3DES
- IDEA
- CAST
- RC5
- Twofish
- Blowfish

The full name of AES is *Rijndael Advanced Encryption Standard.* Rijndael is pronounced *rine-doll* and is a combination of the last name of the two creators of the algorithm: Vincent Rijmen and Joan Daeman. It's the first algorithm that was chosen for use via competition.

Asymmetric algorithms are just like they sound — you use different keys instead of a single key for encryption. These algorithms are also generally known as *public/private key algorithms* because they consist of a private key that the owner keeps and a public key that is shared with others.

These algorithms are considered very secure because you need the two keys to unlock the data. In a way it's like the two keys that are needed to unlock your safety deposit box at the bank. The bank has the private key and you have the public key. Public keys can be handed out to anyone, but only the bank has the private key. You'd really have to go to a lot of trouble to get the private key without getting clobbered by the guards!

The drawback to asymmetric algorithms is that they are very slow. They require a large amount of processing power and can really slow down network traffic.

Again, here's a reminder of the algorithms you'll be looking at:

- RSA
- DSA
- ECC (Elliptical Curve Cryptography)

Why haven't I included PGP in the list of asymmetric algorithms? Well, in reality PGP is a combination of both symmetric and asymmetric encryption. If you have a look at the Advanced Options of PGP, you'll see that all the listed algorithms for use are symmetric: 3DES, AES, CAST, IDEA, and Twofish. The asymmetric part of PGP comes from the use of the public and private keys in the Diffie-Hellman protocol, which is used for the exchange of the keys. The Diffie-Hellman protocol is not used to encrypt the data.

This just goes to prove that you can mix the two types of algorithms and it will work. It may be a method of getting around the drawbacks of the two different algorithm types without too great of a compromise.

Encrypting in the air or on the ground?

That's meant as a bit of joke but it isn't. I'm thinking of Ethernet and the original meaning of the word *ether*. One of the common definitions is "an elastic, massless, medium filling up universal space." That could be the air, couldn't it? So encrypting in the air is simply my bad pun of the day. On the ground, on the other hand, refers to the storage servers sitting solidly on the floor of the server room. In a roundabout way I'm telling you that you can choose to encrypt the data as it flies across the Ethernet wires, or you can encrypt it on your desktop (or intermediate server) and then send it to the storage media. As usual, there are good things and not-so-good things about both choices.

When you encrypt data before sending it to the storage servers (on the ground), it's usually referred to as *static encryption* and it is most commonly a task handled by special cryptographic *NICs* (Network Interface Cards). It's very fast and it doesn't tie up network resources because it's done off-line. When an intermediate device or server is involved, you'll hear it referred to as a *store and forward* process. In that case, the data is sent from the desktop in the clear to an intermediate server, is encrypted on that machine, and when enough encrypted data is stored up, it's forwarded to the final storage server. I've used this on many networks and have rarely run into any huge problems with it. Like I mentioned, it's fast and efficient. The only problem with it, and it is a big problem, is that the encryption key is stored with the encrypted data while it's on the intermediate machine that's doing the encryption. If someone were to gain unauthorized access to that machine, it would be an easy task to decrypt everything he or she could pick up.

The newer versions of Windows (2000 and XP, for example) have cryptographic capabilities built into the operating system. The MS version is called *EFS (Encrypting File System)*. This system works only on drives that are *NTFS* (NT File System) formatted. You can encrypted individual files or you can create encrypted folders and everything dropped into that folder is encrypted.

A more secure way of getting the data securely to the storage server is to encrypt it in the air — of course I mean on the Ethernet connection. This is referred to as *dynamic encryption* and it's very good because you don't have to worry about someone picking up the encrypted data and the key on one machine. It's encrypted as it is transported from the desktop and when it lands on the storage server, the task is complete. It would be very difficult to find the key in this traffic because there would be a number of keys and all kinds of data flying past a sniffer. You wouldn't know which is which.

So, what's the drawback here? Power. Speed. Computational crunching. This sort of scheme requires a lot of CPU processing and on large networks it could easily overwhelm the systems and end up making the traffic flow look like molasses in January.

Dealing with Integrity Issues

So you're saying to yourself that you don't really need to encrypt your data. Okay. You know your business and what's right for you. But have you ever considered that you may need to check the veracity of your applications and data? Did you know that all CEOs have to verify and sign their company's financial records now? Yep. It's a federal law. If their financial statement is wrong, they could go to jail. Wouldn't you want to make sure that the copy you signed and the one that you sent to the government were one and the same?

What about employee records or school records? Haven't we all heard stories of kids who hacked their school's computer and increased their grades? You can do the same with salary records, too. If your company has developed proprietary software, you probably want to make sure that the code hasn't changed because you want to make sure the software sent to customers is the correct version. Changes in software has been known to happen. In the past, software vendors have released applications that had Trojans, back doors, or viruses in them (much to the vendor's embarrassment and chagrin). The software vendors could have saved themselves a lot of time, trouble, and money if they had been identifying their data with a *message digest*.

Message digest/hash

Another word for a message digest is a *hash* and I find it a very appropriate word. The way it works is that you use a specific algorithm like SHA-1 (pronounced "shaw one") or MD5 and run it against the data. The algorithm reads the data, mixes it up a bit, and then spits out a fixed-length of gibberish — it looks like a hash of letters and numbers. Here's an example of a SHA-1 hash:

iQA/AwUBPyWDkun0L7NBhE5LEQJwwwCg0muzqyY67sfu1YKO/wtIbc1+lQIAo
OGt70CU2yZs0vVi7Jcv1LSO65DU=3p8i

The gibberish is the actual message digest, or hash, itself. It's a kind of finger-print of the data. If you send exactly the same data to someone else and they run the same algorithm against the data, they will come up with the exact same hash. That way they know the data has not been changed enroute. It's not possible for the same message and the same algorithm to come up with different hashes. On the other hand, it's impossible to get the same hash for two different data files. Even if you only changed a file by one character, the resulting hash would also change from the original hash.

SHA-1 will always return a fixed-length hash of 20 bytes (160 bits) and MD5 will always return a fixed-length hash of 16 bytes (128 bits).

The way you create a hash is to create small program. You can get SHA-1 and MD5 for free as a *DLL* (*dynamic linked library*) or a *LIB* (*library*) file. Then you write a small program in almost any language you prefer to create the hash. If you're not up to that, there are thousands of sites on the Web where you can download hash programs for free.

Many of download sites include the hash for their programs. After you install the program you can run a message digest algorithm against the downloaded file and compare the hash to the one shown on the Web site. If the two match, then you know you have the real thing. This is done to ensure the integrity of the program.

Keep in mind that MD5 and SHA-1 do not encrypt the data. They use the data to make a fingerprint or snapshot of the data that is given to you as a code. That code is used to determine whether or not the data has been altered. If the data you receive has been altered, you will not get the same code number as the original data.

MACs

Nope, I'm not talking about Apple's products here. I'm talking about a *Message Authentication Code*. MACs are very like message digests except they can be made from most of the complex algorithms like RSA, 3DES, IDEA, and so on. It produces a fixed length output somewhat like a hash, but they are very fiddly to work with. This is because they usually work with one key and you need to share that key with the recipient. That isn't always the most secure, or easiest, way to go. For this reason I'm not going to go into much information on them. The only reason I mention them is that they are part of the next subject.

HMACs

Now this sounds like an air conditioning and heating system. No, sorry, that's HVAC. HMAC stands for *Hashed Message Authentication Code* and it's pro-nounced "*h-mack*". Now, you're asking, what is it for?

Data that has been hashed can be changed enroute. Of course that would mean that the hash the recipient computes would not be the same, but what if the hash had been changed, too? Could a person intercept the data, modify it, create a new hash for the new data, and send it on its way? Yep, entirely possible! So, we need to find a way to make the hash more secure.

You make a hash more secure by combining the data with a secret key and then creating a hash. The intended recipient has been given the secret key by another channel and when she receives the data with the HMAC, she can combine the key with the data and come up with the same result. Voilà, instant data integrity! You can use any symmetric algorithm to create a key and then use SHA-1 or MD5 to create the hash. If you don't know how to create this sort of program yourself, you can buy it from various places on the Web.

Because the hash includes the information about the key in it, a person who hijacks the data has to know exactly which key was used. If an interceptor grabs the data, modifies it, and then creates a hash, there is no way it will come out correctly. That's because he needs that all important key in order to make a correct replication.

Again, the data itself is not encrypted. All you get is a data file, that looks like plaintext, with a bit of gibberish at the end. But, if you want to make this even more secure, there is a way!

You can add a single key to the data and create an HMAC. Then, you encrypt the entire file with your private key and send it on to your intended receiver. You can use PGP keys or you can use a Digital Certificate to encrypt the package. Because the data is encrypted, no one can know what it is by just looking at it. There's no special acronym for this process; it's just one of the ways you can create and use an HMAC.

Tripwire

Tripwire is a software program and not an algorithm. It's a special program that continually creates a hash or checksum of all the data on a server (files and applications) and alerts you when changes have been made. It's one of the standard tools of data security experts and it's been around for quite a while. The freeware version is still available for Linux, but you can purchase Tripwire for other operating systems at `www.tripwire.com`.

This is such a cool program that I urge everyone to at least give it a try. The commercialized product has many different versions now and many more reporting and management features than the freeware version. Plus, you get that all important support.

The one I usually recommend for starters is "Tripwire for Servers." You install it on one server and it seeks out all the other servers on the network. It creates fingerprints of all files and resources; even Windows registry files. Then all the fingerprints are stored in a database. The program continually verifies data and file integrity against the fingerprints database and quickly notifies you of changes. Tripwire now even tells you who made the change as well as what, when, and where the change was made. If you tell the program that the change is okay, it updates the database with another fingerprint.

Remember that Tripwire doesn't encrypt any data; it just creates fingerprints for all your data.

Policies and Procedures

Before you make any major changes in the way you use your network and resources — and adding encryption is a major step — you shouldn't dive right into a solution before you have prepared your Encryption Policies. I know paperwork is such a drudge, but in doing this it will also help you decide what your needs really are.

The questions you need to address in your policy are as follows:

✔ Who is the big boss when it comes to encryption decision making?

✔ What are the responsibilities of the general users, executives, and maintenance staff in regards to encrypting and decrypting data?

✔ Are you going to handle this on your own or outsource?

✔ Who will handle the day-to-day maintenance of the system?

✔ Will your encryption be used internally only or with the outside world?

✔ Which algorithms are you going to use?

✔ What data will always be encrypted?

✔ Is there any data that will be encrypted on an ad-hoc basis?

✔ What rules will a person follow in deciding to encrypt on an ad-hoc basis?

✔ How much training will you give the staff?

✔ Who will be in charge of training?

✔ Will you have staff sign a policy statement that says they understand the rules for encryption?

✔ If a decrypted document is to be printed, how will you make sure that unauthorized personnel can't pick it up off the printer?

↳ How long will you store encrypted documents?

↳ Who is the response team to handle lost keys, lost passphrases, and corrupted data?

↳ Will you need authentication as well as encryption to make sure that only authorized personnel can get access to keys and encrypted data?

Believe it or not, this list could go on for pages! What I've given you are the top level questions. As you answer these, you'll realize that there are more questions to be answered. This is best handled by a small team that occasionally works with others within the company for input. Keep your policies on an internal Web site so everyone has access to them. Also keep hardcopies in a folder in case of network outages.

When you have all of your policies together, you can start working on the procedures. I know a lot of people get these two things mixed up. The difference is that the policies are the rules you need to follow; the procedures are how you will implement and enforce the rules. For example, your company has just named Bob as the Grand Poobah of Encryption Decisions. You need to give Bob some parameters with which to make decisions. Does he do this solely on his own or with help? What help should he seek? Does he have the authority (and budget) to hire a consultant? Blah, blah, blah.

The same sort of things hold true for both the general users and the maintenance team. If someone notices that a decrypted document was printed and is now missing, what do you do about it? Who do you report it to? Again, as you work through your policies you'll realize that some of the questions that come up are actually implementation, use, and maintenance concerns. You should spell out what everyone is expected to do, when they need to do it, and how you are going to handle problems. If you get your policies and procedures started, you'll be surprised how easily the actual rollout happens. You'll save yourself a lot of money in aspirin and you'll be a winner that everyone wants to emulate. Our hero!

Examples of Encryption Storage

There are many different types of encryption storage that will serve anyone from home users to major corporations. There are online encrypted storage "vaults" for individuals to server farms dedicated to encrypted storage. There are also external drives that attach to your computer via firewire or USB. What you get depends upon what you need and what you need will depend upon your requirements.

There doesn't seem to be any industry standard or a vendor solution that tops them all. So, it's really hard to say which is best. Nonetheless, the number of solutions available on the market is mind boggling. So, rather than looking at individual solutions, I'll give you some generic information along with some products you may want to take a look at.

Media encryption

A good practice, especially when you are dealing with laptops or home computers, is to use *media encryption* (disk encryption). This is usually in the form of a special software program that encrypts the entire hard disk. The only portions that are not encrypted are the boot sector, which is need to boot the computer. You can also get external hard drives that automatically encrypt everything that is saved or copied to them. Some of these have a special security device called a *dongle*. The dongle is a physical device that you plug into the port and the cable of the external drive is plugged into the dongle.

Because laptop theft is so common, it's a good idea for every road warrior to encrypt his drives. This will keep strategic information out of the hands of the competition and the customers. If the laptop is stolen, the thief won't be able to read any of the data OR software programs and his only resort would be to completely reformat the hard drive. No, encryption doesn't do anything to prevent theft but it can keep your data out of the wrong hands.

Home users often have lots of sensitive personal financial data stored on their home computers. Because these users are often unaware of the security measures they can take to prevent hackers from gaining access to their home systems, it's a good idea to keep all sensitive information encrypted. This will protect the user against identity theft as well.

Encrypting software programs are usually the choice over hardware encrypting devices because the hardware devices can be very slow to work. Or, if the hardware device is fast, it's likely to be very expensive.

One thing to be aware of that some encrypting software programs store the encryption keys in the encryption software. This is not a good thing because a thief or intruder can conceivably obtain those keys and decrypt all the data. Encryption keys that are derived from a password are also a bad thing. Look for a system that has some type of access control. There are some products that will allow the use of tokens or smartcards for access, too. Whatever the case, be sure to save your key and/or your passphrase is a very, very safe place. I'd hate for you to lose all your data and software programs because you forgot your key!

Here's a short list of some products you may want to look at. I'm not necessarily listing them here as a recommendation; I'm listing them because they give a very broad view of the types of products available.

Pointsec PC is a software encryption program that includes an aspect of authentication. www.pointsec.com/solutions/solutions_pointsec.asp

WinMagic's SecureDoc is also a software program for encrypting hard drives. It has applied for government accreditations and is used by some government agencies. www.winmagic.com/product_info/securedoc/prod_info.asp

NMS for PC is yet another software solution, but this one supports authentication by tokens or fingerprints. It also allows you to set security policies so only the correct data is encrypted. www.carraig.co.uk

WiebeTech makes a lot of hardware products and one of them is an external hard drive that encrypts everything dropped on to it. The product is called Firewire Encrypt. www.wiebetech.com/products/firewireencrypt.html

Last, but not least, is **Decru DataFort**. It's a hardware appliance that sits between the storage servers and the desktop PC. It encrypts everything going in to the servers and decrypts everything coming out. This is definitely something you'll want to consider if you have a very large network and tons of servers. www.decru.com/products/datafort0.htm

Encrypting File System

And then there's Microsoft. In the Windows 2000 and Windows XP (but not XP Home Edition) operating systems, MS has included a little-explored feature called *EFS* (Encrypting File System). Of course your systems have to be using one of these versions of windows to work and it will only work if all the hard drives are NTFS (NT File System) formatted — FAT formatted drives won't work. EFS can be applied on a file-by-file basis, or applied to an entire folder.

EFS works through the use of public and private keys, so if you don't already have a PKI system up and running, you may have to consider it (especially for a large organization.) Each file has a *File Encryption Key* which is encrypted with the user's public key. There are administrative key recovery capabilities you can use if someone leaves the company without giving anyone his key. They type of encryption available varies, depending on what version of Windows you are using. The latest version (Windows 2003 Server) can use DES or 3DES. If you plan on using this, I highly recommend that you read all of Microsoft's Knowledge Base articles on the subject because there are some configurations that won't encrypt properly.

There are also software programs you can use instead of EFS. There's EasyCrypt (www.easycrypt.co.uk) that is sold in England and SafeHouse (www.pcdynamics.com/SafeHouse) that has gotten good reviews. I've seen another product made in England called MadeSafe (www.madesafe.com/us/home) that also has an online "virtual vault" so you can store your encrypted files on their servers so you can retrieve them when you're on the road. Of course there's the reliable PGP (www.pgp.com), too! The commercial version has a feature called PGP Disk which creates an encrypted partition on your drive. All the files dropped on that drive are encrypted.

Again, I am not listing these products as an endorsement because I've only had limited experience with them. However, these products can give you a good idea of what's on the market and to help you with feature comparison.

Secure e-mail

If you don't want to encrypt all your data but are worried about some of the sensitive information contained in e-mail, you can always use PGP and or/S/MIME to encrypt that information.

There is a wealth of information on these two products in Chapter 8, so I won't bore you by going over that same material again.

Program-specific encryption

Many different software programs come with the ability to encrypt their own files; the majority of them are Microsoft products. If you have the more recent versions of Outlook, Outlook Express, GroupWise, PKZIP, and Adobe Acrobat you can encrypt the files made with those programs. Unfortunately, the encryption abilities built into these programs aren't necessarily the safest and strongest, so I don't really recommend them.

Encrypted backup

Backups can be a real pain in the you-know-what, but it's one of those necessary evils of network maintenance. Not all backups need to be encrypted but if your data has a lot of sensitive, proprietary information or contains personal data of individuals, it would be a good thing to encrypt your backup tapes, CDs, or whatever. Imagine going to all the trouble of securing your network only to have someone walk off with a backup tape full of really important stuff.

Encrypted backup can be either hardware or software based. The hardware solutions are likely to have a special crypto chip on board to make the processing faster. If you have your choice, a public/private key system is much better than a secret key system. The reason being is that you occasionally find disgruntled network administrators (who normally have access to the keys) who copy the secret key, steal data, and sell it to competitors. The whole point is that you don't want to put all your eggs in one basket — secret keys are hard to hide and they can be stolen or copied.

There are only two companies in this field that I'm familiar with, so I'll give you their names and URLS for research and comparison. One backup company is called DataVault (`www.datavaultcorp.com/data/security.shtml`) and they specialize in remote backups — you send the data to them across the Internet. (This is a good strategy for disaster recovery, too.) The other company is called ShadowVault (`www.shadowvault.com/Encryption.aspx`) and they have an online system, too. Look at these two companies for the different methods they use.

Chapter 10

Authentication Systems

● ●

In This Chapter

▶ Examining good authentication requirements

▶ Looking at the most common authentication servers

▶ Examining the differences between the different types of authentication protocols

▶ Using digital certificates with authentication systems

▶ A comparison of authentication devices and methods

● ●

*T*he core concept of this book all along has been that encryption isn't really that hard to accomplish — all you need are the right tools and some short lessons. However, what I haven't told you is that encryption can be easy to subvert if you know what you're doing, that is.

Wait! If encryption is effective at hiding and disguising data, then how can it be subverted? Well, when you buy something from an online merchant, are you really sure that you are connected to that merchant? Did you check the Digital Certificate? Did you call the company to verify the details of their Digital Certificate? Does the small lock or key icon in the Web browser really tell you anything about the party you are connected to?

Come to think of it, when you are connected to an online merchant, how do they know that you are really who you say you are? They are trusting the fact that you are giving them personal information, but they have no way of really ensuring that you haven't stolen the credit card you are using for the purchase.

What's missing in the encryption scenario is *authentication* — making sure that you can verify the identity of the person or entity you are dealing with. This isn't really a subversion of encryption itself, it just goes to show that encryption in itself is not a total solution. Digital certificates are used for authentication because the identity of the person or the business has been verified by the company that issued the Digital Certificate. But, these certificates are not foolproof and they can be spoofed. The best thing to do is to combine these certificates with a special authentication system, or use an authentication system *in addition* to the Digital Certificates. Some authentication systems are capable of pretty good encryption themselves. The point is;

you don't want to have to rely upon just one transaction to prove a person's identity. Two identity checks are better and three is wonderful. It's no different than a merchant asking to see two forms of identity before accepting your check in payment for goods purchased. The difference is, no one in cyberspace can see your face. There's a cartoon that I like that illustrates this. There are two dogs sitting at a computer and one says to the other, "On the Internet, no one can tell you are a dog." Too true!

Good authentication (also referred to as *strong* authentication) is based on three requirements:

1. Something you *know*

2. Something you *have*, and

3. Something you *are*

In normal computer transactions, we only incorporate the first requirement of *something you know* which is your UserID and password. Because this can be guessed or stolen, it's not at all secure. In order for authentication to be really secure, you have to add at least one of the additional requirements: *something you have* or *something you are*. Here's and example of the ultimate in strong authentication:

1. A security token (the *have*)

2. Your password or passphrase (the *know*)

3. A fingerprint (the *are*)

The authentication systems I'm about to tell you about all have the ability to include two or more of the good authentication requirements. All this is done in the name of security because it helps to ensure that you are only letting authorized personnel access your network. Of course you should actually *know* these people yourself, or someone in higher up in the organization should have given written approval to add this person to the listed of trusted personnel.

Authentication systems have been around for a long time. Kerberos, for example, has been in use for more than 10 years which is an eon in Internet years. Authentication systems are good at adding an extra layer of confidence in the validity of the identities of users. Most authentication systems offer varying levels of encryption, too, but they are sometimes tricky to set up and they can make the user jump through several hoops in order to make a connection. Unfortunately for online commerce, users generally aren't willing to jump though these hoops just to order a sweater or a coffee maker; they'll go to another site that makes it easier to order.

That's ironic when you consider that we are used to having to prove who we are in daily life to get what we want. We sign for packages at the post office and at home. We show our photo ID when we sign for credit card charges. We present photo ID at airline check-in counters. What we are used to doing in the physical world we are not prepared to do in the virtual, digital world. It would be nice if we all had one form of digital identification that we could use for all online transactions, but it's not likely to happen anytime soon. There are privacy issues to contend with and it would be difficult to come up with an identification scheme that the entire cyber world could agree on.

Common Authentication Systems

There are probably hundreds, if not thousands, of authentication systems on the market. What you need to know is that most of them are based on some core technologies that have been in use for some time now. When you are talking to a vendor about their "new, better, improved" authentication system, ask them what their system is based upon. Chances are that they give you one of four choices: Kerberos, SSH, RADIUS, and TACACS. These are mature technologies that you can trust but it's the configuration of the system and the implementation that makes the difference.

Kerberos

Kerberos is also sometimes spelled as *Cerberus*. (The accepted pronunciation is *KUR-ber-us*.) The name comes from the three-headed dog in Greek mythology that guarded the gates of Hades. (Like Hades really needs to be guarded?) Kerberos is a network authentication system for use on physically insecure networks; that is, a network where you have little or no control of who gets access to workstations or terminals.

Kerberos is a free program (created by MIT and available at their ftp site) and it is also included in many commercial products, including the newer versions of MS Windows. Kerberos works by providing users with "tickets" that are used to identify themselves to other users or computers. It also provides cryptographic keys for secure communication with other users (or computers).

It all starts with a Kerberos server, which is actually a key server. The correct terminology here is a *Key Distribution Center* (KDC). The KDC is a database of all the users, other trusted computers, and their passwords. The users' passwords are encrypted, usually with DES. When a user wants to communicate with another user or another computer, he or she enters his password. Kerberos uses a special algorithm that adds the destination information to the password and changes it into a cryptographic key. DES is commonly used in Kerberos, but it is capable of using other algorithms to accomplish this task.

After the KDC gets the encrypted key from the user, it sets up other keys for the actual encryption of the session — these are normally referred to as *tickets*. Included in the ticket is usually a time restriction so the ticket expires after a certain amount of time. This is done to prevent the use of unauthorized use of a ticket. If one had been intercepted or stolen, chances are that the ticket would not be used during the proper time period, or the origin and destination computers wouldn't match the ticket. The encrypted session will not begin if the KDC detects any anomalies.

Because the KDC holds the master keys and all the access rules, it's imperative that this computer be physically and logically protected. If the KDC is compromised, you lose the integrity of the entire system. A good rule of thumb is to restrict access to the KDC by putting it in a locked room and by controlling access to that room. If the server is ever compromised, then you'll have a list of suspects to start with. It's also a good idea to keep a duplicate KDC in case you run into problem with the main one.

A Kerberos system isn't doing physical identity checks or looking for Digital Certificates from the user. The validity of the system comes from the administrator. Hopefully you wouldn't add a person or a system to the access database (KDC) without first verifying the identity of the person or the veracity of a remote system. If the administrator is adding anyone and everyone who asks for access, then why bother? If that's the case then Kerberos is not acting as an authentication system; it's only acting as an encryption service for remote transactions.

SSH

SSH stands for *Secure SHell* and is one of the darlings of the computer security community that started life as a "secure telnet" service that allowed administrators to work on remote machines without compromising security. It, too, has been around for a long time has matured into a sophisticated product. It's available in both freeware (OpenSSH) and commercial products. It's no longer limited to just telnet; in some ways it can be considered "VPN Lite" because it is able to set up encrypted tunnel sessions for many applications and communications. Be aware of its limitations, though, because SSH is intended for a limited number of encrypted sessions. If you are looking at running thousands of sessions an hour, you may need to look at another product.

SSH requires that both the client (user) and the SSH server have RSA or DSA public keys. The user can create any number of keys for his/her own use and the SSH server program has its own server key which is automatically regenerated for every session, or connection. Encryption starts as soon as the initial connection is made and all traffic is encrypted, including passwords.

Again, the validity of the identity of the users and trusted networks is up to the administrator to handle. Other than UserID and password, SSH does not ask for any other proof of identity. If the administrator is not diligent in checking out who is getting access to which systems, you're still not authenticating your users effectively.

For stronger authentication, SSH can be set up to require the use of security tokens or smartcards, too. It can mesh well with an established PKI system and, to keep processing overhead down, can be configured to trust the Certificate Authority (CA) of the system rather than constantly loading individual keys for sessions.

If you are thinking of implementing SSH, be sure to get the newest version (as of this writing it is SSH2) because the older version had some serious security holes in it. The newer version fixed those problems and added new features and capabilities. As far as the encryption algorithms are concerned, you can choose to use any of the acceptable "strong" algorithms presently in use: DES, 3DES, AES, CAST, IDEA, and Twofish.

For those of you who are running multiple operating systems on your network, SSH has been ported to just about every possible platform you can think of — even Mac OS X. If you're looking for an inexpensive way of encrypting a limited number of sessions daily, then this is a good bet.

Recently there have been a rash of severe security vulnerabilities found with different vendors' implementations of SSH. These vulnerabilities can allow unauthorized persons to gain access to your network and sensitive information. To see if your version of SSH is vulnerable, check the Computer Emergency Response Team (CERT) pages at `www.cert.org/advisories/CA-2002-36.html` to see if your software is listed. If your software is affected, please check with your vendor to see if they have a security patch available for this problem.

RADIUS

Here's an acronym for you: RADIUS. Want to take a wild guess what it translates to? A gold star for those who guessed *Remote Authentication Dial-In User Service*. Just that name itself should give you some indication of how long it's been around — because dial-up accounts became commonplace in any case. It began life as a mechanism for ISPs to control access to their systems and to monitor users' logon times for accounting purposes.

Although RADIUS encrypts a user's password, it does not encrypt the user's name. It's a slightly different creature from most of the mainstream authentication systems in that the initial communications travel over UDP *(Uniform Dataform Protocol)* rather than the normal TCP (Transmission Control Protocol). I'm not going to get deep into the differences in network transmission protocols but it's enough to say that UDP does not have the error correction capabilities that TCP does.

The only thing that RADIUS encrypts is the authentication process; the communications that occur after the authentication has been approved are not encrypted. For that you will need to incorporate IPsec or some other transmission or file encryption to hide everything from view. You can't use a RADIUS system for a VPN, for example.

Because RADIUS was originally built to provide accounting, it gives you excellent logs and reports as to who logged on, when they did, and where they went and what they did after they logged on. That helps to relieve conflict when a user denies they had accessed the system during a certain period and can be used to look for anomalies in users' access (which may indicate a hacking attempt.)

RADIUS needs a database to create the rules for access and to track usage. You can use the database features that come with a RADIUS server or you can choose to connect it to your existing database system.

RADIUS is available as freeware or as a commercial product. If you are unfamiliar with these systems, you might be better off going with a commercial version for the support they offer with the product. In addition, many vendors will also offer upgrades that allow you to add a PKI system and/or encryption capabilities.

TACACS+

TACACS+ stands for *Terminal Access Controller Access Control System*. The "plus" sign is an indication that this is not the original version but is the Cisco implementation along with the changes in security they made to the original protocol.

In many ways TACACS+ isn't that much different from RADIUS. It provides authentication and accounting just as RADIUS does, but it gives you more flexibility in setting up how the authentication is handled. Instead of having one server do the authentication and accounting and auditing, you can split TACACS+ over three servers to do those jobs individually.

Like RADIUS, TACACS+ only encrypts the authentication process. For complete communication encryption you will need to add another system.

Authentication Protocols

Now that I've given you a little bit of information about the different types of authentication servers, you should know that there are different methods of authentication that these servers are able to handle. Authentication protocols vary from the very simple (and most common) UserIDs and passwords that we are all familiar with to more complex and sophisticated systems. Table 10-1 is an overview of authentication protocols.

Table 10-1	Authentication Protocols
Authentication Protocol	**Explanation**
PAP	*Password Authentication Protocol.* This is the one we are all familiar with when we log on to our computers. Not very secure and the password file containing the passwords is only lightly encrypted.
CHAP	*Challenge Handshake Authentication Protocol.* This requires that the server and the workstations have CHAP enabled.

The user enters the UserID and password as usual; then the server and the workstation take over. The server issues a challenge back to the workstation which is information that is unique for this authentication session. The workstation then takes this information and encrypts it using a previously issued password that is shared by both the workstation and server. That password (or other secret) is sent back to the server. The server has the same password or secret and uses it as a key to encrypt the information it previously sent to the workstation. It compares its results with the encrypted results sent by the workstation. If they are the same, the workstation (and user) is assumed to be authentic.

MS-CHAP	Microsoft's implementation of CHAP protocol.
EAP	*Extensible Authentication Protocol.* EAP is a an authentication protocol that supports multiple authentication methods, such as token cards, Kerberos, one-time passwords, certificates, public key authentication, and smartcards.
	In wireless communications using EAP, a user requests connection to a network through the access point which then requests the identity of the user and transmits that identity to an authentication server such as RADIUS.
EAP-LEAP	*Lightweight EAP.* Cisco's proprietary EAP method that only works with Cisco and Apple wireless network equipment.
EAP-TLS	*EAP-Transport Layer Security.* This authentication method requires that a PKI system be in place and that both the servers and the workstations have Digital Certificates. Not only do the servers authenticate the workstations; the workstations also make sure they are connecting to the correct servers via authentication.
EAP-TTLS	*EAP-Tunneled Transport Layer Security.* Basically the same as above, but after the authentication is complete and verified, the communications travel via an encrypted tunnel.
EAP-PEAP	*EAP-Protected EAP.* A new protocol backed by Microsoft, Cisco, and RSA Security that provides mutual authentication. It combines CHAP and EAP.

As you can see, there's a lot to consider here when choosing which authentication method you want to use. Some are easier to set up and use than others. If you decide that you want all your users to use a biometric device (such as a fingerprint scanner), a smartcard, or a security token, keep in mind that you'll have to bear the brunt of the cost of these devices. Most security tokens don't cost very much, but users do lose them and they need to be replaced. Of course you need to provide physical security for these devices as well.

How Authentication Systems Use Digital Certificates

I've mentioned a couple of times that most authentication systems are able to integrate with PKI systems that use Digital Certificates. What I'm about to tell you is a broad generality, but it is a good description of how this combination works. The variances in implementation are due to changes in how the different vendors have configured their systems.

1. An X.509 Digital Certificate is generated. (This can be done by and existing PKI system, or the authentication system can have one of its servers hand this task. The Digital Certificate can also be stored on a smart card or token. When the token/card are slotted in to the client machine, it's available for use.)

2. The Digital Certificate, along with its public key, are added to the key server. (A certificate on a token/card will already have been stored in the key server.)

3. When a connection between a client and a server are initiated (for example), the client sends its Digital Certificate to the server. At this point only the certificate, and not the public key, is sent.

4. The authentication system's server validates the certificate by checking with the key server to see if this certificate is in the key server's list of trusted entities.

5. If something is wrong with the certificate, the connection is dropped.

6. If the certificate is okay, the authentication system validates the certificate.

7. The authentication server creates a session key, encrypts it with public key of the certificate and sends the encrypted information back to the client. (Okay, now we can begin communicating!)

8. The client uses its private key to decrypt the information received from the server and extract session key.

9. That session key is used to encrypt and decrypt the information that is now flowing back and forth between the two systems.

10. Some session keys will have a time limit attached to them and the session will be renewed or dropped after that time period. Other session keys are available for use until the client ends the session.

So, you can see there is a lot of communication back and forth between the client and the server. This takes time to accomplish, but normally it happens so quickly that the user doesn't really notice any lag in time.

Tokens, Smartcards, and Biometrics

Okay. You've decided on which authentication system to use. The next question is: "How are the users going to interact with the system?" Will they only be using Digital Certificates stored on their desktop computers? Or, will they use one of the many physical devices intended to augment the authentication system. To help you decide which to use, I'm going to describe some of the methods and devices, along with the pros and cons.

Digital Certificates on a PC

This is the normal mode of operation and is frequently used in e-commerce. A Digital Certificate and private key are stored on the hard drive of the user's computer. The doesn't usually have to interact with the transaction and is not aware that credentials are being passed back and forth.

Pros

There is certainly a cost savings here because you don't need any additional equipment or software to make this system work. It's easy to implement — certificates can be "pushed" from central servers out to the individual workstations. Finally, most operating systems are able to use Digital Certificates and no extra software is needed.

Cons

It's very easy to sit down at someone else's computer and use their Digital Certificates. (Provided you knew the password needed to log on to the computer.) Depending on the security of the desktop computers, it could be easy to "clone" or copy the private key without the owner knowing anything wrong has happened. Because of this, it might be very difficult to prove that an owner was, or was not, in sole possession of his private key. This really destroys the trust model if the certificates and keys can be stolen or copied.

This is a minor point, but storing Digital Certificates and the keys on a user's PC is very limiting to the user. It means he or she can only work from one PC. If the user moves to another desk with a different PC, the certificates and keys need to be changed, too.

Time-based tokens

These have been around for a long time now. I know the first one I saw must have been in the early 90s! Some Time-based tokens are the size of a very small calculator and others look more like a small paging device. The commonality between the two is that they have a small viewing window in which a number appears. The numbers are picked at random and change every 60 seconds. Most have a countdown indicator to show you how soon a new number is going to be generated.

When you log onto a system with one of these, the system asks for the user's PIN and the random number that appears on their token. This information is forwarded to the authentication system which checks to see that the PIN and the random number are correct for that user. The authentication system and the tokens are synchronized using time.

Pros

The tokens cannot be copied or broken into and, even if stolen, they must be used in combination with a PIN. These devices allow a user to log on to any PC in the office and it is good for remote users who dial-in to the network or connect via a VPN. This is a really simple system and you don't need to spend a lot of time on user education.

There's a lot of support for these systems so you won't have trouble finding an authentication system that works with these tokens. The installation is usually straightforward and it doesn't require a lot of training for the IT staff, either.

One more bonus is the fact that the user is not limited to using just one PC. He can use any PC; even one at an Internet café. That results in a lot of freedom for remote users.

Cons

Because this system is time-based, it's really important that the servers and the tokens have their times synchronized. If a token gets out of synch with the server, the random number shown by the token won't be correct and the user won't be able to log on successfully. Most of these systems are time-limited, too. That means that the connection will automatically be dropped after a certain amount of time has passed. So, if a user is going to be logged on to one PC all day, he or she will have to re-enter their PIN and random number quite a few times during the day. This really irritates users.

There is a small cost involved here. The physical devices cost money and personnel are bound to use them. They are not as expensive as smartcards, but it can get expensive if people are constantly loosing them. The logistics of providing support for remote users can be a pain when they loose theirs, too.

There are no Digital Certificates or other identifying features with these tokens so a user won't be able to encrypt data or digitally sign any documents.

Smartcard and USB Smartkeys

Smartcards look like credit cards except there is a electronic chip imbedded in the card. The USB Smartkeys look like a USB storage drive and can easily be held on a user's key ring. Both devices are capable of storing The UserID, Digital Certificate, and private key. In addition, some devices can also hold a biometric like a fingerprint scan. Both are very sophisticated devices and are well received by users.

A Smartcard needs to have a special reader attached to the PC so it can be read by the computer. The reader can be similar to the card swipe devices seen on department store cash registers, or it can be a special "port" or external reader connected to the PC. The USB Smartkeys only need to be plugged into an existing USB port on the computer. (Some older computers may not have these.)

When a user plugs the device into the PC, the PC reads the information off the device and checks to see that the credentials on the device are valid (e.g., not expired or revoked.) The user is then presented with a "challenge" which is usually a request for their PIN. If the PIN entered is correct, the device is "unlocked" and is ready for use.

All data that is to be encrypted or decrypted is sent through the device, because it is the device that contains the person's private key. This is invisible to the user. As long as the device remains in place, it is kept open for use. If and when the device is removed, the user is automatically logged out and the device is locked. In order for it to be used again, the user has to go through the initial steps again.

Pros

The cool factor is very high and people like to use them. They are easy to understand how to use and don't require a lot of training. The devices cannot be copied or cloned and, if one is lost, it's an easy matter to revoke the Digital Certificate. Therefore, even in the hands of an unauthorized person, they won't work when revoked.

These devices contain two of the authentication requirements: something you have and something you know. When a biometric is included, that also gives you the "something you are" requirement.

This is about as close to a "single sign on" system as you can get which means the user doesn't have to remember a lot of different passwords. In addition, the automatic log-off feature makes these systems very secure.

Because the Digital Certificate and the private key are contained on the device, the user can encrypt, decrypt, and digitally sign documents from any PC he happens to be working from.

Cons

These devices can only be used with compatible operating systems and sometimes need special software. If special software is required, it has to be installed on every machine. If you are dealing with a Business To Business extranet, sometimes the business partners object to having extra software required for their systems to work with yours.

Not all computers have USB ports and you need to have special readers for Smartcards. You also have the cost of the Smartcards or USB Smartkeys themselves. When you look at the costs of the special readers, the devices themselves, and special software to make them work, it can get really expensive — especially for large enterprises. The logistics of supporting remote users can get expensive, too.

Some users get lazy and leave their devices plugged in all the time. This completely circumvents any and all security because anyone could sit down at that computer and appear to be someone he's not.

The entire network and all applications have to be PKI enabled. So, in addition to the initial costs of the devices and readers, you may have to invest in a PKI system, too.

Although these devices have been around for quite a while, there is still a problem with interoperability amongst different vendors. That means that the system you put into place may not work with your customer's system. You also can't mix and match systems and devices. You have to use the same vendor for all systems.

Biometrics

Biometrics are the storing and reading of the physical characteristics of an individual. These include unique characteristics such as fingerprints, eye scan, voice print, or hand shape. The process begins be having the individual report to the department and place where the initial scans are being made. Special hardware and software read the biometrics and store them on a server in a digital format. Special algorithms are used to change the physical characteristics that have been stored into numbers, so a fingerprint doesn't actually look like a fingerprint. The same goes for the other scanned characteristics — a hand scan doesn't look like a hand, and an eye scan won't tell you what color your eyes are.

After the initial scan has been tested and verified, it is stored in an authorization database. When the user wants to log on to a PC, he must use his finger, eye, voice, or hand to transmit the biometric information to the database. This is done with special readers or scanners attached to the PC. For a fingerprint, for example, the user would simply press his finger on a special pad and wait for the system to verify him. In some systems this is combined with a password for stronger authentication.

Pros

There is no special training needed and the users don't need anything special to log in — all they need is themselves. You don't have to worry about the user "losing" his biometric and you don't have to worry about the logistics of replacements. (At least not until clones become a reality!)

Cons

Some biometrics can be duplicated (at least in theory). There is also a wide variance in the reliability and security of different systems. You really have to do your homework to find out which vendor has the most reliable system — some of the vendors will give you suspect data. What you are looking for is the amount of false positives and false negatives a system has.

You need to invest in specially scanning equipment and software to handle the authentication, which can get expensive in a large enterprise. A biometric system itself is not capable of including Digital Certificates. For that you would need a Smartcard or Smartkey system in addition to a biometric system.

For cultural, religious, and societal reasons, you may find resistance among the staff to having their personal data recorded and stored. Some people have a strong bias against these systems and you can't force them to use it.

Chapter 11

Secure E-Commerce

· ·

· ·

When I was little, I used to spend most of December sitting on the living room floor with the Sears or JC Penney catalogs, dreaming of Christmas presents to come. Page upon page was carefully dog-eared and items of particular interest were heavily circled. I'd pray every night that my parents noticed the marked pages. Instead of praying for items now, I can jump to the Web site for whatever I want, bookmark pages of things I like, put together "wish lists" on shopping sites, and generally abuse my credit card to the max.

E-commerce has quickly become extremely commonplace for those who use computers regularly. For people who live far from city centers or large shopping areas, it's a dream come true. They can have items delivered directly to their doors and save themselves day-long trips to major shopping centers. You don't have to limit yourself to shopping, either. You can buy and trade stocks, pay your bills, and generally do all the things that you used to have to get in your car to do. In 2002, e-commerce Web sites generated $14.3 *billion* dollars in revenue.

We're only now beginning to recognize the downside of all this convenience. Some Web sites were not secured, or were not as secure as they could have been, and personal data has been leaking through the seams. We weren't afraid of personal data being publicly available until the con men realized the potential for stealing peoples' identities. As is usually the case, the protectors are one step behind the perpetrators and e-commerce companies have begun to build in more security to their sites.

The news is not all bad, though. Cryptography again saves the day by giving us SSL, Digital Certificates, and other forms of encryption. In this chapter, I go through the most important aspects to setting up a secure e-commerce site.

SSL Is the Standard

Believe it or not but *Secure Sockets Layer* is almost ten years old! Given the fact that most people have only discovered the Internet within the past five years, that says a lot. SSL is also the single-most widely used form of encryption in the world and hardly anyone realizes that it even exists. SSL is a stable and mature technology but that does not necessarily mean that it is the answer to all your e-commerce security problems.

In normal, non-secure Web connections, the Web server acts as sort of a vending machine because it can only handle one request at a time. After it gives you what you asked for, it stops. If you put a dollar in a vending machine for a 35 cent item, the vending machine won't wait to see if you're going to order something else to use up the money left over. Nope, it returns your change and acts as if it has never dealt with you before. The same is true with basic Web transactions. After you pull up a page, the Web server severs the connection and it truly doesn't know you anymore. (That is, unless the Web server used "cookies" to keep track of you. But, that's another subject altogether.)

When you communicate with a Web server you are relatively anonymous to it. A cookie stored on your computer will allow the Web server to track you, but the cookie doesn't usually have any of your personal identification. To the Web server you are just a number, a date and time, and other miscellaneous information.

Because there is no personal information transferred between your computer and the Web server, you would think it would be difficult for someone to obtain that information. But, as I mentioned before, there are always bad guys out there who spend a lot of time trying to trick you. The Web is no different. There are scams and illegal activities on the Web that will either trick you into disclosing your personal information. The scams can be in the form of a Web site that is impersonating another Web site (referred to as *phishing*). There are sites that look like eBay, Amazon, or Paypal, but they're not. At first glance these sites appear to be genuine because they look exactly like the real ones. Often the scammers are using these sites to trick you in to giving them your UserID and password. This has become such a big problem that many of the big e-commerce companies have had to create entire offices just to deal with cases of fraud.

There are other frauds that will hijack the connections between your machine and the Web server (which is a form of a *man in the middle attack* or MITM). These are very hard to spot because you, as the Web surfer, won't notice anything wrong. The person hijacking the connection is hoping to be able to snag some of your personal information flowing across the link. Hijacking is possible because regular Web connections are not encrypted.

SSL was created to try to fix, or mitigate the problems of interception and impersonation. It accomplishes this through the exchange of keys and encryption of the connection. The first implementations of SSL were limited to 40-bit encryption but now most Web browsers are capable of handling 128-bit encryption.

Sometimes an SSL certificate will issue error notices when you access a secure Web page. This happens when the site's Web masters have made a mistake in the way they coded the HTML on that page or it means that page includes links to offsite images or text that are served over HTTP instead of HTTPS. This frequently causes much confusion with users. It doesn't necessarily mean that the security has been breached; it just means that there is an error on the page somewhere.

A typical SSL connection

Before you can start an encrypted session with a Web server, there are a series of transactions and agreements that happen between your machine and the Web server, as shown in Figure 11-1. Most of the time this happens so quickly you don't even realize that something different is going on. Here is an introduction on the exchanges between your machine and the Web server:

- ✔ Your machine initiates the conversation by requesting a secure connection from a site that offers this service.

- ✔ The Web server answers your request by sending its Digital Certificate (and associated public key) to your machine.

- ✔ When your machine receives this information, your browser has a look at its internal information that it holds about certificates and the issuers *(Certificate Authorities)* of Digital Certificates. Your browser compares the Digital Certificate it has received from the to this internal list and then decides whether or not that certificate is trustworthy.

- ✔ If the browser decides the Digital Certificate is okay, then it computes a one-time key *(a session key)* and sends it back to the Web server. This session key is encrypted with the Web server's public key.

- ✔ After the Web server gets the encryption key, the encryption of the communications between the two machines begins. You will note that the next page that appears on your browser starts with *https://* instead of the normal http://. Depending on the type of browser you have, the status bar will also display a small key or a small lock to indicate that the link is secure.

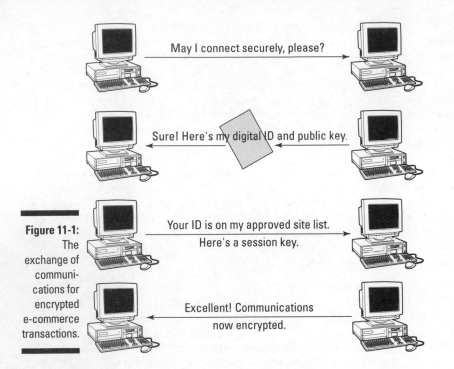

May I connect securely, please?

Sure! Here's my digital ID and public key.

Figure 11-1: The exchange of communications for encrypted e-commerce transactions.

Your ID is on my approved site list. Here's a session key.

Excellent! Communications now encrypted.

If there is a problem with the certificate from the server, your machine receives an alert such as the one shown in Figure 11-2.

Figure 11-2: An invalid SSL certificate alert.

This does not necessarily mean that the Web site is not to be trusted, it's just that the certificate it sent is not on the list of trusted sites in your Web browser. This could be because the certificate was not issued and digitally signed by a mainstream provider of Digital Certificates — like Verisign and GTE CyberTrust, for example. It could also mean that the certificate is a fake and should not be trusted. It's be up to you to do a little investigative work to see if you want to trust the veracity of the Web site and its associated Digital Certificates.

Rooting around your certificates

If you open your browser and go to the settings for Internet options, you'll be able to find the area where the Digital Certificates are stored. In MS Internet Explorer, choose Tools➪Internet Options and then Content tab. Midway down the window you'll see a button that says Certificates. In other browsers, such as Netscape and Mozilla (which are essentially the same), the area where certificate information is stored is under the Preferences command and they are usually under the Privacy and Security section.

When you get to the Certificates dialog box, you'll find a list of *Trusted Root Certificate Authorities*. These are the companies that have issued Digital Certificates to e-commerce companies.

Not all companies that issue certificates will be listed in your browser's Certificates section. The reason there are some companies listed and not others is that there are business relationships between the browser vendors and certain Certificate Authorities. Just because a Certificate Authority is included in the browser's default list does not necessarily mean that their certificates should be trusted more than others. What it does mean is that if you have a problem with a certificate issued and signed by one of these Certificate Authorities, you will probably get more cooperation from them in resolving any problems. Why? Because their reputation and working relationship with the browser vendor could suffer if users are constantly having problems.

When you find the listing of Digital Certificates, you should go to the Certificate Authorities or Root Certificate area and examine the individual certificates. (It's a different procedure for the different types of browsers.) When you open a certificate's description, it will tell you what the certificate is used for. You'll note that some of them will state that they are good for secure e-mail. That's because browsers have e-mail programs built in. What you'll be looking for are the Root Certificates that are used for Server Authentication. That means they are used to validate that SSL Digital Certificates. You also want to check the expiration date of the Root Certificates. If the Root Certificate has expired, you definitely should not trust any certificates coming from that company.

An example of the Certificates included with MS Explorer is shown in Figure 11-3. Note there is an area at the bottom that says Certificate Intended Purposes. This area tells you if the certificate can be used for secure e-mail, client authentication, server authentication, and so on. Some certificates are very limited in what they can be used for and others have a broad range of uses.

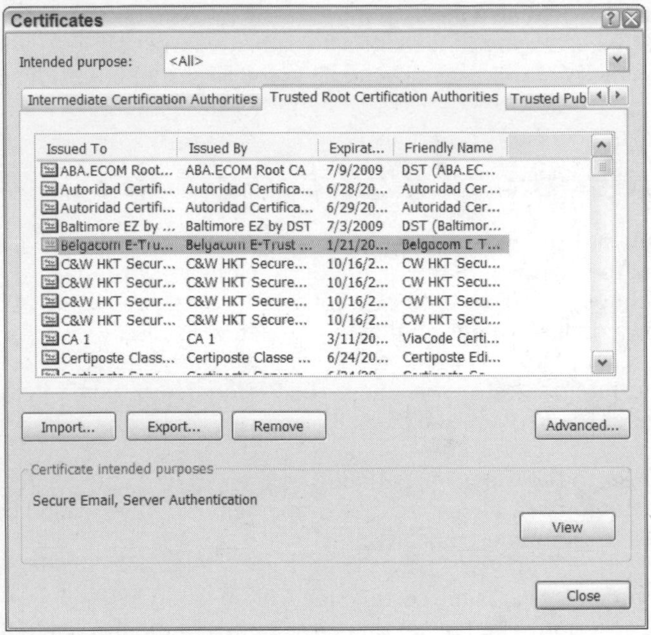

Figure 11-3:
Root
Certificate
uses and its
expiration
date.

The reputation of the companies that issue certificates is all important. It's like trusting a bank. You want to make sure that they've been around for a long time, that they have good business practices, that they are likely to be around for a while, and that they are trustworthy. If you had a choice of two banks, where one was a big established name-brand and the other was located in a storage garage on the outskirts of town and handled its transactions out of a cardboard box, which would you be more likely to give your money to? (Hopefully that's not really a difficult question!)

Likewise when dealing with e-commerce sites. Consider the two examples below:

1. You're going to buy a diamond ring online. You go to the Web site of a famous jeweler in New York City. Their Digital Certificates are good (they were issued by a reputable company and they are they have not been revoked or expired) and are signed by the Root Certificate of a well-known, well-respected Certificate Authority. You find the diamond ring you want, you enter your credit card number on the Web site, and you get your authorization and receipt. If the ring doesn't arrive the next day as promised, how much faith do you have that you will get either your ring or your money back?

2. You're going to buy a diamond ring online. You do an Internet search on "diamond rings" and pick a site at random from the search results. You check up on that company and find an address that places them in Outer Mongolia. You're not sure if there is a real bricks-and-mortar office in Mongolia or if the address is just a mail drop. Their Digital Certificate has not been expired or revoked, but it's been issued by a company called "Hal's Discount Certificates" and there is no Root Certificate in your browser for that company. You check up on Hal's Discount Certificates and discover that the mailing address is in Las Vegas. You order your ring anyway and enter your credit card number on the Web site. When your ring does not arrive the next day as promised, how confident are you that you will get your promised ring or your money back?

Seems like an easy decision to make, right? Well, most of the problems you will run into will be a lot harder to resolve than the examples I have given. There will be a thousand shades of gray in the validity of the Digital Certificates or the Certificate Authorities' Root Certificates. It will be entirely up to you to either place your trust in those sites and certificates or not.

When you are setting up your own SSL e-commerce system, you will need to make these important decisions, too. Is it better to go with the quick and cheap certificates from an unknown Certificate Authority or is it better to bite the bullet, pay the big bucks, and go with the big-name Certificate Authorities? It's an important decision, so make sure you have all the information.

Time for TLS

SSL is a good protocol for protecting and encrypting Web transactions, but it has had it's problems. SSL v3 made a lot of changes in the way authentication is handled and that's the version currently embedded in most Web browsers. But, there's always an opportunity to make things better and *TLS* v1 (Transport Layer Security) was created to do just that. The user won't notice any difference as to whether his browser is using SSL, TLS, or a combination of the both.

The TLS/SSL protocols help prevent communications eavesdropping, tampering, and forgery. Web servers and browsers use the TLS handshake to authenticate each other and to negotiate an encryption algorithm and cryptographic keys before transmitting data. The TLS handshake uses public key cryptography, such as RSA or DSS, to authenticate computers and to negotiate a shared secret. Of course, Digital Certificates are also used.

TLS uses symmetric cryptography, such as DES or RC4, to encrypt the data, such as credit card numbers, prior to transmission over the network. Any message transmissions include a message authentication code (MAC) created with a hash function such as SHA or MD5 to prevent any communications tampering and forgery.

What does TLS do that SSL doesn't? First of all it is comprised of two different parts:

- **TLS Record Protocol:** Ensures that the connection between your machine and the Web server is private by using symmetric data; ensures that the connection is reliable.

- **TLS Handshake Protocol:** An agreement on an encryption algorithm to use before any communications are allowed to continue.

Actually, TLS is a little more complicated than that. It's fairly elegant, too, because it does a lot of conversing and agreeing between your machine and the e-commerce Web server. Another reason TLS is a good solution is that it is an open standard. It's governed by the *IETF* (Internet Engineering Task Force) which is a non-governmental organization that has taken it upon itself to try to create some order out of the Internet chaos. The documents that describe TLS are *RFC 2246* and *RFC 3346* (Request For Comments).

Setting Up an SSL Solution

There are three basic methods of setting up a secure e-commerce Web site using SSL:

1. You can buy a complete SSL solution, including the SSL certificates, from an established vendor. The vendors deliver fully configured servers and all you have to do is build code into your Web site and put it on the box. Most vendors will also offer Web-building solutions as well.

2. You can go to a Web hosting service and basically buy "space" on one of their Web servers that are already set up to run SSL transactions. This is referred to as *Co-Lo's* (pronounced "KOE-loe") which means co-location hosting service. These companies usually have an enormous number of servers situated in what is referred to as a "server farm" (a large, air conditioned computer room) and the service has very fast connection to the Internet. Co-Lo's can also handle your domain name registration and arrange for your SSL Digital Certificates. You usually pay a monthly fee for this type of service.

3. You can build your own solution. You can go from as simple as you please to large and complex. There are open source Web servers and SSL applications, which means they are free. You still need to get your

SSL Digital Certificates and they are a lot more expensive than you would expect. On the other hand, you get what you pay for, too.

What equipment do I need?

You can set up an e-commerce site using SSL for very little investment in equipment. First of all, I'm going to make the foolish assumption that you already have a network that has a fast connection to the Internet. I'm also going to assume that you have a static IP address and registered domain name. If you don't have a domain name and your own IP address, then you'll either have to get them, or you'll have to go with a Co-Lo service. (I address some of the Co-Lo issues in the E-Commerce Managers Checklist.)

Here's a list of what you'll need and what you'll need them for:

- A **server** to use as your Web server/e-commerce site. If you don't expect a lot of traffic, you can even use a desktop machine. On the other hand, it's best to plan ahead and, if you expect your traffic to grow quickly, you're better off getting a server that has enough RAM and disk space to handle a heavy load. (Many SSL applications are open source freeware. Don't pay if the free goods will work for you.)

- A **redundant server** to mirror your Web site. This is to be used in emergencies. If your Web site is hacked, suffers disk failures, or other catastrophes. Believe me, a little money spent on an extra machine will save you thousands in labor and headaches if the worst should happen. Your redundant machine should be configured so you can make an easy switch from one to the other and it does not have to be a top-of-the-line server, either. It just needs to be powerful enough to handle the load until the main server can come back in service.

- A **firewall** to protect your internal network. Your Web server should be have a hardened operating system with all the necessary security patches so that it will be resistant to attack. But, you don't want to put the Web server *behind* the firewall because the firewall would slow down traffic too much. You place the Web server in front of the firewall so that traffic going from your Web server to your internal site is protected from malicious tricks and treats. You can build a firewall using freeware tools or you can purchase a commercial firewall. Whichever the case, the computer you use should be used as the firewall and nothing else.

- A **key server/certificate server** to issue keys and Digital Certificates that SSL needs to operate. This server is on the inside of the network; behind the firewall. While most web servers are capable of handling these transactions themselves, a separate server is a good idea if you expect heavy traffic on your Web server. Having a separate key server gives you an added layer of security because it makes it harder for someone to hack your system and find your keys.

- ✔ A **database server** to hold all the data for the Web server: product pictures, product descriptions, inventory, pricing and orders, customer personal and payment information, and so on. Essentially this is the server that will handle all the back-office type operations that a person would handle if this were a real store. This information should *never* be on the same server as the Web server and, because your business is highly dependent upon this data, the database should be behind the firewall and heavily protected with access controls and other security measures.

- ✔ A **back-up device/server** to store data from the database. This machine may be needed to restore the database, so it must be kept up to date.

- ✔ **Cryptographic accelerator cards**. This is an optional item and is only necessary when you start receiving more than 300-500 page requests per second on your Web server. Because SSL (and TLS for that matter) have cryptographic functions, that means that a lot of the computer's processing power is used to generate cryptographic keys. This processing can significantly slow down the response your customer gets when trying to obtain a secure connection. By installing a crypto accelerator on your Web server, that device takes that load off the server's CPU and the Web site works faster.

The computers I've listed and the jobs they do are really just the minimum for an adequate e-commerce site. If you plan on having a really large and complex site with thousands of combinations of choices, then you would require much more than this. Not only that, but you'll need very talented staff to run it all for you, too. If you don't expect much traffic or if you don't have an IT department, you may want to consider outsourcing your e-commerce site to a Co-Lo.

If you buy a total e-commerce solution (what I call "e-commerce in a box"), you will not need all the hardware that I have just mentioned. There are a number of other decisions you will have to make if you decide to outsource your e-commerce site and I cover those next.

The e-commerce manager's checklist

So you've decided that e-commerce is something your business cannot do without. Maybe you've decided to do it to keep up with your competition and maybe you even have a new approach to e-commerce that will blow your competition away. Whatever the case, you can't handle this undertaking blindfolded — there are hundreds of questions and considerations that need to be addressed. I won't be going into minute detail of all these questions and considerations because that would be better handled in a different book. What I will do, however, is give you the top level decisions that you have to make just to get you on the road to developing your e-commerce site. Table 11-1 is in a checklist format for you so you can copy this page and have it with you as you walk through the steps. For each decision I'll give you the related considerations and consequences.

Table 11-1	The E-Commerce Manager's Checklist	
Question	*Answer*	*The Reason*
What do I need to make SSL run on my site?	Three things: 1. SSL Digital Certificates 2. Qualified Domain Name 3. Static IP Address	An SSL Digital Certificate can only be sold to a "real" business. You have to purchase these certificates from established vendors such as Verisign and GTE CyberTrust. An SSL certificate will not work if it is used on a computer with a shared IP address and none of the vendors will sell you certificate if you don't own the domain name (such as 'widgets.com').
Are there different types of SSL Digital Certificates?	Yes. There are "private" SSL Digital Certificates and "shared" SSL Digital Certificates.	"Private" SSL Digital Certificates are only sold to companies that can prove they are real and can only be used on sites that have a fully qualified domain name and a static IP address. "Shared" SSL Digital Certificates are used when you outsource your e-commerce business to a hosting service or Co-Lo.
How much do SSL digital certificates cost?	The costs for SSL certificates vary greatly. A Verisign certificate for two years will set you back $1595 but a lesser known brand such as Comodo will only cost $199 for three years. Some Certificate Authorities will only charge an annual renewal fee after the initial cost while others are on a strict annual fee. (These fees are for your own, private certificate.)	A lot depends on the reputation of the Certificate Authority and the extra services they provide. There is a very good service and price comparison chart at WhichSSL.. The Web page is `www.whichssl.org/content/table/`

(continued)

Table 11-1 *(continued)*

Question	Answer	The Reason
	If you are outsourcing your e-commerce business to a Co-Lo hosting service, you will probably be "sharing" one of their SSL certificates. This cost is usually disclosed up front and they are much cheaper than having a private SSL certificate.	The WhichSSL site also has information on the reputation of the Certificate Authorities and some of the bait and switch games that are played by some Co-Lo hosting services.
Where do I buy SSL digital certificates?	If you are buying a private SSL certificate, you go straight to the vendor's Web site and place your order online. However, if you are buying more than five certificates, it's best to contact the vendor directly and negotiate a special price.	Prices for private SSL certificates are listed on the vendor's Web site. You can always call the company and try to negotiate your own price, especially if you will be buying a large number of certificates.
	If you are using a Co-Lo hosting service, the fee is payable directly to the Co-Lo.	If you are outsourcing your e-commerce site, your Co-Lo has already negotiated with a vendor for their certificates and the Do-Lo will pass some of that cost on to you.
What documentation do I need to buy SSL certificates?	1. Corporate documents such as a business license or articles of incorporation. 2. Proof of ownership of your domain name. (A 'whois' listing is usually sufficient if it is listed under your company's name.)	An SSL Digital Certificate is a document that testifies that you are who you are. No company in their right mind will sell you a certificate without asking you for proof of identity.
		In this way, the Certificate Authorities are protecting themselves and you against fly-by-night companies who set up shop, take your money, and disappear.

Question	Answer	The Reason
Do I need any special HTML coding in my Web pages to make the SSL certificates work?	Yes, but it's not very difficult to code the link to start an SSL session. A typical hypertext link to begin an SSL session will look something like this: <AHREF="https://www.yourdomain.com/orderpage.htm"> Go SSL Name </a>. Note that the page begins with "https" and not plain old "http."	You can buy special e-commerce programs that are called "shopping carts" for obvious reasons. If you go that route you need to make sure that the vendor is reputable and that the coding won't end up sending credit card numbers to someone in China.
	The coding to begin and end an SSL session is not difficult, but you will also need the coding necessary to handle the ordering and that is much more difficult and requires very experienced staff. The code needs to be written in a way that guarantees security and privacy.	If you are going to handle this yourself, you need someone who is experienced in writing *CGI (Common Gateway Interface)* programs and commands. These programs are especially important because without them your Web server won't be able to talk to the database.
	On the other hand, there are some very good "shopping cart" type programs that have the SSL coding included. If you are working with Paypal or similar, they can provide you with the SSL coding you need, too.	

XML Is the New Kid on the Block

XML stands for *eXtensible Markup Language* and I predict it will soon be as familiar to builders of Web sites as HTML (HyperText Markup Language) is today. XML's reason for being is to add another layer of security to Web page and to make it easier for systems to exchange data . It does this by creating new tags to be used in Web pages and these tags not only define what should be encrypted on a page, but it can also handle different levels of encryption within the same page or document. Along with XML is something called *SSML,* which is Security Sheet Markup Language. Basically SSML is a list of security policies and rules for the XML tags to follow.

By using the tags <secure> and <\secure>, XML tells the browser to encrypt anything that is placed between those tags. The encrypted element is not limited to text, either. You can place a picture, text, or a sound file on a Web page, surround it with the <secure> tags, and it will automatically and instantly be encrypted. The key for encryption is sent separately from the Web page, so the ciphertext and the key never appear together in the same document. The encryption algorithm is decided by a rule you create and it starts working as soon as the page is fully loaded.

SSML is used to set security policies and implementation rules and it works in concert with XML in much the same way that *CSS* (Cascading Style Sheets) works with HTML. The beauty of SSML is that you can have many different levels of encryption within the same page or document. For example, let's say that the Web page is a form that customers fill in with their names, addresses, and other contact information as well as their credit card information. You could choose to encrypt the names and addresses with one algorithm and the credit card information with another algorithm. The security is doubled in that instance because even if one key were discovered or cracked, only one portion of the total information will be disclosed. The attacker would still have no idea which algorithm or key was used to encrypt the rest of the page. If the attacker cracked the credit card number, he would have no idea what the name and address associated with that card was.

XML is a defined standard (RFC 3275), but it's not in general use yet. Some older versions of browsers can't understand XML yet because that ability hasn't been coded into them. The death knell tolls at the fact that HTML and XML don't play well together. In fact, they don't play together at all! If you want, you can create two different versions of the same page with one of those pages using XML. You can code the pages so that they query the browser to see if it can handle XML and, if the browser can't handle XML, your server can automatically send the non-XML page instead.

XML will greatly enhance the security and encryption capabilities of common Web pages and, in particular, pages built to handle e-commerce. Anything that makes the ordering process better gets my vote!

Going for Outsourced E-Commerce

Sometimes you'll find that it's easier and more economical to have the experts do something for you rather than to try to do it yourself. When you decide to outsource e-commerce to a co-location Web hosting service, the agreement is the most important item to get straight. The agreement should answer all of your questions and tell you what guarantees are made by the Co-Lo. Money is almost a secondary consideration because you want things done well first of all.

To help you with your decision, here are the main questions you should be asking. If you don't receive answers that make you comfortable, please try another Co-Lo. It's a very competitive business and especially in metropolitan areas, there are numerous companies offering the same service. Your reputation as a business is at stake here, so make sure you choose a company that will be a good business partner and not just someone who will take your money without regard for good service.

As you read these questions, you'll probably think of others you should be asking. This is not meant to be a comprehensive list of questions; just the top level questions to get you started.

1. Is commercial use allowed with their service? (If they don't allow e-commerce, why bother with them?)

2. Will they handle the procurement of a domain name and SSL certificates for you?

3. Do they have shopping cart software that you can use to help you build your site?

4. Will you have your own servers or will you be sharing a server with other companies? (This is called "virtual hosting" when you share a server with others.)

5. What security mechanisms do they have in place to protect your site? (Firewalls, intrusion detection systems, anti-virus programs, checksums of your files and applications?)

6. Do they have staff on duty 24/7?

7. What guarantees do they make about security and availability?

8. If your site is hacked, who is responsible for what?

9. What is their minimum contract?

10. Do they have references you can check?

11. How much disk space do you get?

12. Are there extra charges for data transfer from your company's network to your servers? (You may want to build your Web site at your company and then transfer all the files at once to your servers at the Co-Lo.)

13. If your site grows, how much does it cost to add extra servers?

14. Do they handle all the software patches or is that your responsibility?

15. What kind of access reports do you get and how often will you get them?

16. Will you have to pay excess bandwidth charges? (If you suddenly have an increase in traffic to your site and they need to upgrade the speed of your connection, is there a charge?)

17. How often do they make full backups of your site?

18. Can you see their security policies and procedures manuals?

19. Will they arrange for a credit card merchant account for you?

20. What is their average uptime on servers? (In other words, do their servers go down very often?)

Some other things you may want to consider are whether or not you provide the equipment for databases or not. Can the database be located at your company office for convenience? And, of course there are the "key" questions — how and where are their encryption keys stored and how do they handle recovery of the keys if they are lost?

Whichever service or company you decide to give your business to, you should think about the future — will they be able to give you more servers and additional bandwidth as your e-commerce site grows? You don't want to get boxed into a corner where you won't be able to serve your customers because your Co-Lo lacks the space and/or the equipment.

When you make your decision, be sure to have your legal counsel go over the agreements and contracts. The type and strength of encryption should be spelled out in detail and you should have the option of changing encryption schemes if the one you are using is found to have serious security problems with it.

Now, with all of this ammunition, you should be able to find a service to help you or go it alone. Have fun with it and be creative but remember the first order of business is to handle all transactions securely. That will help build a good reputation which will surely result in increased sales and good potential for growth. Have fun!

Chapter 12

Virtual Private Network (VPN) Encryption

Sometimes I feel it would be nice to go back to the good ol' days before personal computers could be networked together. Back then, the only threat to your machine was of a physical nature — it could be stolen. My only security measures back then were to cable-lock my machine to the wall, set a BIOS password, and to remove the keyboard and lock it away when I wasn't using the machine. Easy-peasy!

Of course non-networked PCs weren't at all friendly when it came to sharing information and files with other PCs. Remember sneaker nets? That's when everyone kept a large stack of floppies on their desks with which to copy files onto. When you needed to share a file with a co-worker, then you copied your files onto a floppy, put your sneakers on, and walked with the floppies over to your co-worker's desk. Of course that was a good way to exchanged virus-infected files, too.

With computers being connected online all the time — even home computers — the probability that a connection could be hijacked, spoofed, or have all the data captured to a file has become almost inevitable. If it hasn't happened to you, that just means it hasn't happened to you *yet*.

One method of hiding connections is to utilize a *Virtual Private Network* (VPN). Even five years ago VPNs were practically unheard of and now they are as commonplace as mouse pads and flat screens. No longer do you need to have a degree in computer science to be able to figure out how to set up a VPN; the setups and configurations are quite user friendly now. The problems of competing standards and interoperability sometimes rear their ugly heads but, for the most part, VPNs are a relatively easy solution to hiding your data and your connections.

How Do VPNs Work Their Magic?

First of all, a VPN chops the data into chunks called *packets* and then encrypts the packets so that no one other than the intended recipients can read them. Each packet contains *headers* that contain information about the size and type of data, and information to check the authentication and integrity of the data. This is a security measure that ensures that the data has not been changed enroute.

After the data has been packetized and encrypted, the VPN sets up a dedicated channel within which to send the data. This is called *IP tunneling* and is one of the beauties of a VPN. Even though the data is being sent across a public network such as the Internet, the channel cannot be "seen" by unauthorized persons listening in on the line. (Hackers use programs called "sniffers" to intercept network traffic and VPNs can hide a network from these sniffers.)

All of this is accomplished with special software, protocols, and commands that are issued by the VPN equipment. Many (if not most) modern day routers are capable of creating a VPN. In the early days of VPNs, firewalls created a problem because they were unable to "see" VPN traffic and they didn't know if VPN traffic was good or bad traffic. Today's firewalls are not only able to distinguish between encrypted VPN traffic and regular traffic, some firewalls are capable of establishing VPN connections themselves. You need to check with the various vendors to find out which products will suit your needs.

Setting Up a VPN

Generally, you'd use a VPN for three different types of security:

- ✔ **Keeping secrets within a company** — For this you would use an *intranet*, which is a common network infrastructure, across various physical locations; for example, several offices within one building or several buildings may be connected to a data center. With this type of VPN you can segregate departmental networks without having to install new cabling or a new infrastructure. This is effective when you are assigning access to sensitive information based on the "need to know" principle. For example, you can keep the research and development network separate from the general populace of the company. The VPN is transparent to the users and usually does not require special software on the desktop computers for the users to be able to access the VPN.

✓ **Sharing data with suppliers and clients** — For this you would set up an extranet. In this case VPN uses the Internet as the main carrier for data and is generally used when a company has a large number of users and widely dispersed locations. This type of VPN enables customers, suppliers and branch offices to access corporate resources across various network architectures. The mass of users on the Internet are not able to detect the VPN, nor are they able to inadvertently log on, due to the authentication requirements of the VPN. To be doubly secure, a company could also implement IPsec to ensure maximum compatibility and security.

✓ **Creating secret tunnels** — This is for remote users so they can securely log onto your corporate network from their hotel rooms, conference halls, or client locations. The laptops used need to have special VPN client software which is used to initiate the VPN connection and authenticate the user. Again, the traffic is flowing across the Internet to the corporate network, but general users of the Internet cannot see the traffic.

What devices do I need?

When VPNs first hit the market, there were innumerable options; not all of them compatible with one another. Today you basically have three different flavors to choose from: stand-alone VPN appliances, integrated VPN appliances such as VPN-enabled firewalls and routers, or VPN servers.

Virtually all routers sold nowadays support VPNs. Getting the VPN services to work usually means making a few configuration changes in the firewall or router itself.

Stand-alone VPN appliances are generally used when simultaneous VPN connections number in the thousands. If your company serves thousands of customers in various locations around the world, this is something you should consider as it allows you to not only set up an Extranet, but you can control the bandwidth used by various locations as well.

Virtually all network operating systems, such as Microsoft, Novell, UNIX, AS400, and Linux, are all capable of providing VPN services (although the ease of use and the performance will vary greatly amongst systems.). If you have a mix of operating systems, you may have to install VPN client software on some desktop systems for them to be able to successfully log on to the VPN. This option is useful for small companies that have limited resources and a limited number of users or nodes that will need VPN connections.

There is one more solution that I have not listed as one of the major solutions and that is the *managed VPN*. This is a VPN service owned and operated by your telecommunication provider such as Qwest or ATT. They provide the hardware and software to set up the VPN and they monitor your company's connections to ensure availability. The question remains, however, as to how much trust you are willing to place in an outside vendor to manage the security of your sensitive transactions.

What else should I consider?

Because you are probably implementing a VPN to secure your communications, the encryption methods, Certificate Authority capabilities, and encrypted tunneling are some features you should be familiar with before you decide on which type of VPN you ultimately decide upon.

As your VPN vendor if the VPN encrypts all data or is it capable of *selective* encryption? Selective encryption allows you to encrypt only portions of the data or certain types of data, thus freeing up your CPUs for other tasks when needed.

VPNs are able to authenticate two different ways: by data type or by user. If you set up your VPN to only authenticate via data type, any user who is transmitting that type of data will be able (theoretically, anyway) to initiate a VPN connection. If you choose user authentication, you will be able to control which users are able to connect via VPN. The best way is to set your VPN to use both forms of authentication, thus giving you greater security control. However, you need to be sure that your VPN solution actually supports both types of authentication!

If you are planning on using smart cards or other security tokens for authentication, you'll definitely need VPN support for Certificate Authorities to exchange Digital Certificates. Generally, these types of VPN solutions will state that they are "PKI compliant," although you'll have to get the specifics from the vendor to find out what additional hardware and software you will need. Extranets are big users of PKI-compliant VPNs because they are able to create very explicit rules for remote access.

One more thing: It's a common misconception that all VPN tunnels are encrypted. They're not! Some VPN products don't even offer encryption as an option for their tunneling capabilities. Be sure to ask your vendor if their product supports *encrypted tunnel mode* (ETM) if that feature is important to you.

Do VPNs affect performance?

The process of encrypting anything does increase the load on network devices and can potentially decrease overall throughput. However, most VPN encryption is processed very quickly and most users will never notice an appreciable decrease in the speed of their connection. Most performance slowdowns are the result of inconsistent Internet connections rather than the encryption processing.

Where most people notice a decrease in performance is in the use of virtual terminals or applications that are run from a central server rather than the client machine. If a user is transferring humongous files, you'll also see a slowdown. On the other hand, you'd see network slowdowns in these cases whether you were running them over a VPN or not. If this is a problem for you, you can set your VPN with policies that set limits so one user isn't able to gobble up all the network resources.

Don't forget wireless!

Just a quick note for those of you who are struggling to figure out how to protect your wireless network communications — why not try a VPN? Remember that you can encrypt the data as well as the VPN tunnel, so it's an effective mechanism for keeping those snooping ears out of your wireless networks.

Various VPN Encryption Schemes

As you may have figured out by now, not all VPNs are created equal and this applies to their encryption techniques as well. In the Internet world of competing standards, VPNs are no exception — the vendors all tout their solutions as the best. However, some standards have become standard options. These are the VPN protocols that handle authentication, tunneling, and encryption.

PPP and PPTP

Point To Point Tunneling Protocol (PPTP) started life as the *Point To Point Protocol* (PPP). PPP was, and is still used in some places, to allow dial-up users to connect to the Internet. Many ISPs that sell dial up accounts are still using PPP for their connections. but it is not used for VPNs.

PPTP was developed by Microsoft and U.S. Robotics, using PPP as the basis from which to start. The authentication portion of PPTP used Microsoft's authentication protocol, *Challenge Handshake Authentication Protocol* (CHAP) which was a very bad product, indeed. Today's implementations of PPTP should be using CHAP v2 which has closed some of the gaping holes in the original version. (Be sure to check which version of CHAP your product uses!)

PPTP does not encrypt the traffic by default because its main job is to create a virtual tunnel in which to transport the data and to authenticate users. But, it can be configured to encrypt the tunnel as well using the RC4 algorithm. The default configuration for RC4 is 40 bits, which is horribly weak, but it can also be set to run with 128-bit encryption.

Because RC4 is a symmetric algorithm, both the user and the VPN appliance with share the same secret key. That key is thrown away as soon as the session is over. Most Cisco routers are able to handle PPTP but you'll need to check that your particular vendor and model number are compatible with PPTP.

PPTP VPNs are normally used in client-to-gateway or network-to-network connections or for legacy Windows clients. If you have a mix of operating systems, one of the other VPN protocols might work better for you.

L2TP

Layer 2 Tunneling Protocol (L2TP) is actually a combination of the *Layer 2 Forwarding (L2F)* protocol that was developed by Cisco and PPTP which was developed by Microsoft and US Robotics. In the early days of VPNs, it looked as if these two protocols (L2F and PPTP), which were not at all compatible, would duke it out for prevalence in the market. But, the IETF (*Internet Engineering Task Force*) asked that MS and Cisco play nicely and see if they could work together on a product that gave us the best of both their worlds. Thus, L2TP was born.

L2TP is able to authenticate users, create a virtual tunnel, and both encrypt and compress the data traveling within that tunnel. Please note, however, that the tunnel itself is not encrypted; only the data is encrypted. I say that with one caveat: this is only true if you are using a non-Microsoft L2TP set up. If you are using Microsoft products for your L2TP, you must also include IPsec in your configuration because MS's L2TP product does not support encryption.

One of the beauties of L2TP is that it can be used in networks where more than one network operating system is in use. Yes, this means it will operate over IPX, NetBEUI, and IP networks.

IPsec

I'm sure you're familiar with TCP/IP and are aware of the fact that this suite of protocols was developed without a mind towards security. TCP/IP was developed with "openness" in mind. None of the people who worked on its development could conceive of all the different ways it would be used to circumvent security. With security in mind, IPsec was developed. IPsec is an upgrade or enhancement to TCP/IP that provides security features, including encryption capabilities. It's a very good system to use in conjunction with VPNs.

The end-user wouldn't notice the difference between TCP/IP and IPsec, but there are a lot of differences to network administrators. The set up and configuration is not exactly straightforward and the installer needs to have a good understanding of both IPsec and *IKE (Internet Key Exchange)*.

If the installer does not have a good understanding of IPsec, he won't understand what the various configuration options mean. In addition, some of the IPsec terminology has not been standardized and it's easy to misunderstand what a certain configuration mode means.

The Internet Key Exchange (IKE) protocol is an encryption key management protocol which is used in conjunction with the IPsec. IPsec can be configured without IKE, but IKE enhances IPsec by providing additional security features.

IPsec requires the use of either keys or Digital Certificates to be able to work its magic. If you plan to use digital certificates, you'll have to set up a PKI system to handle the creation and dissemination of the digital certificates. On the other hand, if you plan to use keys, these will be symmetric keys and you have to come up with a plan to safely exchange the keys. When an IPsec connection is initiated, the computers exchange information about themselves first. After that information has been passed (and it happens very quickly), the person on the computer originating the connection has to type in the encryption key information. Once this information has been correctly transferred, the data traveling between the systems will be encrypted.

There are also two modes IPsec may use: *tunnel* and *transport*. Transport mode would typically be used where communications terminate at IPsec servers, e.g. an IPsec server talking to another IPsec server. Tunnel mode is more often used when you have desktop computers running IPsec communicating with IPsec servers. Tunnel mode encrypts the header and the payload of each packet while transport mode only encrypts the payload. Only systems that are IPsec-compliant can take advantage of this protocol. For all these systems to be able to communicate with one another, all computers must use a common encryption key or Digital Certificate. Additionally, computers must also have very similar security policies set up.

Combining IPsec with the normal VPN tunneling protocols provides the best solution for most companies because you get a secure, encrypted tunnel as well as encrypted data transport.

Which Is Best?

I wish I could give you an absolute answer on that, but asking "Which is best?" is like asking "How long is a piece of string?" The answer for both these questions is that it depends.

There are so many variables in networks, operating systems, and applications, it's almost impossible to give you an answer without knowing all the details of each and every network configuration possible. Your VPN solution depends on many things. For example, take these factors into consideration:

✔ Is your network comprised of a single operating system or is it a mix of several different operating systems and different versions?

✔ How many remote connections do you want to be able to support simultaneously?

✔ Will your staff, customers, or suppliers be willing to install special software on their systems that will let them connect via your VPN?

✔ Do you intend to require strong authentication of your users with the use of security tokens or smart cards?

✔ Do you expect your network and the number of users to grow substantially within the next year? The next two years? The next five years?

✔ How much money do you have to spend?

✔ Do you have experienced staff to work as customer support for VPN users? In the beginning there will always be a lot of questions and minor glitches to contend with.

Of course I could go on and on with the questions until I've bored you to tears, but you get the general idea. I can't tell you which is best because I don't know your answers to these questions — and there are more questions than this to answer in reality.

Your best bet is to have your IT department draw up a list of your company's requirements and then start talking to VPN vendors. Remember that some of the vendors have been around for a long, long time (in Internet years) because they do have good products and good customer service. Training is always a good thing to get, especially when you are dealing with heterogeneous networks.

Testing, Testing, Testing

Let's say you've done your research, paid your money, and set up your VPN. All is right with the world, right? Well, maybe. Did you remember to test your system to make sure that it's really doing what it is supposed to do? That's an important step that many organizations forget about. It doesn't matter that you've implemented a good encryption algorithm and have long, strong keys that are well protected if you missed a step in your configuration and the encryption isn't working!

You can check with your particular vendor to see what test programs are already included in your system. Most routers include an array of self-tests that are run during startup and periodically during operations. The self-test run at power-up includes cryptographic *known answer tests* (KAT) on the DES, 3DES, and AES algorithms. There are also tests for SHA-1 and on Diffie-Hellman. Another set of tests checks the random number generator (RNG).

If, for some reason, your vendor has not included cryptographic testing for your VPN and no testing software programs you can use, first of all I'd question the validity of the vendor and their product. Secondly, you can always do a search on the Internet for "known answer tests" and you'll have more than enough data to get you going.

Chapter 13

Wireless Encryption Basics

· ·

In This Chapter

▶ Looking at the weaknesses of wireless encryption

▶ Learning some of the attacks on wireless and wireless encryption

▶ Implementing protection measure for your wireless network

· ·

*W*ireless networks are quickly becoming ubiquitous — they're in airports, at coffee shops, bookstores, and even pizza parlors advertise wireless *hotspots* now. Hotspots are locations where wireless access is available for use by the general public. (Check out `http://intel.jiwire.com` to find a listing of hot spots near you.) Some hotspots are free and some charge a time-based fee. We also use wireless networks in our homes because they free us from having to string Ethernet cables up stairs, down stairs, and between walls. Businesses love them for the same reason. You can now sit in a long meeting and, with your laptop, still be in touch with your team via e-mail or Instant Messaging (IM). You can watch your favorite show on TV and browse the show's Web site from the comfort of your living room couch. Who would have ever thought that radio waves could be so much fun?

There is a downside to all this convenience, though. I hate to even mention it because it seems like offering you candy and then telling you, "No, no, *bad* wireless, bad!" What's the downside? Number One, there is no built-in default security and, Number Two, the encryption scheme for wireless is almost worse than useless. In short, it's a total mess.

Wireless networks use radio waves to transmit data and that's one of their greatest advantages. A special box, called the Wireless Access Point, is connected directly to Internet. The Access Point (or AP, for short) broadcasts its location via an antenna and any computer that has a special wireless network card can pick up these broadcasts and use them to connect to the Internet, too. However, because they use radio waves, almost anyone with an wireless network card can pick up the network traffic. That includes areas outside your physical location. If you have a laptop with a wireless network card, you can walk the streets of any major metropolitan area and find open (unsecured) wireless networks. Your wireless network card actually does the looking for you. When the card finds a strong signal, it automatically tries to connect.

There are security measures you can take to hide your wireless broadcasts and limit unauthorized access. However, these security measures are not foolproof (or hack proof). For example, if businesses have changed their network broadcasts and employed *WEP* (Wired Equivalent Privacy) encryption, there are at least ten freeware and shareware software programs on the Internet that will help hackers or freeloaders to find your network, figure out the encryption keys, and log on to your network without authorization. This is such a widespread problem that there are literally thousands of companies (perhaps more) who are sharing their Internet and network bandwidth with freeloaders and hackers and they don't even realize it. If you have a wireless network at home, you may be sharing it with your neighbor and not know it, either.

Like most Internet applications and services, security and encryption was almost an afterthought with wireless networking, and the solutions offered at present are a band-aid at best, and offer a false sense of security at worst. There are changes in the works to make security and encryption better, but they are slow in coming. Additionally, any changes that are made will be for the new products — the chances that better security and encryption will be backwards-compatible are practically nil. What that means is that companies who already have large wireless infrastructures will have to replace almost all of their equipment. I don't see that as being very likely because executives hate to allot money for security upgrades.

So, let's have a look at what WEP has to offer. I'll discuss some of the configuration challenges, how WEP is cracked, and some suggestions for making your wired network more resistant to unauthorized logons.

Why WEP Makes Us Weep

There are a number of inadequacies with WEP that makes using it difficult and easy to configure it incorrectly. You can tell the Access Point to enable WEP, but if you don't manually configure all the wireless network cards on the desktop and laptop computers, it won't work — and you won't know it's not working. There are no dialog boxes or error messages that tell you that you've something wrong and the only way to test your wireless network for security holes is to try to hack it yourself.

Hacking your own network is a good way to test the security of your systems. Most hacking tools are available for free on the Internet and those that charge a fee are incredibly cheap. Most of these hacking tools are not very user-friendly and you need to have a good understanding of the technology before you can use these tools accurately and efficiently. A caveat here, too: Never try to hack your network unless you really know what you are doing. Hacking tools are capable of damaging your network. If you need help, there are computer security consultants who are more than willing to help you. Many of them are considered to be *White Hat Hackers* (the good guys) and they are proficient in what is called *penetration testing*. The normally use the same tools the hackers do, but they know what they are doing and will let you know if any of that testing could damage your network. You should look for someone who has a CISSP (Certified Information Systems Security Professional) accreditation or other, similar certifications.

But, enough of that — I'll get back on track with the subject of wireless encryption.

No key management

WEP is sort of a kindergarten version of a PKI system. Any PKI system worth its weight has a good key management system — keys are securely generated, are of adequate length and randomness, can be expired or revoked, and not everyone gets the same key. But, with WEP all computers are configured with the same keys and all the default keys that come with wireless access points are well known by hackers and are posted on the Internet. That's like having all the front doors of houses in your neighborhood use the same key — and then putting copies of that key on grocery store bulletin boards. Yeah, you've locked your doors, but anyone who cares to look for the key can get in without trouble.

The second big problem with WEP is what I mentioned before — all the wireless network cards have to be manually configured with the same keys as the access point. That means you have to sit down in front of each machine, start the configuration program, and manually enter a series of numbers. This has to be done manually because there is no way of "pushing" the keys automatically to the desktop and laptop computers. Good key management also requires that the keys be changed on a regular basis to keep them from being guessed or cracked. Well, if you have 300 computers in your office, that means you will have to sit down in front of every one of those computers every time you change the keys. Not only is this a chore and the chances of making a mistake are high, but no one is going to do that! Imagine you have thousands of users in a building with dozens of access points. A real nightmare scenario if you want to do good key management.

One last thing while I'm on the subject of keys — WEP will let you set a key with all zeroes. How hard would that be to guess or crack?

Poor RC4 implementation

In general, RC4 is a good algorithm. It's used in most of the e-commerce encryption. But, even a good algorithm can be made to work in a bad way and that's what has happened with WEP.

As I mentioned before, when an algorithm starts generating a key, it takes some random data to start it off first. RC4 starts with an *initialization vector (IV)* which is a series of random bytes added to the front of the encrypted data. In WEP the initialization vectors are too small (only 24 bits) and they are reused. That's like saying, "I'm going to start this message with ABCD, the next message will start with EFGH, and then I'll use ABCD again." If you use a scheme like that, it's not going to take long before an attacker will figure it out.

And last but not least of the mistakes made with WEP is the fact that the first three bytes of the key are sent in the clear. So now an attacker can easily snag the IV and 3 bytes of the key with no hassles whatsoever. All the attacker needs to do is to collect a few megabytes of encrypted data flying through the air, let his encryption cracking program do some calculations, and voila! — he has the key. And, did you know that you can get programs on the Internet that will crack a WEP key in seconds? Yes, sometimes it's that easy.

Authentication problems

An access point can be set to *Open Authentication* which allows everyone to log on, or it can be set to *Shared Key Authentication*. If you configure your access point to restrict access by enabling Shared Key Authentication, you will inadvertently give eavesdroppers so much information about the shared keys, that they will be able to crack the keys and join your network anyway. What a conundrum — If you allow Open Authentication, any attacker can join the network because there is no challenge. If you allow Shared Key Authentication, any attacker can *eventually* join the network with more information about your encryption than he would have had with Open Authentication.

In this case I usually recommend using Open Authentication and make changes to other parts of the access configurations. Later in this chapter there are examples of some concrete steps you can take to secure your network.

Not everything is encrypted

WEP can give users and administrators a false sense of security because they incorrectly assume that, when WEP is implemented, everything on the network is encrypted. Wrong again. The network does its authentication by sending out data in the clear and then waiting for responses. This assists the possible attackers or unauthorized users in identifying the network names, authorization methods, and information about keys. Here's a look at some of the data that is sent in the clear:

✔ **Beacons:** These are continually broadcast by the access points with the SSID *(Service Set Identifier)* and the *Media Access Control* (MAC) *address* Basically, these are the names of the networks and the physical identification of the computer's network card. These items are sent via the access point beacons so desktop and laptops computers can find the network to join it. This data is not encrypted when WEP is enabled on the wireless network.

✔ **Probes:** Desktop and laptop computers that want to join a wireless network will send a request for a probe packet from the access point. If the access point allows the request, it responds with an answering packet that contains information about the network. This data is not encrypted when WEP is enabled.

✔ **Ad-Hoc Packets:** These are packets allow the clients to speak directly to one another without having to go through the access point; like when one person is sharing a folder with another person. These packets don't contain beacon data and are usually considered data packets by the network, but they aren't always encrypted.

If you decide to use WEP, and I strongly urge you to do so, even though there are numerous problems, you must remember to make WEP *required*. Many administrators turn on WEP without making this distinction and don't realize that, if a desktop or laptop computer doesn't have its WEP keys, that computer is sending data in the clear. Again, that false sense of security is rearing its ugly head again.

WEP Attack Methods

When the majority of people logged on to networks via modems, hackers created software that automatically had their computer dial thousands of phone numbers in a series; looking for a modem to answer. These software programs were called *war dialers*. Taking a page from that book, hackers and freeloaders looking for wireless access points now engage in *war driving, war walking,* and *war chalking*. War driving and war walking are simply moving from place to place (like a city's business district) with a laptop equipped with a wireless network card, a strong antenna, and wireless hacking software. They use their laptops to look for corporate and private wireless networks they can log on to. When wireless networks are found, the hackers sometimes leave some War chalking marks on the sidewalk or the building to indicate the location of a wireless network and other useful information. War chalking is just like it sounds. The hacker uses everyday chalk that can be found in any toy store. The marks are coded symbols. Most people on the streets never notice them and, if they did, have no idea what the symbols mean.

Finding wireless networks

You can walk around the downtown area with a laptop equipped for wireless networking and find networks with no problem at all. The wireless network card looks for networks to log on to and, when it finds one, automatically tries to log on. On totally unsecured networks there isn't even a UserID or password required. If the network card finds more than one network, it will either log on to the one with the strongest signal or ask the user which network to log on to. I guarantee that if you walk around the downtown area of any major city, you'll always find an unsecured, unencrypted network within a few blocks.

War drivers use their cars and war walkers just roam the sidewalks on foot. They equip their laptops with special wireless search and hack programs with names like *AirSnort, NetStumbler, Kismet, and WEPCrack*. These programs are not too difficult to figure out and most are available for free on the Internet. I must mention at this point an important fact:

If your company is using wireless networks and is not attempting to restrict access to the wireless network, then war driving and war walking are not crimes! If someone can find your network with no special software or equipment and log on to it, you'd have a hard *time prosecuting them for unauthorized access.* It's like leaving your door unlocked and having an "Open" sign on the door.

With many businesses implementing wireless hot spots (wireless networking hosted by the shop), the wireless hacking programs make it easy to get around any security the shops have implemented on their wireless networks. Because many of the shops are operating their networks on a pay-peruse model, the wireless hacking programs could quickly make operating wireless networks a losing proposition. If all your customers are using hacking programs to log on to your hot spot, you obviously are not getting any income from it.

A slightly disturbing development is the fact that some stores and restaurants are using wireless networking for ordering and payment. The management is certain their networks are secure, but it would not be difficult for a slightly skilled war driver to get on to their network and adjust pricing for himself, give himself free products, and/or open their network to others. Hacker magazines and Web sites can and do list vulnerable wireless networks without fear of retribution. Check out www.wardriving.com for a quick taste of what you're up against.

War chalking

It's often been reported that hobos during the Great Depression made marks on buildings, trees, and sidewalks indicating whether or not an establishment was friendly towards them. If a particular household would give a hobo a meal for doing some yard work, for example, someone would mark the side of the house or something nearby to let others know this fact. The marks were unobtrusive and owners often didn't even realize they were there. There is a good web site at www.slackaction.com/signroll.htm, which gives good examples of the symbols the hobos used.

War drivers have created their own symbols to indicate to others not only are there wireless networks nearby, but the symbols often have important information as to how to log on to protected wireless networks. They've called this *war chalking*. You can buy large sticks of chalk, intended for children to create sidewalk art, in almost any drug store or toy store. The chalk is cheap and it's easy to carry a large piece in your pocket.

I have seen these marks myself on sidewalks in San Francisco and New York, so I know this is not rumor. So, even if you have implemented WEP correctly and made other changes to ensure the security of your wireless network, you may want to walk a few blocks in every direction to see if there are war chalking marks. If you do see some, it might be a good idea to make some changes to your wireless security, including changing the encryption keys. Of course it wouldn't do any harm to erase any of these symbols you happen to find, either.

Figure 13-1 shows an example of some war chalking marks and explanations of what the symbols mean:

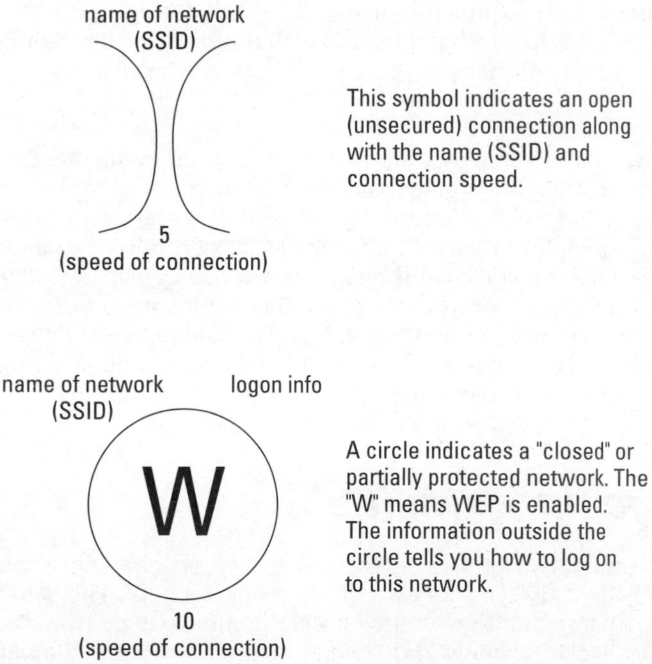

name of network
(SSID)

This symbol indicates an open (unsecured) connection along with the name (SSID) and connection speed.

5
(speed of connection)

name of network   logon info
(SSID)

Figure 13-1:
Some war-
chalking
symbols and
their
meanings.

W

A circle indicates a "closed" or partially protected network. The "W" means WEP is enabled. The information outside the circle tells you how to log on to this network.

10
(speed of connection)

Wireless Protection Measures

Here's a quick and dirty listing of some of the important (and fairly easy) things you can do to make your network less visible to war drivers and to implement WEP or other encryption schemes:

Look for rogue access points

Because wireless access points are very cheap, the temptation for employees to install their own access point is very high. In fact, they may be sitting right on top of the CPU box and you haven't even noticed them. Rogue access points can expose your network to outsiders and circumvent security measures such as firewalls and intrusion detection systems. This is the sort of problem that makes war chalking symbols appear outside buildings.

First of all, make it a policy that unauthorized access points are a big no-no and installing them is grounds for termination. That lets your staff know that you mean business.

Secondly, get one of the free war driving software programs I mentioned earlier and use it yourself to find rogue access points. There are even programs you can easily run on a PDA. One that has gotten good reports is called WaveRunner. I mention this because walking around the office with a PDA is a lot less obtrusive than walking around with a laptop. With a PDA device your staff may not realize what you're up to. Otherwise they may turn off their access points so you won't find them.

On the other hand, you may want to send out an announcement to all staff telling them that you are going to conduct a search for unauthorized wireless access points and will confiscate any you find. You may want to offer amnesty to get staff to turn in their wireless access points before you start your search. Tell the staff that they have a few days grace period in which to turn in their access points and there will be no punishment or terminations. After that period though, there will be (and should be) some sort of penalty to show that you are serious about this. I'm all in favor of giving people the opportunity to do the right thing first.

Change the default SSIDs

Although this isn't strictly an encryption technique, changing the default SSIDs can help "hide" your network from casual lookers. The SSID is basically the network name that the wireless access point broadcasts. It's a well-known fact (among hackers, anyway) that vendors often use their company name as the SSID. For example, the company LinkSys uses the SSID of "linksys." It doesn't take a brain surgeon to find networks using the default names. You'll need the access point's manual for instructions on how to change the SSID.

When you change the SSID, try to choose a name that's not totally obvious or too generic. For example, if your company is 123 Company and that name is on the door of your offices, don't change the SSID to "123 Company." That would be one of the first names a hacker would attempt to try. Likewise, names like "finance" or "personnel" or "marketing" are far too easy and obvious for someone to guess. So, try to be a little more creative and give your networks names that only mean something to you.

In addition to changing the default SSID you can also disable the "broadcasting" feature of the SSID. The broadcast feature means that the access point is sending out the name of the network to any wireless card that is trying to log on. If you disable this feature, a user will have to manually enter the name of the network and the network card won't find it automatically. The various wireless access point vendors have different methods of accomplishing this task, so you'll have to refer to your user's manual to see how to make these changes.

Turn on WEP

You have to do more than just turn on WEP; you also have to check a box that says something like "make WEP required." That ensures that WEP must be enabled on all desktop and laptop computers, too. Again, refer to your user's manual to figure out how your system handles this.

While I'm on this subject, I want to mention that it's important to change the default keys for WEP on your system. You'll need to refer to your manual again. In any case, when you've changed the keys, you have to go around to all the desktop and laptop computers and manually enter those same keys into those computers.

And one more thing on WEP: always use the strongest encryption possible. As of this writing it's 128-bit encryption. You'll have to make sure that all the wireless network cards in your computers are able to handle that level of encryption as some of the older ones were limited to a using a much smaller key size. If your systems can handle it, it doesn't cost you anything to use the strongest encryption, so why waste your time with weaker encryption? Even with WEP cracking tools, it would take a hacker quite a bit longer to figure out 128-bit keys. He may just move on to an easier target and leave your system alone.

Position your access points well

If you install your access points near windows and walls, you can be sure that the wireless signals "leak" to the outside and can be found by others. The best thing to do is to locate the access points as close to the center of the building as possible. There's a number of software programs and devices that can help you with this and one of them is called the Ekahau Positioning Device. You can find more information about this at www.ekahau.com. You want to position your access points so people outside the building can't find the signals, but your staff inside the office do need to be able to find the signals. If you place the access point too securely (like behind steel doors), no one will be able to log on.

Buy special antennas

Yes! You can buy special antennas that will shield and/or shape the wireless signals. With these antennas on your access points, you can direct the signals, limit them to certain areas, and shield them from walls, windows, and doors. Check with your local electronics store and try talking to some of your local ham radio enthusiasts. Ham radio operators usually know more about radio waves and tuning antennas than you ever thought possible.

Use a stronger encryption scheme

This would mean that you would need to hire someone who has a great amount of experience in the field because it's not something even the best network administrators are used to doing. Special programs would need to be created to affect the way the access points and the clients communicate and the encryption algorithms and keys that they use.

Use a VPN for wireless networks

VPNs are much better at authentication and encryption than WEP. If you already have VPNs set up for the rest of your network, it's not much of a chore to set it up for wireless networks. Just make sure your access points are all behind your firewall and then set up your VPN scheme. You can be guaranteed of better authentication and much better encryption that way.

There are a few companies that are making special software to help hide your network from freeloaders. Bluesocket (www.bluesocket.com), NetMotion Wireless (www.netmotionwireless.com), and Net-Screen Technologies (www.netscreen.com) even make specialized wireless VPNs. If your wireless network deals with a lot of sensitive information, this is something you really should look into.

Employ an authentication system

RADIUS servers were designed to support stronger authentication for remote users so, in this case, they are a good marriage. There is more information about RADIUS and other authentication systems in Chapter 10, so you should check back there for the software and hardware you will need.

Part IV
The Part of Tens

The 5th Wave   By Rich Tennant

"Our automated response policy to a large, company-wide data crash is to notify management, back up existing data and sell 90% of my shares in the company."

In this part . . .

In this part are the lists and lists and lists of good things to do and good things to get — crypto Web sites, terminology, and tips on software. It's kind of like the Christmas package that you've been waiting for. All good things come to those who wait, right?

Chapter 14

The Ten Best Encryption Web Sites

● ●

*T*hank goodness for the Web! You can use it to research even the most obscure interests and facts, and I use it quite a bit when writing books on technical subjects. In writing this book, I came across some really good sites that might interest you. Some of the sites are fairly elementary but interesting, and others delve into the subject a bit more deeply.

Mat Blaze's Cryptography Resource on the Web

www.crypto.com contains a little bit of everything. There are research papers, discussions of the government's use of cryptography, and links to RFCs (Requests For Comments) of interest. What's particularly interesting is the article at www.crypto.com/masterkey.html, which details the algorithm used to create master locks for regular door locks. If you know the algorithm, you can create a master key to open almost all locks!

The Center for Democracy and Technology

www.cdt.org/crypto is a non-profit organization which lobbies the government on cryptography issues — in particular, the right for citizens to use strong encryption to protect their work and/or their networks. It's interesting reading as the government regards strong encryption as a "munition" and controls the export of strong encryption. If you do business with companies or individuals overseas, you may want to have a look at this site to see if any of the government's restrictions apply to you.

SSL Review

The site used to be called Which SSL.org and has recently changed its name to SSL Review. The URL is `www.sslreview.com`, and it gives you all you need to know, and more, about SSL. One of my favorite parts of this site is the side-by-side review of the major digital certificate vendors which includes the costs and other factors.

How IPsec Works

Although this site is actually part of Cisco's main site and is Cisco-specific in it's explanations, it has some very good information for those of you considering implementing IPsec. The URL is a long one, so here it goes: `www.cisco.com/en/US/tech/tk583/tk372/technologies_tech_note09186a0080094203.shtml`. Because IPsec hasn't been as widely implemented as the vendors (and security experts) may have hoped, it is available as a feature in many products. You may want to look at these pages before you jump into it feet first.

Code and Cipher

`www.certicom.com/resources/codeandcipher/volume1/issue1/index.php` is Certicom's educational newsletter on what's new in cryptography. You can subscribe to their newsletter, which comes out quarterly, to keep up with the latest trends and vulnerabilities.

CERIAS — Center for Education and Research in Information Assurance and Security

`www.cerias.purdue.edu/about/history/coast_resources/cryptography` has plenty of links to white papers, reports, studies, techniques, and products and vendors. CERIAS is a well-respected organization at Purdue University and is a wonderful resource for other security-related subjects as well.

The Invisible Cryptologists — African Americans, WWII to 1956

www.nsa.gov/wwii/papers/invisible_cryptologists.htm is a project by the NSA (National Security Agency) to let us in on declassified information. I found the chapters of this section particularly interesting about some of our unsung heroes of WWI and the Cold War.

Bruce Schneier

www.schneier.com. No book on cryptography would be complete without mention of Bruce Schneier; one of the most well-known cryptographers of the age. His books are almost required reading for those who are serious about the subject and you can subscribe to his newsletter: CryptoGram online.

North American Cryptography Archives

www.cryptography.org first has you fill out a form stating that you are an American and that you will not be exporting information about strong encryption overseas. From there you are presented with a smorgasbord of links and information about algorithms, history, books, research, you name it. It would take you weeks to go through all the information on this site alone!

RSA's Crypto FAQ

www.rsasecurity.com/rsalabs/faq/index.html has everything from basic information to highly technical and complex papers — take your pick! RSA is one of the most respected vendors of cryptographic software and encryption solutions and they have tons of information regarding how-tos. I find that getting the information you need from their site a bit difficult via their navigation links, so I usually use their Search window to find what I want. However, the Crypto FAQ is a good place to start.

Chapter 15

The Ten Most Commonly Misunderstood Encryption Terms

• •

*L*earning the lingo of a new technology is often the toughest part of the process. Have you ever had a meeting with some techno-geeks and found yourself just sitting there with your mouth open while your brain silently implodes? Chances are that you were simply ignorant of the terminology they were using and the geeks were engaged in the techno equivalent of rams butting heads. It's a wonder to watch, but it sure doesn't get you anywhere!

I'll go into some of the terms you're likely to have thrown at you and deconstruct them. The next time the geek-speak thing happens, you'll be able to understand them and play their game, too.

Military-Grade Encryption

Beware of this one! Basically, the only people who have "military-grade" encryption are the intelligence agencies such as the NSA and some segments of the government and they are not about to share this technology with the average consumer!

What this person *might* be referring to is encryption that is endorsed and/or tested by government agencies for commercial use.

Trusted Third Party

This refers to a Certificate Authority or similar entity who has been entrusted to store and distribute public keys. Some well known trusted third parties are Verisign, RSA, and Entrust. There are many more commercial Certificate Authorities, but you can also set one up for your own use within your organization.

X.509 Certificates

This is a standardized format for digital certificates. Since certificate servers are basically databases, it made sense that all certificates contain the same fields for information; making it easier for the certificate servers to manage the storage and distribution of certificates. A certificate that complies with the X.509v3 standard will contain the following information: version, serial number, signature algorithm ID, issuer name, validity period, subject (user) name, subject public key information, issuer unique identifier, subject unique identifier, extensions, signature on all the fields.

Rubber Hose Attack

When an algorithm is considered practically unbreakable, someone will always remind you that it is susceptible to a rubber hose attack. What? In simple terms, a rubber hose attack simply means beating up your adversary with a rubber hose (or other threatening object) until he/she breaks and gives you the secret key or password. Inelegant, but effective (not that I recommend it, however!)

Shared Secret

When two or more parties use the same key for encryption and decryption. Symmetric algorithms use a shared key for this purpose.

Key Escrow

To many, "escrow" is a bad word, but it needn't be. You are probably familiar with the escrow process when buying a house — the bank holds some money back "just in case" it is needed. Key escrow is the secure storage of a person's private key and/or passphrase "just in case" it is needed. Say an important person in a company suffers a medical emergency and is unable to communicate information about his private key and passphrase. The company may have a serious need for that information. If the key and passphrase were escrowed, that information would be available in an emergency.

Initialization Vector

Even with good algorithms we need to make sure that there is no way that any messages begin with the same sequence of characters. For example, if every encrypted message began with the characters 234kngaeo9i, it could give an attacker enough information to begin cracking the message.

The trick then, is to make sure that all encrypted messages begin with a unique sequence in the first byte of data. To do that, a sequence of random bytes is appended to the front of the plaintext before encryption by a block cipher, or used as a part of the first step in a block cipher procedure that uses some form of chaining.

Alice, Bob, Carol, and Dave

These names represent the cryptographers' convention of identifying who sends the message, who receives the message, who intercepts the message, etc. Instead of saying "A sends a message to B" and so forth, cryptographers have personalized the process by stating that "Alice sends a message to Bob."

I chose to break with convention in this book and use Boris and Natasha — simply because they are more fun!

Secret Algorithm

Run, hide, and don't deal with anyone who promises to protect your data by using a "secret" algorithm. Cryptographers found out a long time ago that it was better to make their algorithms public so they could be thoroughly with out bias. Many algorithms have been pulled from use after they were publicized and the testers found problems with them.

A secret algorithm has not been rigorously tested by the cryptographic and hobbyists' communities and, therefore, you can't possibly know if there are hidden problems with it.

Steganography

Steganography is similar to cryptography. Cryptography means *secret writing*, and steganography means *covered writing*. The trick with steganography is that it hides data in plain sight. How can that be? Some historical steganographic tricks include tiny pin punctures made in selected characters in a newspaper article or writing in invisible ink. More modern uses of steganography include hiding text in one pixel of a picture or hiding a file in an MP3 music file. Steganography can be used alone or in conjunction with cryptography.

Chapter 16

Cryptography Do's and Don'ts

• •

*P*eople make mistakes all the time. Airlines crash due to human error, people discover thousands of dollars deposited to their bank accounts — a mistake in data entry by a human, and cars run out of gas because the driver forgot to check the fuel gauge. It's a wonder we manage to do anything right at all given our propensity for making mistakes.

Studies have also shown that most hacks against computer networks could have been avoided — if only someone had installed a security patch or made simple changes in a configuration file. Given that you probably won't be too surprised to hear me say that encryption often fails because someone forgot to do something — or they did something incorrectly. I can't possibly cover all the configuration ins and outs in a simple list, but I can help you avoid some of the pitfalls by giving you some simple tips on what to do and what not to do. Therefore, without further ado. . . .

Do Be Sure the Plaintext Is Destroyed after a Document Is Encrypted

Many, many people make this mistake! They go to all the time and effort to encrypt a document before storing it or sending it off to someone else, and then they save the unencrypted document on their personal hard drive or on a file server. If an unauthorized person gained access to the file server or the personal computer, all the security of the encryption is lost. Not only that, but if the attacker has both the encrypted document and the plaintext document, he could figure out what your key is.

The commercial version of PGP has a feature that allows you to thoroughly destroy a plaintext document by erasing the file and totally scrambling the bits numerous times. Other commercial and freeware programs have this capability, too, but always use one that you trust and not just something you found on the Web.

If you must store a document in its plaintext form, move the file to a server that it not connected to the network.

Do Protect Your Key Recovery Database and Other Key Servers to the Greatest Extent Possible

You know what a gut-wrenching feeling it is to discover that you have lost your key ring — your house keys, car keys, mailbox key, key to your mother's condo, key to your pied d'tierre in the south of France. When you lose your keys you just know that someone is going to steal your car and enter your house. Not only that, but it's a pain and a half to replace all the locks and get new keys. It's not that much different if an unauthorized person gets your encryption keys.

If your encryption keys are stolen because someone has gotten them off your server, your first job is to secure the server so that it can't happen again. This means physical access to the server as well. Then you have to revoke all the existing keys and generate and issue new ones. Don't forget to tell the staff what has happened, too, and why these steps are necessary.

Don't Store Your Private Keys on the Hard Drive of Your Laptop or Other Personal Computing Device

For the same reason that you need to secure your key servers in the company office, you need to make sure that people's private keys are adequately protected on their workstations and laptops. Laptops are particularly vulnerable to theft and, if the private key is left on the hard drive in a default location, it makes it child's play to use that key.

When keys are generated, the cryptosystem often saves the private keys in a default location on the hard drive. Hackers and other attackers know exactly where to look for these keys and they know how to search the hard drive for keys that are stored in different directories than the default. The best thing to do is to have keys stored on some sort of removable media such as a USB keychain drive. You can password protect the USB drive as well.

Do Make Sure Your Servers' Operating Systems Are "Hardened" before You Install Cryptological Systems on Them

All operating systems, as they come installed from the factory, have numerous security holes in them. "Hardening" the operating system means changing all the vulnerable default settings and installing security patches that come from the vendors. Some operating systems are better than others as far as security goes, but Windows systems are notoriously bad when it comes to security.

You want to make sure your key servers other important servers of your encryption system are hardened so they aren't so easily hacked.

Do Train Your Users against Social Engineering

Social engineering is just a euphemism for "con job," and it happens every day. Employees get calls from someone purporting to be from the IT department and are asked to give up their passphrases and keys, amongst other things. Employees do this because they are afraid to challenge authority.

Give your employees permission to challenge anyone who asks them to do something that may compromise security. Tell your employees what needs protecting and what doesn't. In that way you make everyone aware of potential problems and you create a large team of "cyber cops" who are working for you instead of against you.

Do Create the Largest Key Size Possible

Most cryptosystems give you the option of creating keys of almost any size, starting with 40 bits and working up to over 4,000 bits. The difference in protection is like the difference in strength between a nylon cable tie and a reinforced steel lock. Which would you choose to lock up a bike, for example?

I don't know why vendors give you the choice of using outdated and unsafe small keys when larger key sizes are clearly better. Since it costs you nothing to create a larger key, always choose the largest key size possible. It will do a better job at protecting your data.

Do Test Your Cryptosystem after You Have It Up and Running

Most people are content to set up an encryption program and just leave it at that. What they forget to check is that the system actually encrypts data correctly. The most common problem is that the encryption program is not actually creating an initialization vector that is random enough.

Check with your vendor for software to test your system or search the Web for software that can do this for you.

Do Check the CERT Advisories and Vendor Advisories about Flaws and Weaknesses in Cryptosystems

SSH v.2 has been considered for years to be one of the most effective means of encrypting occasional remote communications. Given that, the number of security vulnerabilities found recently is really surprising. What that tells us, however, is that just because something is free of vulnerabilities or flaws when you install it, doesn't mean that something wrong won't be found later on. It's sort of like recall notices for problems with cars and trucks.

Although it doesn't seem like a priority, it really is important to check the CERT (www.cert.org) web site, security sites, and vendor sites for alerts on problems with encryption systems. When an alert is announced, there is usually a patch or a workaround to fix the problem. You should take care of those as soon as possible.

Don't Install a Cryptosystem Yourself If You're Not Sure What You Are Doing

As with any program installation, if you don't know what you are doing, you can really muck up the program badly. Usually there are numerous dialog questions to answer during the installation as well as directory location and other decisions to make. With a cryptosystem this is not the time to chuck the manual and try to do it on your own. If you install the program incorrectly, chances are your encryption won't work correctly either.

Read the manual, call your vendor support, read up about potential problems on the Internet before you install a cryptosystem. If you can, find someone who has a large amount of experience with these types of systems and hire him or her short term to help you out.

Don't Use Unknown, Untested Algorithms

As I have mentioned before, if an algorithm is unknown or secret, that means it hasn't been tested to see if it can be broken or not. If you come across an algorithm you've never heard of before, do some research on the Internet to see if anyone else of note is using it. Believe me, if you want opinions on something, the Internet is the place to find it.

One last word on unknown algorithms: If it hasn't been tested and your not sure of the reputation of the person who created it, how can you be sure it's trustworthy. In this day and age of Internet scams, I wouldn't put it past someone to release an "algorithm" that's really a Trojan program to be used to break the security of your system. Buyer beware!

Chapter 17

Ten Principles of "Cryptiquette"

· ·

*W*hen use of the Internet and e-mail became commonplace, most people had no awareness of the subtle do's and don'ts in correspondence. From that developed what we refer to now as "Netiquette" — things like not writing an e-mail in all caps (which is the Internet equivalent of shouting for attention) and not spamming mailing lists. Whenever a group of humans congregate, there are always subtle and not-so-subtle rules of how to compose yourself. Encryption is no exception.

A good friend of mine, Dave Del Torto (also known as *DDT*) gave a talk at a Defcon conference many years ago and introduced the concept of "criptiquette." I was impressed with the common-sense rules he gave and I have his permission to publish them here (with some of my own interpretations). Thanks, Dave!

For those of you who would like to contact Dave, he runs a non-profit organization that brings encryption technology to underdeveloped nations suffering from human rights abuses. He and his organization provide PGP, equipment, and training to human rights workers so they can communicate without fear of the government snooping on their e-mails. The organization is www. cryptorights.org and Dave's address is xo@cryptorights.org. (He is extremely busy and may not answer right away.)

If Someone Sends You an Encrypted Message, Reply in Kind

There's a reason the person sent you the message in an encrypted format, even though it may not be evident to you. Respect your friend's efforts by replying with an encrypted message.

Don't Create Too Many Keys

Especially with PGP, those of us who use it often search key servers for keys for the people we want to send something too — only to find that there are

3 gazillion keys for that person. Finding out which one to use is a real pain. Therefore, if you are using public/private keys, please make sure that you keep the number of keys you use to a minimum and make it easy for people to recognize which ones they should use.

Don't Immediately Trust Someone Just Because He/She Has a Public Key

Anyone can generate a pair of keys, especially with PGP. Just because you see the public key of someone you know, or someone you wish to correspond with, doesn't necessarily mean that key really belongs to that person. You should always verify, verify, verify keys with your correspondents before you send encrypted messages to them.

Always Back Up Your Keys and Passphrases

Losing your keys and your passphrases is a royal pain for everyone involved. Always, always, always back up your keys and your passphrases to some type of removable media. (And don't keep the passphrases and the keys on the same drive, floppy, or CD.) Save your keys and passphrases as plain, ordinary text files (.txt) without fancy formatting and name them something other than the obvious. "Recipes" is a good filename as is "To Do List." They are not something that draws immediate attention to them like a file called "Natasha's Private Keys" does.

Be Wary of What You Put in the Subject Line of Encrypted Messages

The point of this is to not draw unnecessary attention to the message. If the encrypted message contains the projected sales figures for a new product, don't put in the subject line, "Projected Sales Figures for Next Year." You're only asking for trouble if you do that. Use a phrase that is meaningful to you and your recipient, but not to the entire world.

If You Lose Your Key or Passphrase, Revoke Your Keys as Soon as Possible

Nothing is more frustrating to the sender and receiver than to exchange messages that can't be decrypted. It's a waste of time and effort, too.

If you lose your key or your passphrase, revoke your key as soon as possible. Key servers won't always update this information immediately, so you should also notify the people you correspond with the most. Include your new key (in ASCII format) in your message so those people won't have to search key servers for your new key.

Don't Publish Someone's Public Key to a Public Key Server without His/Her Permission

If a person has not published his or her key on a public key server, there may be a reason for this. Don't assume the person forgot and do it for himself or herself. That person owns the key and let him or her do with it what he/she pleases.

Don't Sign Someone's Public Key Unless You Have Reason To

This pertains to PGP more than anything else. If you were to search for Phil Zimmermann's key and then look at all the people who have signed his key, the list is enormous. If you talk to Phil, he'll admit that he has no idea who most of these people are. The only reason you should be signing someone's public key is either because that person asked you to, or because you are assigning a high level of trust on your own PGP keyring. For heaven's sake, don't sign keys for people you don't know!

If You Are Corresponding with Someone for the First Time, Send an Introductory Note Along with Your Public Key

If you are intending to send an encrypted file or message to someone who is not expecting anything from you (maybe you've never contacted this person before), send them an introductory message with your public key and explain what and why you are sending this message. Give the person time to read the message, too. Some people aren't religious about reading their e-mail on a daily basis and you have to give that person a reasonable amount of time to read and digest the message. It also gives that person an opportunity to add the key to their key chain.

Then, when you send the message, you can be reasonably comfortable that it will be successfully decrypted and read. Nothing is more irritating that to receive an encrypted message from someone you've never heard of and then have to search various key servers to find the correct key!

Be Circumspect in What You Encrypt

You don't need to encrypt everything you send. If it's just a friendly message saying "Hi, how are you?" chances are that you can forget sending it encrypted.

Chapter 18

Ten Very Useful Encryption Products

*I*t would be wonderful for me to come up with a list of the best encryption products but, like everything else, "best" is an objective term and can't be applied too well in this case. It's like asking car buffs which car is best or asking a football fan which team is best. It's a good way to start an argument that can last all day!

Instead of the best, then, I decided to give you a list of some very useful products that you can try for free or for very little money. That's always a good deal, isn't it?

PGP: Pretty Good Privacy

This is the poor man's entry to encryption products. You can get the free version, called GnuPG at www.gnupg.org or you can get the commercial version at www.pgp.com. If you're new to this and not sure if you want to use it long-term, you may want to try GnuPG first. The commercial version of PGP integrates with many e-mail programs and has other great features such as PGPDisk, which is a neat feature to encrypt disk drives or USB drives.

Both forms of PGP have large user communities and lots of resources available on the Web to help you.

GAIM

GAIM is the name of a new program that will encrypt all your online chatter. Worried that people are reading what you write in AIM, ICQ, IRQ, MSN, Jabber, and more? Then download this neat little puppy and hide your messages from others. http://gaim.sourceforge.net (Please note that there is no "www" in the URL.)

madeSafe Vault

This is an online privacy and encryption vault in which to store your most sensitive files. The company also makes a number of home and small business related products which are sold mainly as "privacy" products, but really are encryption products. One of the neat things their products do is, after the data is encrypted, it is then stored in various places on the hard drive and not in one contiguous space. That makes it harder for someone to even find all the encrypted data. The company is based in England and their prices are in Pounds, but they do have a neat product with a good interface. www.madesafe.com/uk/products/Vault.htm

Password Safe

This is a cool little bit of software — and free — that will store all those thousands of passwords in one little place and keep them all encrypted so no one can steal them. Made by the infamous cryptographer, Bruce Schneier, Bruce no longer supports this program because he has made the source code available for others to review and change as required. You can get this program at http://passwordsafe.sourceforge.net

From my experience this program is easy to use and it doesn't interfere with other programs.

Kerberos

This is one of the encrypting authentication systems I told you about earlier in this book. It's free and it's also being included in many off-the-shelf programs such as Windows XP. If you want to give it a try yourself, please read the FAQ first (www.faqs.org/faqs/kerberos-faq/general). After you've at least perused the FAQ and gotten a feel for what Kerberos is all about, then go to the MIT site, fill out the request form (which just asks if you are a US citizen) at http://web.mit.edu/network/kerberos-form.html and then download the program.

OpenSSL and Apache SSL

If you are planning on creating a Web site for e-commerce, then SSL is a must and is available at the Open SSL site at www.openssl.org. There's everything you need there, including a FAQ, instructions, and download sites.

The Apache software group has been known for years as the creators of the most secure Web server around for UNIX or Windows machines. Also check out their free version of SSL, found at www.apache-ssl.org.

SafeHouse

SafeHouse has made drive encryption programs for Windows platforms for years. This is a cool product because the encryption and decryption is "invisible" to the user — there's no need to mount or unmount a special drive or partition, the product does it all for you. They also have a free version for you to try out. www.pcdynamics.com/SafeHouse.

WebCrypt

If you have a Web site or are in the business of creating Web sites, then you know how easy it is for people to steal your code and your pictures. The WebCrypt product will encrypt your Web pages so all your hard work isn't just thrown out the window. Check them out at www.moonlight-software.com/webcrypt.htm. The product works on Windows, Macs, and Linux platforms.

Privacy Master

This is an easy to use program for home users to encrypt any private information and be able to set the level of security for files and documents. Privacy Master used to be known as PrivacyMaker and is sold through a new company. You can find it at www.secureaction.com/encryption.

Advanced Encryption Package

This is too cool! You can send an encrypted file to someone even if that person doesn't have the same encryption package you have! This program creates self-extracting encrypted files that you can send to others. There are lots of other features, too. Available at www.secureaction.com/encryption.

Part V
Appendixes

In this part . . .

Here you get some extra stuff that I thought you would be interested in that didn't really fit in other chapters of the book. I've put together a fairly comprehensive list of common terms and some information on import and export regulation on encryption technologies. I hope you find all of it useful!

Appendix A

Cryptographic Attacks

*Y*ou would think, after all the work cryptographers put into testing their algorithms for holes, that modern crypto systems would be hard to break. Well, in a sense it is hard to break these well-developed systems if you go at it with a sledgehammer approach. However, most of the modern attacks find ways to simply circumvent the security in an algorithm or crypto system instead of finding ways to "break" them. Because we are human, we sometimes make mistakes in software and hardware that makes it easier for attackers to find the weaknesses in a security mechanism.

Sometimes crypto attacks are made easier because the vendor made a simple mistake in creating the encryption program. This has happened more often than you'd care to know. There are tons of people out there with time, energy, and spare computers around who love to find holes in crypto programs, and when they do, they take a fair amount of delight in publishing their results. If you do an Internet search on "cracking crypto" or "attacking cryptography," you'll find hundreds of highly technical papers and lots of freeware that will do the job for you.

That's not to say that encrypting your data and messages is a bad thing. It's certainly more secure than not encrypting it. In fact, in one well-known case, an e-commerce site went to all the trouble of setting up SSL to encrypt credit card numbers for purchases, but they stored those numbers unencrypted on the Web server. The attackers did not need to attack the SSL sessions, they just found a path into the Web server and stole the credit card numbers with no problem. Sometimes smart people do dumb things. It's up to you to try to play it smart.

Without further ado, I present some of the common attacks you are likely to come across in your reading or discussions about cryptography.

Known Plaintext Attack

Basically, this attack means that you know what some of the plaintext is in the encrypted data. For example, in an e-mail message, you know that there will be a return e-mail address. If there is a Word document attached to the e-mail, you know that there will be a file with the ".doc" extension somewhere in the ciphertext.

The compression programs like PKZip and WinZip have been proven to be fairly vulnerable to this type of attack. The compressed, encrypted files are usually protected with a password or passphrase. If you were to try to use brute force the key or the passphrase it would probably take you a couple of months to finally crack it. But, many zip programs allow you to view the contents of the zipped file without unzipping it. That will give you the name of the encrypted file, which is your *known plaintext*. To make things even easier, there is a freeware hacking program called *pkcrack* that will make things much easier for you.

I won't go into the step-by-step details on how pkcrack works, but it is able to crack a passphrase or encryption key in fewer than ten minutes.

Other known plaintext attacks are much more sophisticated and can take much longer. I haven't seen any freeware on the Internet that is a general purpose crypto cracker for plaintext attacks. Most attackers write their own programs to do this because there are so many variables involved: the plaintext, the type of algorithm used, the length of the key, and the length of the passphrase. These attacks usually take the known plaintext, create a series of ciphertexts based on the plaintext, and then do a comparison evaluation to try to find the key.

Chosen Ciphertext Attacks

In this attack, Boris has somehow acquired some encrypted data and he doesn't know what it means. Usually this data is captured off a network connection with a sniffer. Boris has two ways to try to crack the ciphertext:

✔ He can send the ciphertext back to the victim and social-engineer the victim to decrypt it and send it back. With both the ciphertext and plaintext, Boris can figure out the key.

✔ He can try to find some plaintext that is probably included in the ciphertext and work backwards from there.

This sort of attack is usually tried against e-mail that has been encrypted with a public/private key combination.

Chosen Plaintext Attacks

This is very similar to *known plaintext* except that the plaintext is not known; the attacker is only guessing. The attacker chooses a bunch of words or phrases that he guesses might appear in the ciphertext. He encrypts his list of words and phrases and compares that to the ciphertext. Again, this takes a fair amount of computational energy on the part of the computer (or computers) involved.

This can also be done by spamming the target with the same message over and over, intercepting the encrypted response to these messages and comparing what you get. WEP encryption for wireless networks is very susceptible to this type of attack and the attacker can obtain an entire set of keys in a matter of a few hours.

The Birthday Attack

Did you know that if you gather 23 people in a room, the chances of two of them having the same birthday is greater than 50 percent? It's one of those strange but true facts that seem impossible. In cryptography, when an algorithm produces the same key or ciphertext string more than once, it's called a *collision* and cryptanalysts rely upon the fact that there are bound to be collisions in ciphertext.

If an attacker or cryptanalyst finds the same string of ciphertext more than one time in data, the chances are greater that the key can be obtained and the data read. In the past, some algorithms have proven to be very susceptible to collisions and were therefore no longer used.

Man-in-the-Middle Attack

This is perhaps the most famous of all attacks and it is carried out quite frequently with some success. This attack is possible with public/private key encryption and SSL transactions. Scary, huh?

A *MITM (man-in-the-middle)* attack is done by sitting on the network and monitoring traffic between two people (or two computers). You can sniff and capture the traffic and, when the conditions are right, enter the traffic stream and pretend to be one of the two people. Here's a quick and easy scenario as to how this might happen.

Boris wants to send a message to Natasha, so he asks Natasha for her public key. Natasha complies by sending her public key to Boris, but unbeknownst to either of them, Igor has intercepted the key. Then Igor sends his own public key to Boris by pretending to be Natasha. (It's very easy to forge headers in e-mail so it appears you are someone else.)

Boris then sends Natasha an encrypted message with Igor's public key. Boris doesn't know it's not Natasha's key, so he has no worries.

Igor intercepts the return message encrypted with his own key and reads the contents. Then he changes the contents, encrypts the message again with Natasha's key (which he had intercepted previously), and sends it on to her. Natasha reads the message and assumes it is from Boris. Neither Boris nor Natasha realizes anything has gone wrong.

This type of attack is the most common type used against public/private key systems. An improvement in the security comes from signing the keys. When the keys are signed by a certificate authority, Boris and Natasha can check the signing properties of the keys to see if they match what the certificate authority has as the properties. If the properties don't match, then something is definitely wrong.

But, people don't take time to check things out and are quite willing to accept things at face value. This type of attack is also known as *hijacking*.

Timing Attacks

This is a bit obscure, but you can also break crypto by watching the amount of time a system takes to encrypt messages. If Boris captures enough traffic over a long period of time and then computes the differences in timing, it will give him enough data to start figuring out the key.

In 1995, a 22-year-old cryptographer did that to the RSA algorithm and quickly made headline news with his discovery.

Rubber Hose Attack

And now, for something completely different! If you don't have the computing power or the time to try a brute force attack — that is, trying every possible combination of keys there could possibly be — you can always revert to the *rubber hose attack*.

This is quite easy, but I strongly recommend against it because it entails using a length of rubber hose to beat the passphrase out of your target. Physical violence is not considered a hacker's tool. I doubt that many cryptographers or cryptanalysts use this methods, but I wouldn't put it past the CIA!

Electrical Fluctuation Attacks

This is a relatively new method of attack and it's very similar to the timing attack. Instead of gathering data to deduce the amount of time it takes to encrypt the data, an electrical fluctuation attack measures the small fluctuations in power consumption to figure out the key. This was discovered in 1998 by the same fellow who figured out how to conduct timing attacks.

In order for an electrical fluctuation attack to work, Boris would need to have physical access to a cryptographic smart card or other hardware with the secret key hardwired into the device. Boris would attach a type of electrode to the device and then measure the differences in the amount of electrical current used when the device is encrypting something. If Boris gathers enough of this data, he can eventually figure out the key.

Major Boo-Boos

The number one boo-boo that people make when implementing encryption software or other crypto systems is that they forget to adequately protect the keys! Admininstrators have been found to leave encryption keys on Web servers — in directories that allow anyone to access them. Keys are also often stored on desktops and laptops in default locations, on servers, and on databases. If you know what you are looking for, secret keys, private keys, and public keys are very easy to find. Another mistake people make is not restricting access to their computers. For example, say Boris has stolen a laptop from a traveller at the airport. Boris boots the machine; there's no password, and he finds and copies the keys. He can now easily impersonate his victim in e-mails and with authorization mechanisms that allow remote connections to the corporate network. Additionally, if the keys have been stored on some sort of removable media such as a floppy or USB drive, the media is not usually password protected. On top of that, the keys are very often kept in a folder that says "My Keys." That's like leaving your house keys under the front door mat!

Another boo-boo is that people will save their passphrase in a text file and store it either on their desktop/laptop machine or on removable media. That's fine except they will name the file "My Passphrase."

As I have mentioned before, people have a hard time coming up with passphrases that are appropriately long and complicated. If you create a passphrase that does not have an adequate mixture of upper and lower case letters and characters, it can be cracked. Hackers and attackers use simple programs that have dictionary words built into them as well as slang words, peoples' names, place names, and obvious combinations of words. When an attacker runs one of these programs, more often than not he can get hundreds of passphrases in under an hour.

Some systems don't ensure that plaintext is destroyed after it's encrypted. This data can be stored in a swap file, in RAM, in temporary files, or even in the same location as the encrypted data. Whatever the case, these systems are leaving plaintext on the hard drive where it can be found by others. If an attacker can get to the plaintext files, he doesn't need to bother with the ciphertext, and you've done nothing to really secure your data.

Some encryption programs suffer from poor design. I have seen systems that use a special window for the user to type his passphrase, but the program didn't dump that data when the window was closed. The only way you will know that this is happening on your system is to check.

Sometimes the encryption program will temporarily store your passphrase in a cache for a certain amount of time so you don't have to keep typing it every time you send an e-mail. PGP 8.x uses this feature. Alhtough this is a cool feature, it's possible that the cache would still be open and usable when the user leaves for the night. To make sure others can't take advantage of a cached passphrase, be sure to set the cache to expire in a short period of time.

People lose authentication tokens all the time. They are usually the size of a credit card, but you have to have it in front of you or insert it in the computer to use it. People leave their tokens on desks and they leave them in computers. It doesn't take a genius to be able to pick one up with sticky fingers. If your token is lost or stolen, report it immediately. If you are the administrator, revoke the old token immediately and issue a new one. Some tokens are only protected with a short PIN, which is not very secure.

Some programs allow "bad" algorithms to be used. A case in point is Microsoft Windows (many versions). There is a setting in the operating system that tells Windows which algorithms to accept and which not to accept. There is a lengthy discussion on their site about it. The URL is http://support. microsoft.com/default.aspx?scid=kb;en-us;Q245030. It's much better if you get an expert to help you out with this, otherwise you could seriously mess up your operating system and the way it handles crypto.

Of course, there are lots of different boo-boos that vendors and users make with cryptography, but they mostly fall into the types of problems I've mentioned above. As long as you have a good passphrase, use as long as key as possible, and keep your keys safely stored, you'll bypass a lot of common problems.

Appendix B

Glossary

● ●

A5: The encryption algorithm used for GSM telephones. These telephones are mainly sold in Europe.

AES: *Advanced Encryption Standard.* A block cipher that was chosen through a competition of the world's greatest cryptographers. It is approved for government use by NIST and is assumed to be good for the next 20 years before a replacement needs to be found. Also known as *Rijndael (rine-doll)* for the two people who created the algorithm.

Algorithm: A set of mathematical step-by-step rules, or a recipe, for the encryption and decryption of data.

ANSI: *American National Standards Institute.* An organization that evaluates and publishes standards for various industries, including the computer technology industry.

ANSI X9.17: The standard for the exchanging (or sharing) of the key for the DES algorithm.

Application Encryption: A program that uses an algorithm to encrypt data. PGP is an example of an application that has encryption built-in.

Asymmetric Algorithm: An algorithm that produces two keys; a public key and a private key. The public key is shared with others and the private key is kept safe by the owner. The term "asymmetric" has to do with the fact that there are two different keys — it does not mean that the algorithm is lopsided.

Authentication: The process of making sure that a person is really who he says he is, or that a computer is really the computer it's supposed to be. It's like being asked for your driver's license before you can cash a check. Computers use encrypted keys or encrypted communications to exchange proof of identity.

Back Door: Usually a design flaw in software that allows unauthorized access into a system by those who know the secret.

Block Cipher: An algorithm that encrypts data and cuts the data into small chunks and encrypts the chunks one after another. The "chunk" is a block of data and the algorithm decides how large those chunks are. This term was not invented by Lucy in the "Peanuts" comic. (You blockhead, Charlie Brown!)

Blowfish: A symmetric block cipher invented by Bruce Schneier. Publicly available on the Internet.

Browser: Your Web browser such as Internet Explorer, Mozilla, Netscape, or Opera. All browsers now have the capability to exchange data with another computer via an encrypted link. Although this term is also applied to shoppers who are not actively purchasing goods in a particular shop, that has nothing to do with cryptography.

Brute Force Attack: It's like trying to break into a building by all possible hard attack methods: picking the locks, breaking the windows, breaking down the doors with a sledge hammer, or using bombs. In cryptography, a brute force attack is used when the attacker knows nothing about the encryption. He will start with easy guesses first and then build up to sophisticated methods. Brute force attacks in cryptography usually entail using lots of computers that try to guess each portion of the key or the encrypted message.

CAST: A block cipher developed by Carlisle Adams and Stafford Tavares (CAST) and patented by Entrust. It is available for public use.

CERT: *Computer Emergency Response Team.* A special team that has been formed to deal with computer emergencies of all sorts. Some companies form their own teams and other companies rely upon commercial CERTs. There is also a central CERT at Carnegie Mellon University in Pennsylvania. That CERT sends out alerts and information about new computer attacks and fixes.

Certificate: (See Digital Certificate.)

Certificate Authority (CA): A company or a specially built computer within a company that generates and controls Digital Certificates and the accompanying keys. This is also referred to sometimes as a "trusted third party" because it is supposed to be an unbiased yet powerful authority.

CHAP: *Challenge Handshake Authentication Protocol.* Largely used in Microsoft products, CHAP is a two-way password authentication scheme.

Checksum: A numeric value assigned to data to be used as an indicator of change made to the data. An algorithm changes the data into numbers, goes through a number of computations, and then assigns a single, long number as the checksum. If the checksum of the data you receive is not the same checksum as the person who sent it, then something got changed in transit. Also known as a "fingerprint," checksums are used to check the integrity of data. Checksum is also what many people do with their checking accounts at the end of the month.

CIAC: *Computer Incident Advisory Capability* (pronounced "sigh-ack"). This is an organization formed by the Department of Energy to track and report on computer security problems.

Cipher: The word cipher is very often confused with the word "code." A cipher is closer to an algorithm. It does not know the "semantics" of the text or data it is converting; as far as a cipher is concerned, it's just a blender of sorts. It's the part of the algorithm that replaces one letter with another character. (Also see Code.)

Cipher Block Chaining: Also known by cryptographers as *CBC,* this is like "shuffling" the encrypted blocks of data with one another to come up with different ciphertext. Using cipher block chaining makes it much harder for someone to try to break an algorithm.

Ciphertext: The encrypted form of data. Ciphertext does not have to be text, it can be any form of data including pictures and music.

Client: Usually a desktop computer or a laptop. This is opposed to "servers." Servers provide data, services, and resources to the client computers. Just think of clients as customers in a restaurant and the servers as waiters, and you'll get the meaning. Client can also refer to a software program that runs on a desktop computer or a laptop. This type of program is normally used when the server is sending a special type of information that can't be understood by other programs.

Code: A code is just a set of rules to represent meaningful information in another way — this doesn't necessarily imply secrecy. A code does deal with symantics and can tell the difference between a letter and a number. Morse code and programming code are two good examples.

Cracking: An action to try to break the security of a computer system, software program, algorithm, encrypted data, and so on. For instance, attackers will try to crack the key to encrypted data so they can decrypt it and see what it says. This has nothing to do with the eating of Maryland crabs, contrary to popular belief.

Cryptanalysis: The examination of encrypted data to try to discover how the data was encrypted. Cryptanalysts will try to find the key or some plaintext in the encrypted data so they can unlock it. In a way, this is similar to "cracking," but it is usually done by well-meaning folks employed by the NSA. (And, yes, because they are in Maryland, many do eat crabs.)

Cryptography/Crypto: The art or science of finding ways to hide or change data. The main goal of cryptography is to maintain secrecy – it's a way to transform plain data (pictures, music, text, software, and so on) from a recognizable form to an unrecognizable form and back again. Cryptography is also the technical field of creating methods of changing data into an unrecogniz-able form and then reversing the process to make it recognizable again.

DES: *Data Encryption Standard.* A popular symmetric key algorithm that was created in 1975. It is usually replaced now with 3DES, which is much stronger than the original algorithm.

Diffie-Hellman: An algorithm created by Whitfield Diffie, Martin Hellman, and Ralph Merkle to solve the problem of how to share a secret over an unse-cured line without compromising the secret. This became the basis for public/private key exchange.

Digital Certificate: A computer file that contains information about a person or a computer, along with a public encryption key. Digital Certificates have a standard format for the information contained so it can be used in many dif-ferent encryption programs. A Digital Certificate is issued by a Certificate Authority. The Digital Authority usually has strict regulations about who or what may receive a Digital Certificate. Identities are usually verified by the Certificate Authority, which implies a greater degree of trust.

Digital Signature: A checksum created by an algorithm, combined with a person's public key, that is based on a block of data and the person's private key. The result is a character-based string that is included with the data when it is sent. If the data has been changed en route, it will be reflected in a changed digital signature. A digital signature is used to guarantee that the data was sent by the person who claims to have sent it. In one sense it can be considered a type of notary stamp to prove authenticity.

Digital Signature Standard: This is also referred to as *DSS* and is the algo-rithm used to create digital signatures. DSS was developed by the NSA and approved by NIST.

ECC: *Elliptical Curve Cryptosystem.* A relatively new and unique form of encryption that uses mathematical curves over defined fields to create a public/private key pair.

Encipher/Encrypt: Changing plain data *(plaintext)* into an unreadable or unrecognizable form *(ciphertext)*.

Exclusive Or: (See XOR.)

Export Control: Laws and regulations to prevent products or technologies from being exported from the United States when exportation of that informa-tion is not in the best interest of the country. The United States considers cryptography to be munition and therefore controls the export of some encryption methods and products.

FIPS: *Federal Information Processing Standard.* Rules and regulations adopted by the federal government for computer systems, computer security, and the implementation of cryptography.

FORTEZZA: A PCMCIA card that contains the SKIPJACK encryption algorithm. This is mainly used by government agencies and some law enforcement agencies to encrypt e-mail. This term is often confused with *foccacia,* which is actually a type of Italian bread and has nothing to do with cryptography.

GOST: A symmetric block algorithm developed in the former Soviet Union.

HASH: A type of checksum that produced a fixed string of characters from a section of data that is used as a "fingerprint" of the data. If the data has not been changed, you will always get the same hash; if it has changed by only one character, the hash will not be the same as the original.

IDEA: The *International Data Encryption Algorithm* was developed in Switzerland and is one of the algorithms that is used in PGP.

IETF: The *Internet Engineering Task Force* is a large open international community of network designers, operators, vendors, and researchers concerned with the evolution of the Internet architecture and the smooth operation of the Internet. It is open to any interested individual.

IKE: This stands for *Internet Key Exchange* and is used by the protocol *IPsec* (secure IP) for key management.

IP: *Internet Protocol* carries individual data packets on a network. It allows the packets to be routed through multiple networks until it reaches its destination.

Ipsec: A network security protocol that uses encryption to protect data as it is moving through the network.

ISAKMP: *Internet Security Association Key Management Protocol* was the basis for IKE and is still used in many networking environments. ISAKMP defines payloads for exchanging key generation and authentication data.

KDC: Stands for *Key Distribution Center* and is the basis of the Kerberos authentication system. It is a device or computer that allows two computers to encrypt the traffic flowing on the network between them. Not to be confused with *KFC,* which is fine to eat on a 4th of July picnic.

KEK: A *Key Encryption Key* is used to encrypt other keys such as session keys or data keys. A KEK does not encrypt any of the data itself, it just sets up the environment so that encryption can begin.

Kerberos: An authentication protocol, developed at MIT, that uses session keys. Available commercially and in the public domain.

Key: The data created by an algorithm that causes a cipher to begin the encryption and decryption process. Keys are associated with the algorithm that was used to create it.

Key Escrow: The storing of copies of encryption keys so they can be used if the original key is lost or corrupted. This is very difficult to do securely.

Key Fingerprint: A unique string of characters that is used to authenticate a key. This is done by creating a hash of the key. Usually used by PGP users to verify that the parties are using the correct keys for encrypting and decrypting communications.

Key Length: The size of a key represented in bits. The larger the number of bits, the stronger the key is.

Key Management: The process and procedures uses to safely store and distribute keys. It also makes sure that keys are sent out in a secure manner so they won't be compromised.

Key Pair: A set of keys created by an asymmetric algorithm: the public key and the private key.

Key Recovery: A method of hiding parts of keys in different places so a key can be reassembled if the original key is lost or corrupted. Key recovery usually involves the use of multiple storage locations and multiple passphrases to complete the recovery process.

Key Splitting: A security measure that splits a key up amongst a number of people so no one person on his own can use the key. All members of the group must participate in order for the key to be used.

Keyring: A program or file that holds a set of keys.

LDAP: *Lightweight Directory Access Protocol.* A protocol used in databases to allow simple search and access operations for data that is usually hard to index — phone numbers, addresses, and now used for encryption keys.

MAC: *Message Authentication Code.* A one-way hash that uses a single key. The key is used to verify the hash.

MD2: *Message Digest #2.* Developed by Ron Rivest, it's a 128-bit one-way hash.

MD4: *Message Digest #4.* Another one-way hash developed by Ron Rivest, but later found to be very weak. It was replaced with MD5.

MD5: *Message Digest #5* is an algorithm used to create a hash.

NIST: *National Institute of Standards and Technologies* is a government agency that establishes national standards.

Non-Repudiation: A process that, once completed, makes it extremely difficult for someone to deny that they were involved in the process. It's a method of ensuring that someone sent a file or encrypted a file without "reasonable doubt" that they did so.

NSA: The *National Security Agency* is an intelligence agency responsible for intercepting communications and developing crypto systems for the security of national secrets. This agency employs the largest number of cryptographers in the world.

Oakley: A protocol for a session key exchange that is a hybrid of the Diffie-Hellman scheme.

One Time Pad: Also known as *OTP,* this is one of the older but most secure forms of encryption. A person creates a pad of completely random characters and then uses that pad to replace the characters in a message, one by one. If the pad is never used again, it is nearly impossible to break.

One Time Password: A security mechanism in which a password is only used one time and never again. These passwords are usually generated by a small card-like device that is synchronized with an authentication server.

One Way Hash: Also known as a *one way function,* this is the same as a message digest or a fingerprint. It's called "one way" because the algorithm creates an encrypted string that cannot be decrypted. The encrypted string is used for comparison only.

PAP: *Password Authentication Protocol.* This protocol allows users to authenticate with one another but does not prevent unauthorized access.

PCMCIA: Stands for *Personal Computer Memory Card International Association.* It's a plug-in slot for peripheral devices such as modems and wireless network access cards. There are also PCMCIA cards that store crypto functions and keys.

PGP: Short for *Pretty Good Privacy,* this is cryptographic protocol for encrypting e-mail. PGP uses RSA and IDEA algorithms and comes as a complete software package.

PKCS: *Public Key Cryptography Standards.* This is a standard for keys that was created by RSA and describes how public/private keys can interoperate with various algorithms.

PKI: *Public Key Infrastructure.* A system that uses public and private keys for encryption and decryption, but also checks to make sure that the correct keys are being used for any transaction.

Plaintext: Data that is in its original form and has not been decrypted. Also, it's the data after decryption has taken place.

Private Key: One of a pair of keys created by an asymmetric algorithm that are mathematically linked to encrypt and decrypt data. This key belongs to one person (or computer) and is kept safely secret. (Also see Public Key.)

PRNG: *Pseudo Random Number Generator.* A process or algorithm that generates a random sequence of numbers. A good PRNG will make it nearly impossible to guess what the next number or numbers in a sequence might be. Used in key generation in algorithms.

Protocol: In computer technology, a protocol is an accepted set of rules for computer communications or the transference of data. A protocol goes into a detailed level of instructions for the behavior of any software, hardware, which ports to use, and so on.

Public Key: One of a pair of keys created by an asymmetric algorithm that are mathematically linked to encrypt and decrypt data. This key can be shared with anyone and everyone without fear that it will give any clues as to what the private key might be. (Also see Private Key.)

RADIUS: *Remote Authentication Dial-In User Service.* A protocol developed to help secure remote access to networks by persons, computers, and other networks. Originally developed to secure modem banks, it is now used to secure remote network connections.

RC2: *Rivest's Cipher #2 or Ron's Cipher #2.* Named after Ron Rivest, this is a block cipher that uses a 40-bit key that is considered very weak.

RC4: *Rivest's Cipher #4.* This is a stream cipher that is widely used in commercial products and especially in e-commerce transactions.

Reusable Passphrase: A passphrase that can be used over and over, with no limitations. Most passphrases are reusable.

Revocation: The retraction or cancellation of a certificate and its associated keys.

RNG: *Random Number Generator.* An algorithm or cryptographic device that can create true random numbers. True random numbers are often generated by physical and natural events that cannot be predicted and occur randomly.

RSA: Stands for *Rivest, Shamir, Adelman,* which are the last names of the three men who created the RSA algorithm and the RSA company (RSA Data Security). The RSA algorithm creates public/private keys and can be used to create a digital signature (among other activities).

Salt: Random data that is mixed in with a password to help foil dictionary attacks on passwords.

Secret Key: The key created by a symmetric algorithm. This key is used to both encrypt and decrypt data.

Seed: A random value that is added to an algorithm to help begin the generation of a pseudo random number. (See PRNG.) This is not to be confused with the seed generation used in tennis tournaments.

Server: Usually a large and powerful computer used to store and disseminate large amounts of data and/or services to desktop computers and laptops on a network (clients). Servers are also used for storage and important applications.

Session Key: A key that is only used for a short period of time: a session. The key is normally used to encrypt data between two machines only and is thrown away when the session is complete.

SHA-1: *Secure Hash Algorithm #1.* An algorithm used to create a one-way hash. It's similar to MD4.

SHTTP: *Secure HyperText Transfer Protocol.* This is a change to the regular HTTP, which is used to display Web pages. SHTTP adds cryptological services to HTTP for the encrypted transmission of sensitive data over the Web.

SKIP: *Secure Key Interchange Protocol.* This protocol is used in the IPsec headers. The headers contain information about keys that are being exchanged over the network. The header contains information such as what type of key is included, its destination and source, and the application associated with it.

SKIPJACK: A block cipher developed by NSA and often used in hardware crypto devices.

S/MIME: *Secure Multipart Internet Message Extensions.* This protocol is added to e-mail programs so e-mail can be encrypted and the contents kept secret.

SMTP: *Simple Mail Transfer Protocol.* The protocol used to transmit e-mail between servers. SMTP traffic is not encrypted.

Snake Oil: A derogatory term used to describe marketing language that is deceptive and misleading, often stating that the encryption or crypto device does more than it is able to do.

Sniffing: A method of listening in on network traffic and capturing it. A special sniffer program is run on a computer on the network and captures and stores the information it was told to save. Very similar to eavesdropping. Hackers use these programs to capture UserIDs, passwords, encryption keys, and other important data.

SSL: *Secure Sockets Layer.* A cryptologic protocol that is added to data at the socket layer so a secure, encrypted link can be established and maintained. This protocol is often added to applications and is primarily used to protect Web communications.

Stream Cipher: A symmetric key cipher that encrypts data bit by bit rather than cutting the date into chunks like a block cipher does.

Symmetric Algorithm: An algorithm that creates a single key to both encrypt and decrypt data. This is sometimes called a "secret key" algorithm because the key is never supposed to be made available to the public and must be kept secret.

TACACS+: *Terminal Access Controller Access Control System.* Does the title somehow give you an idea that this protocol is used to control access to something? It is. It was developed by Cisco and is used to authenticate and authorize remote access by persons or machines.

TCP/IP: *Transmission Control Protocol/Internet Protocol.* A suite of protocols used for networking that has become the de facto standard. Even networks that use other networking protocols will include TCP/IP so other networks can communicate with them.

TLS: *Transport Layer Security.* This is a draft version of a new security protocol to replace SSL.

Token: A hardware device that is used to authenticate its owner to computers and applications on a network. A token can be a one-time password generator, a physical device that plugs into a socket, a smart card that is run through a reader, or another similar device.

Triple DES: Also known as 3DES, this algorithm is basically the same as DES except that it encrypts each block of data three times instead of once.

Twofish: A new symmetric algorithm that was one of the runners up to become the new AES algorithm for government use. It is freely available on the Internet.

Validity: The level of confidence a person has that a key actually belongs to the person who presented it.

Verification: Comparing a digital signature created with a private key to its public key. This proves that the information was sent by the person who actually digitally signed the data.

VPN: *Virtual Private Network.* A VPN provides an encrypted link on an otherwise unprotected network such as the Internet. It allows remote computers or networks at a distance to connect to another and protect their communications with encryption.

Web of Trust: The scheme used by PGP where individuals "sign" other people's public keys to give an indication of the key's validity.

X.509: A public key certification specification as part of a directory system that stores and distributes public keys.

XOR: Stands for *eXclusive Or;* it is a mathematical function of comparing bits from the data to random bits created by the algorithm. It's used to indicate whether the bits of the two strings match.

Appendix C

Encryption Export Controls

In This Appendix

▶ Getting down to the nitty-gritty of export controls

1n times of war, the military and the government use encrypted messaging and file transfers to exchange data to and from the war zones. In addition, almost all diplomatic messages are sent encrypted to protect the national interests. Cryptography played a huge role in World War II and during the Cold War as both sides spent large amounts of resources trying to break the encryption codes of the "other" side. Because cryptography is important to the national security, it's only common sense that the government would like to keep their methods secret. But, the government goes a bit further than that; they also control what encryption products can be exported to other countries. What is a little surprising to most people is that cryptography — algorithms and encryption methods and technologies — is considered "munitions" by the government. That's right — cryptography falls into the same category as guns, land mines, and bombs. Or at least it used to until the rules were changed in 2000.

What does this mean to the common lay person? It means that if you develop encryption technologies, you may have to register your products with the U.S. government and obtain permission to ship your products to certain countries.

A funny thing happened in the mid-1990s when I was working in a lab that tested a relatively new product — firewalls — for compliance and certification. One firewall company that was seeking certification was located in Israel. That company would send us fully configured firewalls on Sun Microsystems boxes. These were new, state-of-the-art Sun boxes and not outdated, obsolete products. The firewall software on the boxes was developed and owned by the Israeli company; they just happened to have installed them on an American owned computer.

After testing and certifying the firewalls, we normally sent the firewall boxes back to the vendors. However, in the case of the Israeli company, they had incorporated one of their encryption products in their firewall. Because that encryption was stronger than companies in America were allowed to export, we were not allowed to send their own Sun boxes back to them! Yes. Every time the product failed testing, the Israeli company had to send us another completely new box to test because we couldn't send their own boxes back to them. It was a total farce, but those were the government's rules.

What a shame! It was silly to let those Sun boxes go to waste, so the only thing we could do was to reconfigure them and use them in our own lab. (I'm not sure the Israeli company realized they were funding the expansion of our lab facilities by default!)

Because strong encryption is able to hide the communications and data transfers of important data, the U.S. government controls what type of encryption products can be exported and which countries we are allowed to export to. There's a vast bureaucracy of offices, agencies, and lots of paperwork that goes along with all this. The export restrictions used to be horribly strict — such as the restriction against foreigners downloading Web browsers that incorporate 128-bit encryption — but the rules and regulations are slowly loosening up.

Ironically, the government was due to vote on relaxing the export regulations even further when the September 11, 2001, terrorist attacks happened. The vote was dropped afterwards. There has been some talk in Congress that terrorists are using encryption to hide their messages and, with the fear-mongering going on, it will probably be a number of years before we see any new relaxation regulations come about.

Reading and actually understanding the government's regulations on import and export of encryption technologies is a nightmare. The documents are full of conditional clauses and "wherefore's" and "where as's." Indecipherable as an encrypted message itself! My best advice is to hire good legal counsel if your company is involved in this aspect of the industry. Although a lot of the regulations have been relaxed (like, you can register your product after the fact that you've already sent it overseas), paradoxically, the regulations have made some filings more difficult.

There are a number of agencies, offices, and so forth to deal with now. In a nutshell, here are the main cast of characters and their corresponding Web sites:

✔ Wassenaar Agreement: www.wassenaar.org

   This is an international agreement/treaty on export controls for conventional arms and dual-use goods and technology (meaning: encryption products).

   (You can click on the different flags to view the export regulations for that country.)

✔ U.S. Delegation to the Wassenaar Agreement: www.usun-vienna.rpo.at/wassenaar

   These people represent the United States for the Wassenaar Agreement.

✔ Bureau of Industry and Security: www.bxa.doc.gov

This agency handles the export of sensitive goods and technologies.

✔ U.S. Department of State, Directorate of Defense Trade Controls: www.pmdtc.org

If your company exports encryption, you have to register with this group.

✔ Export Administrations Regulations Marketplace: http://bxa.fedworld.gov

There are links to other sites and information about export regulations.

So, what are some of the export regulations? Here's a quick list of some rules and regulations you should follow. Remember not to take this as legal advice. If in doubt whether or not you or your company need to comply with export regulations, consult your lawyer.

✔ **Your company does not have to file with the government if:**

- You are sending encryption to a U.S. company or subsidiary overseas. (There are exceptions — like countries we don't have good relations with.)
- The encryption is only for short-range wireless transmissions.

✔ **You *do* have to notify the government if:**

- Your product is a "mass market" product with symmetric key length not exceeding 64-bit algorithms.
- Your product is not "mass market" but it uses key lengths less than or equal to 56 bits for symmetric algorithms, 512 bits for asymmetric algorithms, and 112 bits for elliptic curve algorithms.

✔ **You have to undergo a review process with the government if:**

- Your products are "mass market" products with symmetric key lengths exceeding 64-bit algorithms.
- Your products do not qualify as "mass market" but employ key lengths greater than 56 bits for symmetric algorithms, 512 bits for asymmetric algorithms, and 112 bits for elliptic curve algorithms.

So, as you can see, the rules are not exactly straightforward and some of the language is quite confusing. That's why it's best to work with a lawyer or other encryption export specialist if you're engaged in sending algorithms or encryption products overseas.

In the list of agencies and links above, there is a checklist to follow to help you figure out whether or not you have to file anything with the government. I didn't find that the checklist was that helpful, so I haven't included it here.

Index

• R •

Notes

Notes

Notes

Notes

Notes

Notes

FOR DUMMIES®

The easy way to get more done and have more fun

PERSONAL FINANCE

0-7645-5231-7

0-7645-2431-3

0-7645-5331-3

Also available:

Estate Planning For Dummies
(0-7645-5501-4)

401(k)s For Dummies
(0-7645-5468-9)

Frugal Living For Dummies
(0-7645-5403-4)

Microsoft Money "X" For Dummies
(0-7645-1689-2)

Mutual Funds For Dummies
(0-7645-5329-1)

Personal Bankruptcy For Dummies
(0-7645-5498-0)

Quicken "X" For Dummies
(0-7645-1666-3)

Stock Investing For Dummies
(0-7645-5411-5)

Taxes For Dummies 2003
(0-7645-5475-1)

BUSINESS & CAREERS

0-7645-5314-3

0-7645-5307-0

0-7645-5471-9

Also available:

Business Plans Kit For Dummies
(0-7645-5365-8)

Consulting For Dummies
(0-7645-5034-9)

Cool Careers For Dummies
(0-7645-5345-3)

Human Resources Kit For Dummies
(0-7645-5131-0)

Managing For Dummies
(1-5688-4858-7)

QuickBooks All-in-One Desk Reference For Dummies
(0-7645-1963-8)

Selling For Dummies
(0-7645-5363-1)

Small Business Kit For Dummies
(0-7645-5093-4)

Starting an eBay Business For Dummies
(0-7645-1547-0)

HEALTH, SPORTS & FITNESS

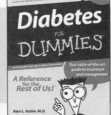

0-7645-5167-1

0-7645-5146-9

0-7645-5154-X

Also available:

Controlling Cholesterol For Dummies
(0-7645-5440-9)

Dieting For Dummies
(0-7645-5126-4)

High Blood Pressure For Dummies
(0-7645-5424-7)

Martial Arts For Dummies
(0-7645-5358-5)

Menopause For Dummies
(0-7645-5458-1)

Nutrition For Dummies
(0-7645-5180-9)

Power Yoga For Dummies
(0-7645-5342-9)

Thyroid For Dummies
(0-7645-5385-2)

Weight Training For Dummies
(0-7645-5168-X)

Yoga For Dummies
(0-7645-5117-5)

Available wherever books are sold.
Go to www.dummies.com or call 1-877-762-2974 to order direct.

FOR

DUMMIES®

A world of resources to help you grow

HOME, GARDEN & HOBBIES

Feng Shui For Dummies
0-7645-5295-3

Gardening For Dummies
0-7645-5130-2

Guitar For Dummies
0-7645-5106-X

Also available:

Auto Repair For Dummies
(0-7645-5089-6)

Chess For Dummies
(0-7645-5003-9)

Home Maintenance For
Dummies
(0-7645-5215-5)

Organizing For Dummies
(0-7645-5300-3)

Piano For Dummies
(0-7645-5105-1)

Poker For Dummies
(0-7645-5232-5)

Quilting For Dummies
(0-7645-5118-3)

Rock Guitar For Dummies
(0-7645-5356-9)

Roses For Dummies
(0-7645-5202-3)

Sewing For Dummies
(0-7645-5137-X)

FOOD & WINE

Cooking For Dummies
0-7645-5250-3

Cookies For Dummies
0-7645-5390-9

Wine For Dummies
0-7645-5114-0

Also available:

Bartending For Dummies
(0-7645-5051-9)

Chinese Cooking For
Dummies
(0-7645-5247-3)

Christmas Cooking For
Dummies
(0-7645-5407-7)

Diabetes Cookbook For
Dummies
(0-7645-5230-9)

Grilling For Dummies
(0-7645-5076-4)

Low-Fat Cooking For
Dummies
(0-7645-5035-7)

Slow Cookers For Dummies
(0-7645-5240-6)

TRAVEL

Italy For Dummies
0-7645-5453-0

Hawaii For Dummies
0-7645-5438-7

Las Vegas For Dummies
0-7645-5448-4

Also available:

America's National Parks For
Dummies
(0-7645-6204-5)

Caribbean For Dummies
(0-7645-5445-X)

Cruise Vacations For
Dummies 2003
(0-7645-5459-X)

Europe For Dummies
(0-7645-5456-5)

Ireland For Dummies
(0-7645-6199-5)

France For Dummies
(0-7645-6292-4)

London For Dummies
(0-7645-5416-6)

Mexico's Beach Resorts For
Dummies
(0-7645-6262-2)

Paris For Dummies
(0-7645-5494-8)

RV Vacations For Dummies
(0-7645-5443-3)

Walt Disney World & Orlando
For Dummies
(0-7645-5444-1)

Available wherever books are sold. Go to www.dummies.com or call 1-877-762-2974 to order direct.

FOR DUMMIES®

Plain-English solutions for everyday challenges

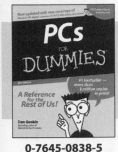

COMPUTER BASICS

PCs For Dummies
0-7645-0838-5

The Flat-Screen iMac For Dummies
0-7645-1663-9

Windows XP All-in-One Desk Reference For Dummies
0-7645-1548-9

Also available:

PCs All-in-One Desk Reference For Dummies
(0-7645-0791-5)

Pocket PC For Dummies
(0-7645-1640-X)

Treo and Visor For Dummies
(0-7645-1673-6)

Troubleshooting Your PC For Dummies
(0-7645-1669-8)

Upgrading & Fixing PCs For Dummies
(0-7645-1665-5)

Windows XP For Dummies
(0-7645-0893-8)

Windows XP For Dummies Quick Reference
(0-7645-0897-0)

BUSINESS SOFTWARE

Excel 2002 For Dummies
0-7645-0822-9

Word 2002 For Dummies
0-7645-0839-3

Office XP 9 in 1 Desk Reference For Dummies
0-7645-0819-9

Also available:

Excel Data Analysis For Dummies
(0-7645-1661-2)

Excel 2002 All-in-One Desk Reference For Dummies
(0-7645-1794-5)

Excel 2002 For Dummies Quick Reference
(0-7645-0829-6)

GoldMine "X" For Dummies
(0-7645-0845-8)

Microsoft CRM For Dummies
(0-7645-1698-1)

Microsoft Project 2002 For Dummies
(0-7645-1628-0)

Office XP For Dummies
(0-7645-0830-X)

Outlook 2002 For Dummies
(0-7645-0828-8)

Get smart! Visit www.dummies.com

- **Find listings of even more *For Dummies* titles**
- **Browse online articles**
- **Sign up for Dummies eTips™**
- **Check out *For Dummies* fitness videos and other products**
- **Order from our online bookstore**

Available wherever books are sold. Go to www.dummies.com or call 1-877-762-2974 to order direct.

FOR

DUMMIES

Helping you expand your horizons and realize your potential

INTERNET

The Internet FOR DUMMIES
0-7645-0894-6

The Internet ALL-IN-ONE DESK REFERENCE FOR DUMMIES
0-7645-1659-0

eBay FOR DUMMIES
0-7645-1642-6

Also available:

America Online 7.0 For Dummies
(0-7645-1624-8)

Genealogy Online For Dummies
(0-7645-0807-5)

The Internet All-in-One Desk Reference For Dummies
(0-7645-1659-0)

Internet Explorer 6 For Dummies
(0-7645-1344-3)

The Internet For Dummies Quick Reference
(0-7645-1645-0)

Internet Privacy For Dummies
(0-7645-0846-6)

Researching Online For Dummies
(0-7645-0546-7)

Starting an Online Business For Dummies
(0-7645-1655-8)

DIGITAL MEDIA

Digital Photography FOR DUMMIES
0-7645-1664-7

Photoshop Elements 2 FOR DUMMIES
0-7645-1675-2

Digital Video FOR DUMMIES
0-7645-0806-7

Also available:

CD and DVD Recording For Dummies
(0-7645-1627-2)

Digital Photography All-in-One Desk Reference For Dummies
(0-7645-1800-3)

Digital Photography For Dummies Quick Reference
(0-7645-0750-8)

Home Recording for Musicians For Dummies
(0-7645-1634-5)

MP3 For Dummies
(0-7645-0858-X)

Paint Shop Pro "X" For Dummies
(0-7645-2440-2)

Photo Retouching & Restoration For Dummies
(0-7645-1662-0)

Scanners For Dummies
(0-7645-0783-4)

GRAPHICS

PowerPoint 2002 FOR DUMMIES
0-7645-0817-2

Photoshop 7 FOR DUMMIES
0-7645-1651-5

Macromedia Flash MX FOR DUMMIES
0-7645-0895-4

Also available:

Adobe Acrobat 5 PDF For Dummies
(0-7645-1652-3)

Fireworks 4 For Dummies
(0-7645-0804-0)

Illustrator 10 For Dummies
(0-7645-3636-2)

QuarkXPress 5 For Dummies
(0-7645-0643-9)

Visio 2000 For Dummies
(0-7645-0635-8)

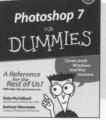

Available wherever books are sold. Go to www.dummies.com or call 1-877-762-2974 to order direct.

FOR DUMMIES®

The advice and explanations you need to succeed

SELF-HELP, SPIRITUALITY & RELIGION

Sex For Dummies
0-7645-5302-X

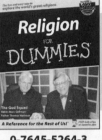

Parenting For Dummies
0-7645-5418-2

Religion For Dummies
0-7645-5264-3

Also available:

The Bible For Dummies
(0-7645-5296-1)

Buddhism For Dummies
(0-7645-5359-3)

Christian Prayer For Dummies
(0-7645-5500-6)

Dating For Dummies
(0-7645-5072-1)

Judaism For Dummies
(0-7645-5299-6)

Potty Training For Dummies
(0-7645-5417-4)

Pregnancy For Dummies
(0-7645-5074-8)

Rekindling Romance For Dummies
(0-7645-5303-8)

Spirituality For Dummies
(0-7645-5298-8)

Weddings For Dummies
(0-7645-5055-1)

PETS

Puppies For Dummies
0-7645-5255-4

Dog Training For Dummies
0-7645-5286-4

Cats For Dummies
0-7645-5275-9

Also available:

Labrador Retrievers For Dummies
(0-7645-5281-3)

Aquariums For Dummies
(0-7645-5156-6)

Birds For Dummies
(0-7645-5139-6)

Dogs For Dummies
(0-7645-5274-0)

Ferrets For Dummies
(0-7645-5259-7)

German Shepherds For Dummies
(0-7645-5280-5)

Golden Retrievers For Dummies
(0-7645-5267-8)

Horses For Dummies
(0-7645-5138-8)

Jack Russell Terriers For Dummies
(0-7645-5268-6)

Puppies Raising & Training Diary For Dummies
(0-7645-0876-8)

EDUCATION & TEST PREPARATION

Spanish For Dummies
0-7645-5194-9

Algebra For Dummies
0-7645-5325-9

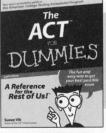

The ACT For Dummies
0-7645-5210-4

Also available:

Chemistry For Dummies
(0-7645-5430-1)

English Grammar For Dummies
(0-7645-5322-4)

French For Dummies
(0-7645-5193-0)

The GMAT For Dummies
(0-7645-5251-1)

Inglés Para Dummies
(0-7645-5427-1)

Italian For Dummies
(0-7645-5196-5)

Research Papers For Dummies
(0-7645-5426-3)

The SAT I For Dummies
(0-7645-5472-7)

U.S. History For Dummies
(0-7645-5249-X)

World History For Dummies
(0-7645-5242-2)

Available wherever books are sold. Go to www.dummies.com or call 1-877-762-2974 to order direct.

FOR DUMMIES®

We take the mystery out of complicated subjects

WEB DEVELOPMENT

Creating Web Pages FOR DUMMIES
0-7645-1643-4

HTML 4 FOR DUMMIES
0-7645-0723-0

Dreamweaver MX FOR DUMMIES
0-7645-1630-2

Also available:

ASP.NET For Dummies
(0-7645-0866-0)
Building a Web Site For Dummies
(0-7645-0720-6)
ColdFusion "MX" For Dummies (0-7645-1672-8)
Creating Web Pages All-in-One Desk Reference For Dummies
(0-7645-1542-X)

FrontPage 2002 For Dummies
(0-7645-0821-0)
HTML 4 For Dummies Quick Reference
(0-7645-0721-4)
Macromedia Studio "MX" All-in-One Desk Reference For Dummies
(0-7645-1799-6)
Web Design For Dummies
(0-7645-0823-7)

PROGRAMMING & DATABASES

C++ FOR DUMMIES
0-7645-0746-X

XML FOR DUMMIES
0-7645-1657-4

Access 2002 FOR DUMMIES
0-7645-0818-0

Also available:

Beginning Programming For Dummies
(0-7645-0835-0)
Crystal Reports "X" For Dummies
(0-7645-1641-8)
Java & XML For Dummies
(0-7645-1658-2)
Java 2 For Dummies
(0-7645-0765-6)
JavaScript For Dummies
(0-7645-0633-1)
Oracle9i For Dummies
(0-7645-0880-6)

Perl For Dummies
(0-7645-0776-1)
PHP and MySQL For Dummies
(0-7645-1650-7)
SQL For Dummies
(0-7645-0737-0)
VisualBasic .NET For Dummies
(0-7645-0867-9)
Visual Studio .NET All-in-One Desk Reference For Dummies
(0-7645-1626-4)

LINUX, NETWORKING & CERTIFICATION

Red Hat Linux 7.3 FOR DUMMIES
0-7645-1545-4

Networking FOR DUMMIES
0-7645-0772-9

A+ Certification FOR DUMMIES
0-7645-0812-1

Also available:

CCNP All-in-One Certification For Dummies
(0-7645-1648-5)
Cisco Networking For Dummies
(0-7645-1668-X)
CISSP For Dummies
(0-7645-1670-1)
CIW Foundations For Dummies with CD-ROM
(0-7645-1635-3)

Firewalls For Dummies
(0-7645-0884-9)
Home Networking For Dummies
(0-7645-0857-1)
Red Hat Linux All-in-One Desk Reference For Dummies
(0-7645-2442-9)
TCP/IP For Dummies
(0-7645-1760-0)
UNIX For Dummies
(0-7645-0419-3)

Available wherever books are sold.
Go to www.dummies.com or call 1-877-762-2974 to order direct.

 WILEY